OZARK
TROUT
TALES

OZARK TROUT TALES

A FISHING GUIDE FOR THE WHITE RIVER SYSTEM

STEVE WRIGHT

WHITE RIVER CHRONICLE, PUBLISHER

First printing 1994
Second printing 1997

Layout and design by Walker Design Group

Cover photo by Don House, House Photoworks

Inside photos by Steve Wright, except where otherwise noted

Library of Congress Catalog Card Number: 94-90589

ISBN 0-9638832-9-1

ACKNOWLEDGEMENTS

This book would not have been possible without Mark Blackwood, Jim Gaston, Kirk Dupps, Joe Fennel, Richard Ferrell, Bob Still and John Tyson. I will be forever grateful for their belief in this project and in me.

Thanks to the Arkansas Game and Fish Commission and the Missouri Department of Conservation, especially AGFC trout biologist John Stark and assistant Darrell Bowman, whom I bothered on a weekly basis during the writing of this book.

A special thanks to Bill Butler, whose cabin on the White River at Rim Shoals is the perfect writer's retreat - no television, no telephone (until recently) and a bookcase stocked with the works of A.J. McClane, Ernest Hemingway, Lee Wulff, Izaak Walton, Zane Gray, Henry David Thoreau, Norman Maclean and Randy Wayne White.

Tim Walker deserves sainthood for following my plodding steps through the completion of this project. I almost killed us both.

Finally, this book wouldn't have been near as much fun to write without the hospitality of new friends, like Jerry and Katy Nixon, and all the anglers, guides and outfitters along the White, North Fork and Little Red rivers who were so willing to show off their favorite trout rivers and share some Ozark trout tales.

TABLE OF CONTENTS

Page 15

Page 20

Page 37

TABLE OF CONTENTS

CHAPTER 3

Bull Shoals Tailwater (White River)

Page 46

Page 58

Page 72

TABLE OF CONTENTS

Page 80

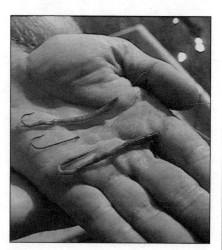

Page 85

Page 121

CHAPTER 4

Norfork Tailwater (North Fork River)

CHAPTER 5

Greers Ferry Tailwater (Little Red River)

TABLE OF CONTENTS

Page 136

Page 161

Page 167

"The fisherman is a natural story-teller. No man's imagination plays more pranks than his, while he is tending his reels and trotting from one to another, or watching his cork in summer. He is ever waiting for the sky to fall. He has sent out a venture. He has a ticket in the lottery of fate, who knows what it may draw? He ever expects to catch a bigger fish yet. He is the most patient and believing of men. Who else will stand so long in wet places? When the haymaker runs to shelter, he takes down his pole and bends his steps to the river, glad to have a leisure day. He is more like an inhabitant of nature. The weather concerns him. He is an observer of her phenomena."

— *Journal of Henry David Thoreau*, Feb. 9, 1852

PREFACE

There are two things you never hear in the Ozarks - meat frying and the truth. That's what they used to say, anyway, when this area of northern Arkansas and southern Missouri was seen as a tough, unforgiving land.

You don't hear that expression around here now. Headlined by all the goings-on in Branson, Missouri, there's no shortage of meat to fry in the Ozarks.

As for the truth, let's start with the author's photo on the back cover. No, I didn't catch that fish. As Arkansas Game and Fish Commission trout biologist John Stark likes to point out, I didn't even net the 37-inch brown trout as it tried to escape his electrofishing boat that night on the White River.

But I did hold it long enough for a picture, before it went back into the Bull Shoals Tailwater. And, in a way, it represents some of my research, one more big-fish story.

In September 1993, I began traveling up and down the White, North Fork and Little Red rivers gathering information about trout fishing.

I had two goals when I started. The first was to present practical how-to techniques on trout fishing in the Ozarks. The second was to document the relatively brief and almost miraculous history of the White River, North Fork River and Little Red River as trout streams.

One year after Bull Shoals Dam was built on the White River, I was born 125 miles downstream at Batesville, Arkansas. Those of us who've grown up with the five U.S. Army Corps of Engineers hydropower dams in place on these rivers tend to overlook the effect they had.

The dams and the recreational opportunities they created were the engines of change in the Ozarks. Those engines, for better or worse, are roaring now.

Fishing provides just another example. There are no official rankings on this, of course, but the White River System has been among the best fisheries in the United States for three different species in the last 50 years.

First, it was known for smallmouth bass, before dam construction wiped out the smallmouth habitat. After the dams were built, the White River System was known for growing giant rainbow trout, before fishing pressure knocked them out. Now it's No. 1 for brown trout, having produced two world records from 1988 to 1992.

I hope as you read through this book you'll get a feel for that change and how quickly it has come upon us. And I hope you'll get a sense of what unique fisheries these are.

One thing that hasn't changed in the Ozarks is the friendliness of the people. All my adventures on the rivers have been at the side of someone who knew what he was doing and didn't mind sharing it. This book is almost as much about people as it is about trout fishing.

Fishing should be a challenge. Pick and choose from the smorgasbord of techniques offered and find a new challenge.

And keep in mind, the biggest challenge will be allowing these rivers to realize their potential.

— Steve Wright
Fayetteville, Arkansas
October 1994

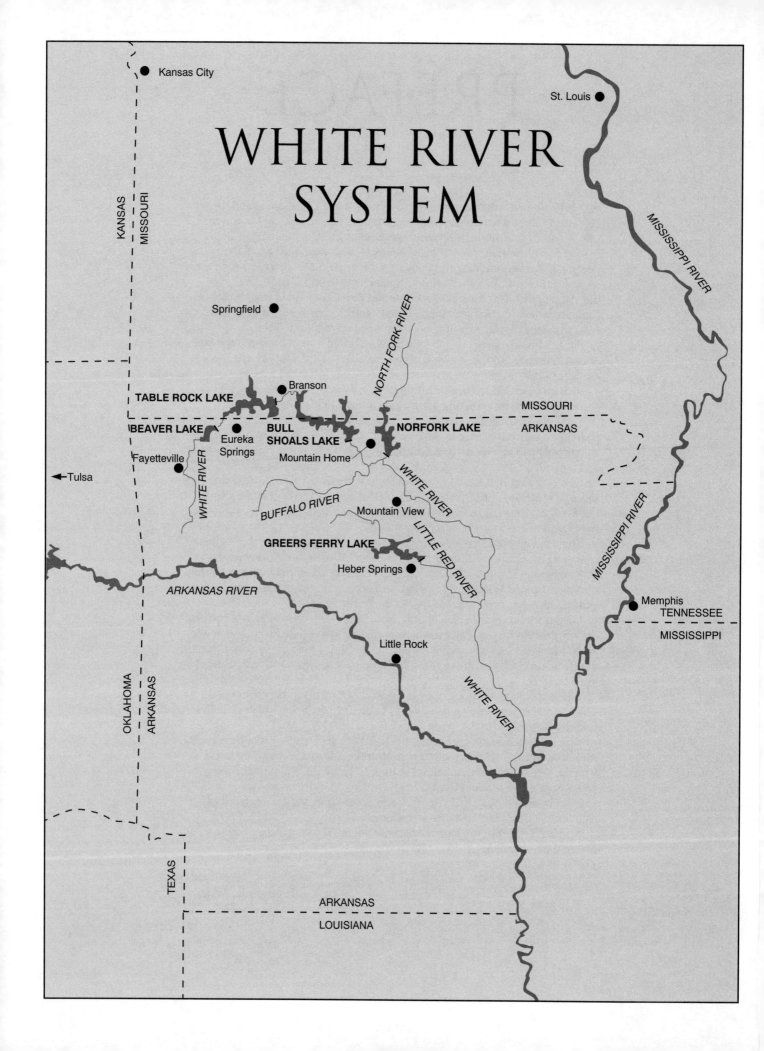

INTRODUCTION

How The Whole Dam Thing Got Started

Man's attempt to control nature came swiftly and powerfully to the Ozarks. Within a quarter century - from 1941 to 1964 - the U.S. Army Corps of Engineers built five major dams in the White River Basin. Three are on the White River - Beaver, Table Rock and Bull Shoals - and two are on major White River tributaries - Norfork Dam on the North Fork River and Greers Ferry Dam on the Little Red River.

An "Ozark Coast" was the result, as 6.5 million cubic yards of concrete backed up 200,000 surface acres of water behind five dams, all located within 200 miles of each other. Suddenly, a hilly land with no natural lakes of any size took on a new personality. And trout became a trait of that change.

The five dams are operated as a system - the White River System. When the lakes are in flood stage, water releases from the dams are coordinated within this system. Although the dams are in the Ozarks, the focus is also on delta farmlands bordering the White River in eastern Arkansas. By coordinating water releases from

OZARK TAILWATER TROUT HABITAT	
Tailwater	**Miles**
Beaver	8
Table Rock	22
Bull Shoals	101
Norfork	5
Greers Ferry	32
Total	**168**

the five dams, most floods in the entire White River Basin are prevented. In essence, the White River System is one big buffer zone between man and nature.

This whole dam thing began when Congress approved and President Franklin Roosevelt signed the Flood Control Act of June 28, 1938. The White River Basin attracted attention because it had been hit by four major floods between 1898 and 1927.

In that 1938 act, flood control was the only justification for building these major impoundments throughout the country. The Flood Control

Act of 1941 added hydropower generation and "other beneficial uses" as purposes for the projects. The broader plan helped "sell" the dams to the public and justify the high construction costs.

Why Trout?

Green trout are native to the Ozarks. That's an Ozark nickname for smallmouth bass. Real trout - rainbows, browns, cutthroats, etc. - aren't native to this area, but the "green trout" expression would serve as an ironic indicator of things to come.

Fishing didn't figure into the discussion about whether or not to build major impoundments in the Ozarks. The destruction of warmwater fisheries habitat resulted in this great trout experiment. It's an important point to remember. Ozark tailwater trout are an experiment.

Norfork Dam became the first of the five White River System impoundments. Its construction took place during World War II.

The dam was completed and Norfork Lake began to fill in 1944. This also signaled the beginning of a major decline in Ozark smallmouth bass stream habitat.

Water drawn through all the White River System dams comes from intakes located several feet below the surface of the lakes. Tailwater temperatures range from 42 to 65 degrees during the year, but are usually in the 50-degree range. Smallmouth bass prefer water temperatures in the 60- to 65-degree range for spawning.

The North Fork River had been considered one of the best smallmouth bass streams in the country. With Norfork Dam in place, the tailwater stream below it became too cold to suit the smallmouth.

Trout stockings were simply mitigation for the loss of warmwater habitat in the tailwaters below the dams.

The trout experiment started in July 1948 when the Arkansas Game and Fish Commission stocked 600 rainbow trout 4 to 6 inches long in the Norfork Tailwater.

One year later, anglers were catching 2- and 3-pound trout. Two years later, 6- and 8-pound trout were coming from the Norfork Tailwater, and it was obvious the trout were surviving and thriving.

This experiment included the transfer of aquatic vegetation from Ozark spring-fed streams to the Norfork Tailwater. It proved to be as successful as the trout stockings. Vegetation introduced in 1952 and 1953 was well established by 1954. The vegetation improved both fish cover and trout food sources, in the form of aquatic invertebrates.

The first experimental trout stocking of the Bull Shoals Tailwater took place in 1952. It included 1,800 brown trout and 16,000 rainbow trout, all 6 to 8 inches long. Survival and growth rates were found to be similar to those at Norfork.

These results and a growing reputation of the White and North Fork rivers as trout fisheries resulted in another major step in the mitigation process. In 1955, Congress authorized construction of the Norfork National Fish Hatchery. Two years later, the hatchery was completed and by 1962 it was supplying 1.8 million trout for the White and North Fork rivers.

By this time, trout fishing had taken hold. Early records indicate that during one September week in 1957, White River anglers caught 34 trout weighing between 7 and 13 pounds. Arkansas didn't start keeping official records for trout until 1959. The rainbow trout state mark fell four times in five months, increasing to 15 pounds, 3 ounces, and two state record brown trout were landed.

The successful experiments at Norfork and Bull Shoals would be repeated below Table Rock, Beaver and Greers Ferry dams.

A world class trout fishery had been brought to the Ozarks and suddenly there were fewer complaints about the decline of the native "green trout," the smallmouth bass.

Float Trip Tradition

If you say someone is "as busy as a guide on a riffle," they'll know what you mean in the Ozarks. Float fishing trips are so much a part of the Ozark experience they've worked themselves into the language.

The Ozarks is the birthplace of commercial float fishing, and the White River is the stream that popularized it. Commercial operations began in the early 1900s. By 1941, when a White River outing was featured on the cover of Life magazine, float fishing had become one of the top tourist attractions in the Ozarks.

"Every second you were floating, you were looking up at God's wallpaper," is the way one man described it.

Before the dams were built, float trip options were almost endless. They could vary from one day to several weeks. The construction of Powersite Dam near Branson, Missouri, in 1913 put one minor obstacle in place, but a 210-mile float trip from Forsyth, Missouri, to Batesville, Arkansas, was still possible.

Branson's Jim Owen earned a reputation as the king of the float trip outfitters. He owned several dozen wooden johnboats and employed over 30 fishing guides.

In the 1940s, an 18-mile float trip from Forsyth to Moore's Ferry cost $22.50. Another common Owen-outfitted trip started at Beaver, Arkansas, and ended at Branson - 65 miles in 10 days.

Multi-day float fishing trips meant boat-loads of manpower and gear. A

Conveyor Belt Tough On Hunting Dogs

Although construction of Bull Shoals Dam provided jobs in the area, it proved to be a difficult time for Flippin, Arkansas, residents. Crushed rock used in concrete for dam construction came from a quarry on Lee's Mountain, northwest of Flippin.

Blasts from the quarry damaged most businesses in downtown Flippin and many residences.

At the time of its construction, Bull Shoals was the fifth-largest concrete dam in the United States. The tremendous amount of crushed rock needed would have required round-the-clock truck traffic from the quarry to the dam.

Instead, a seven-mile conveyor belt system was set up between the two sites. It was reported to be the longest such conveyor belt ever constructed.

Just like the blasts from the quarry, the conveyor belt caused some problems, specifically for raccoon hunters. Coon hunting is a long-time Ozark tradition and a good dog is considered a valuable possession. But once the conveyor belt began operating, it got tough to tree a coon in Marion County.

"It ruined a lot of good coon dogs," said Forrest Wood, the founder of Ranger Boats and a lifelong resident of Flippin. "Coons learned they could get on that conveyor belt to get away from the dogs. Several dogs had to be locked up. They just couldn't stand it."

IMPORTANT DATES IN THE WHITE RIVER SYSTEM

1913 Powersite Dam completed, forming Lake Taneycomo.

1938 President Franklin Roosevelt signs the Flood Control Act of 1938, giving U.S. Army Corps of Engineers authority to build dams on free flowing streams.

1941 Jim Owen's White River float trips, based in Branson, Missouri, are featured on the cover of Life magazine. Norfork Dam construction begins. Commercial power generation starts in 1944.

1947 Bull Shoals Dam construction begins. Commercial power generation starts in 1952.

1948 Arkansas Game and Fish Commission experimentally stocks 600 rainbow trout (4-6 inches long) in the Norfork Tailwater in July. Within one year, 2- to 3-pound trout are caught. By the end of the second year, 6- to 8-pound trout are caught.

1954 Table Rock Dam construction begins. Commercial power generation starts in June 1959. Two more power generation units go on line in 1961.

1955 On August 4, Congress authorizes construction of the Norfork National Fish Hatchery as mitigation for the loss of the native warmwater fishery in the White River Basin. Construction is completed in 1957.

1958 Jim Owen announces his float trip service will cease operations in Branson, Missouri, as, first, Bull Shoals Dam ended White River float trips below Forsyth and, now, Table Rock Dam has done the same to the White River above Branson.

1959 During the first year of record-keeping, Arkansas' rainbow trout mark is broken four times from June 11 through Oct. 2 - increasing from 11 pounds, 3 ounces to 15 pounds, 8 ounces. Two state record brown trout are caught - 10 pounds, 13 ounces, then 12 pounds, 2 ounces.

1959 Greers Ferry Dam construction begins in March. The overall project is completed in July 1964.

1960 Beaver Dam construction begins in November. Commercial power generation starts in May 1965, and the overall project is completed in June 1966.

1963 Hydropower generator Nos. 5-8 go on line at Bull Shoals Dam, completing construction of the project that began in 1947.

1968 Arkansas' record rainbow trout for the first time comes from the Greers Ferry Tailwater when David Kitchens lands a 15-pound, 8-ounce fish.

1970 Missouri's record rainbow trout for the first time comes from Lake Taneycomo when Charles Gott catches a 13-pound, 14 3/4-ounce fish.

1972 Troy Lackey lands an Arkansas and North American record brown trout weighing 31 pounds, 8 ounces from the Bull Shoals Tailwater.

1977 Leon Waggoner breaks Lackey's records with a 33-pound, 8-ounce brown trout from the Bull Shoals Tailwater.

1985 Arkansas' cutthroat trout record is broken four times, increasing from 3 pounds to 9 pounds, 9 ounces.

1988 August proves to be the best month for big brown trout in Ozark history as three 30-plus-pounders are caught in the North Fork River, near its confluence with the White, including a new state and world record 38-pound, 9-ounce fish by Huey Manley.

1991 Marty Babusa sets a new Missouri brown trout mark with a 23-pound, 4-ounce fish from Lake Taneycomo.

1992 Howard "Rip" Collins sets new world and state brown trout records with a 40-pound, 4-ounce fish caught in the Greers Ferry Tailwater.

1994 Kevin Elfrink breaks the Missouri brown trout record with a 24-pound, 15-ounce fish from Lake Taneycomo.

Photo courtesy of Arkansas Game and Fish Commission

Howard "Rip" Collins of Heber Springs, Arkansas, caught this 40-lb., 4-oz. brown trout from the Greers Ferry Tailwater in 1992.

commissary boat, packed with food and tents and manned by a cook, preceded the anglers. The commissary boat's supplies might include a cooler and a couple hundred pounds of block ice, plus a few live chickens, which would be butchered along the way.

A typical Ozark johnboat comfortably held two anglers and a fishing guide, and a float trip would include as many as 10 fishing boats. At noon, the cook prepared a shore lunch for the anglers along a gravel bar. They'd meet again at the end of the day, when tents were pitched and everyone enjoyed another shore-cooked meal.

Overnight float trips continue to be a part of the Ozark tailwater trout fisheries, although one-day floats and overnight stays at resorts have overtaken them in popularity.

You can still arrange some form of an overnight float trip on any of these Ozark tailwaters. But because of its 100-mile length and lack of influence from any downstream dams, the Bull Shoals Tailwater remains the place where original Ozark float fishing traditions are strongest.

There is, of course, one part of the tradition that can't be duplicated in the Ozark tailwaters - smallmouth bass fishing. You'll still find smallmouth bass in some places - especially in the White River near the mouths of Crooked Creek and the Buffalo River - but in nowhere near the numbers that made the smallmouth bass the No. 1 gamefish in the Ozarks.

Once the large hydropower dams were built, Ozark float fishing had been forever changed. In 1958, Jim Owen shut down his float fishing service in Branson.

In a letter to former customers, Owen wrote: "The building of Bull Shoals Dam took away all of my wonderful floating water on the lower White River and the just completed Table Rock Dam has done the same to the floating water on the upper White River."

Owen's floating water was replaced by lakes, but the float fishing tradition would survive in the tailwaters below the dams.

Twenty-foot fiberglass johnboats, like those pictured here, retain many of the same characteristics of the original wooden johnboat design.

Johnboat Another Part Of Ozark Tradition

The johnboat, like commercial float fishing, is an Ozark original. Similar in shape and function to the pirogue, johnboats are long, narrow and shallow. That shape allowed one person to pole a cargo-laden boat through shoals.

Before automobiles and railroads came to the Ozarks, johnboats were the main mode of transportation. Everyone who lived along the river owned a johnboat or two. The boats were tied to trees along the bank with a long rope, to allow for the rise and fall of the river. It was common practice to borrow a neighbor's boat when needed.

Johnboats stayed in the water out of necessity. The first johnboats were made of raw pine boards. Once placed in the river, the boards would swell from absorbing water and form a seal. If taken out of the water, the boards would gape open as they dried.

Johnboats could be as long as 30 feet, but were usually only 18 to 24 inches wide. A new boat might weigh 300 pounds. After it had been in the river, it would swell to over twice that weight.

The modern johnboat design is credited to Owen Swinney of Winona, Missouri, in 1919, according to "McClane's New Standard Fishing Encyclopedia." Swinney's boat was made of pine boards 20 feet long and 18 inches wide. The sides flared 130 degrees and the hull tapered fore and aft, creating a bow and transom that were about a foot wide at the bottom and two feet wide at the top.

Today's version of the johnboat is rarely made from wood. Fiberglass and aluminum are the most common materials. Rather than a pole, it's powered by an outboard motor.

The 20-foot fiberglass johnboats routinely used on the Bull Shoals Tailwater carry the most similarities to the original johnboat design. The long, narrow boat's ability to negotiate shallow water remains a valued trait.

The Hatchery System

Cold water released from the five major hydropower dams in the White River System creates ideal habitat for growing trout, but not for natural reproduction. Although trout growth rates average a half-inch a month and more, reproductive rates are limited, especially for rainbow trout. Hatcheries, therefore, are the lifeblood of the Ozark tailwater trout fishing.

Six hatcheries - three federal and three state - work in coordination to produce nearly three million trout per year for stocking in the 168 miles of the White River System. The hatcheries actually turn out more trout than that, but some are sent to other waters.

No two hatcheries in this system are alike. They range in size from huge to tiny.

Norfork National Fish Hatchery, for instance, has the highest production of any coldwater hatchery in the U.S. Fish and Wildlife system. It produces about two million trout per year, ranging in size from 5 inches to 12 inches. Three-quarters of those are stocked in Arkansas as 9-inch fish.

But some 6-inch trout are transferred to the Arkansas Game and Fish Commission's Centerton Hatchery. Although this relatively small facility is mainly concerned with warmwater species, it includes two spring-fed raceways that are used to grow the 6-inch trout from Norfork Hatchery to 12- and 14-inch trout for stocking in the Beaver Tailwaters.

Shepherd of the Hills Hatchery in Missouri is the only one in this system that continues to raise trout from brood stock. The other hatcheries receive eggs or fingerlings that are then raised to stocking size trout.

The primary state-operated hatcheries supplying trout for the White River System are Spring River and Centerton in Arkansas and Shepherd of the Hills in Missouri.

Federal hatcheries include Norfork and Greers Ferry in Arkansas and Neosho in Missouri. The federal hatcheries are under the direction of the U.S. Fish and Wildlife Service.

Spring River Hatchery is one of only a few hatcheries in the world that grows trout in deep silos, rather than raceways. Mammoth Spring supplies the water.

Spring River Raising Trout In The Round

Spring River Hatchery near Mammoth Spring, Arkansas, is easily the most unusual among those that supply trout for the White River System. In fact, there are only a handful of facilities like it in the world.

Rather than long, shallow, rectangular raceways, the Spring River Hatchery grows most of its trout in deep, round silos. Each of the 36 silos holds 22,000 gallons of water and measures 13.5-feet deep and 17.5-feet in diameter. (The hatchery has 14 raceways, too.)

"Theoretically, it would take three (50-foot by 8-foot) raceways to equal one silo," said Melissa Jones, who became manager of the Arkansas Game and Fish Commission's Spring River Hatchery in 1985. "There is no other facility like this in the United States.

"The water is the key. You won't find many places anywhere that have this volume of water available."

Two-and-a-half miles upstream from the hatchery, Mammoth Spring feeds the Spring River with nine million gallons per hour of 58-degree water. The combination of silos and water creates an unusually efficient trout hatchery.

"We don't have to pump the water (to the hatchery), cool it, nothing," Jones said.

The AGFC didn't have to build the Spring River Hatchery, either. That was done by Marine Protein, Inc., in 1972. It planned to market rainbow trout for tablefare. The Kroger grocery chain based in Cincinnati, Ohio, bought the hatchery. In 1985, Kroger left the commercial trout market and donated the hatchery to the AGFC.

You'll still here Arkansas anglers refer to "Kroger" trout, as the freshly-stocked fish from the Spring River Hatchery are easily identified. They won't have the brilliant colors of rainbow trout that have been in the river long, but they won't have the partial fins found most other hatchery-stocked trout, either. Trout raised in raceways tend to hold on to the concrete bottom with their pelvic fins, which are grated and scraped; silo-raised trout don't suffer fin abrasions. Also, Spring River Hatchery trout are 12 inches long, while most Norfork Hatchery stockers are 9 inches long.

Spring River Hatchery's mandate from the AGFC requires a minimum of 500,000 12-inch rainbow trout per year. They are grown from 5-inch trout, which come from the Norfork and Greers Ferry hatcheries.

The Water

If you worship Ozark streams, the tiny community of Boston, Arkansas, is a mecca. You can stand at the now abandoned Boston Post Office and consider yourself at the beginning of the White River. The mountain that Boston sits atop also spawns War Eagle Creek and Kings River, both within a stone's throw of the White River's start. A few miles away, flowing off the hilltop in another direction, begins the Buffalo River.

Think of it this way. If you placed your hand on a map, with fingers spread wide, but all pointing in a northerly direction, your index finger represents the White River, your second finger is War Eagle Creek, your third finger is the Kings River, your little finger is the Buffalo River and the back of your hand is the Ozark mountain where Boston is located.

Less than 50 miles away, to the southeast, about where your wrist would be if still spread on the map, are the beginnings of the Little Red River.

For most of its 720 miles, White River runs in a southeasterly direction toward the Mississippi River. But first it must gather its tributaries. It takes a long, circuitous route in doing so.

The White River first heads west. Follow Highway 16 a few miles toward

If you worship Ozark streams, the tiny community of Boston, Arkansas, is a mecca.

the town of Pettigrew and you'll begin to notice a tiny stream that grows in size the farther you travel. White River doesn't really look like a river until it has flowed 40 miles and been joined by its Middle and West forks, near Fayetteville, Arkansas. Now it's flowing north and meets War Eagle Creek at the headwaters of Beaver Lake.

White River starts turning to the northeast and snares Kings River at the headwaters of Table Rock Lake. From the north of the White River Basin, the James River joins the White in Table Rock Lake.

The White River is headed due east by the time it reaches Branson, Missouri. After another short northern jog, it begins its southern descent back into Arkansas.

Below Bull Shoals Dam, White River catches Crooked Creek, then Buffalo River, which at one time was commonly called the Buffalo Fork of the White River. By this point, the White River has traveled 334 miles,

almost half its total length, and the Buffalo has flowed 150 miles. From beginnings less than five miles apart, the two rivers meander almost 500 miles before they join.

Eleven miles downstream from the White-Buffalo confluence, North Fork River, on its southern descent from Missouri, spills into the White.

In one sense, rivers are like people in being known for the company they keep. That helps explain the water quality of the White River and its previous reputation as a smallmouth bass stream.

A list of the top five smallmouth bass streams in Arkansas, would include Crooked Creek, War Eagle Creek, Kings River and Buffalo River. Therefore it should come as no surprise that the White River was known as one of the best smallmouth bass streams in the country, before the dams began changing its character.

The White and Little Red rivers don't meet until both have become warm, Mississippi Delta streams, near Augusta, Arkansas. But, like the White, the Little Red was previously known for its smallmouth bass and the river's three main tributaries - South Fork, Archey Fork and Middle Fork - are all typical Ozark streams containing smallmouth bass.

War Eagle Creek begins on the same Madison County hillside that spawns White River, Kings River and Buffalo River.

The Land

Two old Ozark expressions accurately describe the geology here: Our mountains ain't so high, but our valleys sure are deep; and, Ozark mountains go down instead of up.

Geologically speaking, there are no mountains in the Ozarks. It's common to read that the mountains here are among the oldest in the world, older than the Alps, but that isn't accurate. This area wasn't formed the same way as the Alps, Rockies, Appalachians or even Ouachitas, which are all the result of continental collisions.

The Ozark region was a shallow sea bed that was lifted to form a flat plateau, not a jutting mountain range. The Ozark Dome, a broad, asymmetrical uplift centered in southeastern Missouri, was then carved by water.

The glaciers of the Ice Age didn't engrave the Ozarks, but their effects did. Rainfall increased and dissected the sedimentary rock - limestone, dolomite, sandstone and shale - that dominates the area, creating these deep valleys. In addition, water made its way underground, forming thousands of caves, sink holes and springs.

During a float trip down the White River, you will pass bluffs that reveal the geological history of the Ozarks like an open book. At the bottom appear the limestone and dolomite of the Ordovician Period (500 million years ago). Stacked upon it are the limestone and chert layers of the Mississippian Period (350 million years ago) capped by the sandstones and shales of the Pennsylvanian Period (300 million years ago). The trip back in time, again, provided by water slicing its way through rock.

As a result, this is a special place. The rivers don't all flow south, as is the pattern in glaciated land, but spread out, like the branches of a tree, in all directions, following a path of least resistance through the soluble rock.

And the same quality that made pioneer life so tough here - a soil too thin for extensive farming - can be credited with helping produce clear streams.

Photo courtesy National Park Service

The same scraggly, gnarled cedar trees commonly seen clinging to Ozark bluffs have been living there for centuries and may survive for centuries to come.

Ancient Trees Living Along Ozark Bluffs

When you float down an Ozark stream and look up at a gnarly cedar tree clinging to a rock bluff, you could be viewing the same tree Henry Rowe Schoolcraft saw when he explored the Ozarks in the early 1800s. In fact, when Schoolcraft saw it, that scraggly old cedar tree may have been a couple hundred years old.

"If you're fishing on the White River, I guarantee you're looking at these trees just like our first European settlers saw them," said Dr. Dave Stahle.

Stahle heads the University of Arkansas tree ring laboratory. Tree growth rings are an archive of natural history. By taking pencil-sized corings and counting annual growth rings, Stahle can determine weather conditions during the lifetime of a tree. The information provides both a chronicle of the past and a baseline in studying future climate changes, like global warming.

In his Ozark studies, Stahle has discovered 600-year-old eastern red cedar trees and 400-year-old post oaks and white oaks. He expects to find even older living trees.

"We like to say the oldest trees that ever lived in the eastern deciduous forest are still alive today," Stahle said.

Another tree ring scientist determined that a dead red cedar tree found along Jack's Fork in Missouri lived from 1185 to 1976 - almost 800 years.

"That's why I believe the oldest red cedar in the Ozarks is still out there," Stahle said.

Although the Ozarks was one of the most heavily timbered lands at the turn of the 20th century, there remains thousands of acres of old-growth forest. You just have to know where to look for it. The oldest trees are frequently found on the most marginal sites - like south-facing upper slopes in Ozark hill country.

Rather than the massive size you'd ordinarily expect from ancient trees, these are thin and scraggly. Growth is slow and the wood is dense. A 10- to 24-inch diameter white oak might be 200 to 400 years old on these sites. Appearance and location have been the keys to their survival.

"A lot of people think this is second growth because it's not very big," Stahle said. "But when the pioneers and industrial loggers went through these forests, they didn't cut down everything. They didn't cut the poor stuff."

Now, the poor stuff is proving to be rich in information for scientists like Stahle.

WHITE RIVER

BEAVER TAILWATER

Small Trout Fishery Has Big Impact

Of the White River System's five U.S. Army Corps of Engineers-built dams, Beaver Dam was the last to be be completed, and it forms the shortest section of trout water - about eight miles. However, this short trout fishery may become the most important in the White River System in terms of its influence on the future.

The Beaver Tailwater was the first in Arkansas to receive special trout fishing regulations. In 1988, the Arkansas Game and Fish Commission introduced a 16-inch minimum length limit on brown trout and reduced the daily creel limit to two brown trout.

From a trial basis on Beaver, those regulations were added to the Bull Shoals Tailwater, Norfork Tailwater, Greers Ferry Tailwater and Spring River trout fisheries in 1990.

The Beaver Tailwater is also the site of a habitat restoration project, begun in 1994, that could have an even bigger impact on the other Ozark trout fisheries.

◀ **Ray Smith releases a trout caught in the Beaver Tailwater, which includes about eight miles of trout habitat.**

Although Dam Site Park provides plenty of public access for bank fishing, a boat comes in handy.

So in spite of its small size, the Beaver Tailwater has already had a major impact on Arkansas trout fisheries, in terms of regulations, and could be another influence, in terms of habitat restoration.

It might be more accurate to say that the Beaver Tailwater's influence is a result of its small size. It is easily

monitored. Experiments that might not be feasible in a larger fishery are accommodated at Beaver.

"We stocked Beaver with brown trout for two years under no special regulations," said Mark Hudy, who became the state's first trout biologist in 1985 and served in that capacity until 1989, when he took a job as a fisheries biologist in Virginia's George Washington National Forest. "It didn't work. It didn't meet our objectives.

"Then we did two more stockings of brown trout under the 16-inch regulation and it worked. It showed a real dramatic increase. We took that as a pilot and used it across the state, where we thought it would work."

The Beaver Tailwater has produced some 10-pound brown trout and a 20-pounder was caught and released in an AGFC electrofishing sample in 1994. In its early years, it produced a few 10-pound rainbow trout, too.

But, because it is so narrow and short and fishing pressure continues to increase as the northwest Arkansas and southwest Missouri areas grow, this tailwater fishery does not have the trophy potential, under current regu-

BEAVER TAILWATER AT A GLANCE

Location: Between Beaver and Table Rock lakes on the White River, northwest of Eureka Springs, Arkansas. It is 17 river miles from Beaver Dam to the Arkansas-Missouri line.

Road Mileages to Beaver Dam

Little Rock, Ark.	187
Tulsa, Okla.	157
Shreveport, La.	353
Memphis, Tenn.	294
Kansas City, Mo.	227
St. Louis, Mo.	309
Dallas, Texas	427

Length of Trout Waters: Generally considered to be about eight miles, from Beaver Dam past the Houseman Access, but some trout will also be scattered in the next few miles to the town of Beaver, for which Beaver Lake is named. Local anglers think there are big brown trout and rainbow trout that stay in the deep, cool holes in the lower section of the river year around. Houseman, however, is the farthest downstream trout stocking site, and stocking during summer months is discontinued there at times because water surface temperatures often exceed 75 degrees.

Dam: Commercial power generation began in May 1965. The overall project was completed in June 1966 at an estimated cost of $46.2 million. There are two hydroelectric power generators in Beaver Dam. The dam forms a 28,000-acre lake at the power pool level of 1120 feet above sea level. Beaver Dam was the last of the U.S. Army Corps of Engineers dams built on the White River.

Trout Stocking: First trout were stocked in 1966. The 1994 Arkansas Game & Fish Commission stocking schedule called for 60,000 9-inch rainbow trout, 25,000 12-inch rainbow trout, 10,000 brown trout and 25,000 cutthroat trout.

Fishing Regulations: Daily limit is six trout, including not more than two browns or cutthroats. Brown trout daily limit is two with a 16-inch minimum size limit. Cutthroat trout limit is two with a 16-inch minimum size limit. No size restrictions on rainbow trout.

Catch-and-Release Zone: (As of January 1, 1995) Catch-and-release fishing only with barbless-hook artificial lures from Dam Site Park Camping Area C to 100 yards above Parker Bend Access (1.0 mile).

Scenic Views: For a quick overview of the Beaver Tailwater, take Highway 62 west out of Eureka Springs. After crossing the White River on 62, turn left on Highway 187, which crosses Beaver Dam and eventually connects back with Highway 62. Inspiration Point, located on Highway 62, provides a scenic overlook of the Beaver Tailwater, as does the U.S. Army Corps of Engineers-built overlook at the dam (south side, opposite the powerhouse).

Power generation information: Call the U.S. Army Corps of Engineers Table Rock Dam powerhouse at 417-336-5083 for a recorded message of current conditions. For a 24-hour forecast, call the Southwest Power Administration recorded message center at 918-581-6845 and press #12 for Beaver Dam.

Historical note: Pea Ridge National Military Park, site of the largest Civil War battle west of the Mississippi River, is located about 20 miles from Beaver Dam, on Highway 62 in Benton County. The three-day battle was fought in March 1862 by 26,000 men. It ended any chance the Confederacy had for taking control of Missouri. After the battle most Union and Confederate troops moved east across the Mississippi River for other campaigns.

lations, that the other areas do. More so than the other four White River System tailwaters, this is a put-and-take fishery. For that reason, the catch-and-release zone established beginning January 1, 1995, could produce quick results in the Beaver Tailwater.

The lack of big fish numbers should not, however, detract from the beauty of the Beaver Tailwater. Like the others in the Ozarks, its primary natural features are tall, limestone and sandstone bluffs overlooking flat gravel bars - classic Ozark float trip scenery. But, unlike the other Ozark tailwaters, there are no commercial or private docks on the river banks.

> **"One thing a lot of people don't consider is that the areas where you do have easy access will also have the majority of the fishing pressure."**

When Beaver Dam's two hydroelectric power generators are off, the White River is reduced to a trickle. There are several places where you can stand on one bank and cast a line all the way across the stream.

When the power generators are on, water rises rapidly in the narrow river channel and the gravel bars are submerged. The rise and fall in water level is particularly dramatic in the Beaver Tailwater, and, thus, discourages dock-building. There isn't a commercial dock in the Beaver Tailwater's trout habitat, the first being at Holiday Island.

Another unique trait of the Beaver Tailwater is the influence upon it from Table Rock Lake. When Table Rock's level rises above the "normal" or "power pool" mark of 915 feet above sea level, it starts backing up into the Beaver Tailwater.

When Table Rock hits the 916

level, you can run a johnboat powered by a 10-horsepower motor all the way to Beaver Dam during periods of no power generation.

As Table Rock rises above 916, you'll begin to see larger and larger boats in the Beaver Tailwater, and it becomes a part of the lake.

On the other hand, when Table Rock drops to 915 feet, few boats can get past the shoals at Parker Bend during periods of low flow. Most of the time, the boats you see on the Beaver Tailwater will be canoes, whose occupants are on a float trip from the dam to Spider Creek or Riverview resorts.

The White River System is best experienced from a boat. That holds true for the Beaver Tailwaters, even though it is a narrow stream at low water and has a great deal of public access land. With the addition of Bertrand Ramp in 1994, there are public boat ramps in the upper, middle and lower section of the tailwater.

A canoe or johnboat allows anglers to move downstream, hitting the main areas and some not so accessible spots in between. A boat can be used more as a means of travel from bank- and wade-fishing spots in the first five miles of the river, then can be used to fish from in the lower stretch of the river, where the water is too deep to wade and there is less public access.

"One thing a lot of people don't consider is that the areas where you do have easy access will also have the majority of the fishing pressure," said John "J.R." Robey, manager of Spider Creek Resort. "For a guy to spend eight hours on the road getting here, then sit around fishing from the bank, well, I think he's a damn fool."

The short length of the Beaver Tailwater can be an advantage if you want to pursue several species of fish. Options include: trout in the upper reaches of the tailwaters, white bass and walleye in the middle section, black bass and crappie around Holiday Island, and black bass (largemouth, spotted and especially smallmouth) in the Kings River, which empties into Table Rock Lake in Missouri. It's only 30 miles from Beaver Dam to the mouth of the Kings River.

Trout habitat added to the Beaver Tailwater must be able to withstand high volumes of water, like those created when the floodgates are opened at the dam.

Habitat Project Could Be Model For Future Fisheries Improvement

In 1990, during a major flood, the gates were opened at Beaver Dam for 10 straight days. A water force of over 50,000-cubic-feet-per-second scoured the Beaver Tailwater, eroding banks, removing aquatic vegetation and washing gravel into the deeper holes in the stream bed. As a result, the trout population in the Beaver Tailwater took a nosedive.

But the story may have a happy ending, and the Beaver Tailwater may become a testing ground for improving fishery potential in the White River System. Initial studies took place in 1993 and work began in 1994 on a multi-year project that will improve trout habitat in the Beaver Tailwater. The project quickly received notice by the American Fisheries Society, earning its Fisheries Management Conservation Achievement Award for 1993-94.

Few habitat improvement projects of this magnitude have been undertaken in a tailwater trout fishery, and it is the first of its kind in the White River System. Initial estimates put a price tag on the project of $150,000. Among the groups funding it are the Arkansas and Tulsa chapters of Trout Unlimited, the national Trout Unlimited organization, Arkansas Game and Fish Commission, Arkansas Soil and Water Conservation Commission, Southwestern Power Administration and U.S. Army Corps of Engineers.

"This will most definitely be a model for the future," said AGFC assistant chief of fisheries Larry Rider. "We'll get a real good test in the Beaver Tailwater. Then we've got areas in the White River below Bull Shoals Dam and in the North Fork River where habitat could be enhanced."

Through stream habitat renovation, such as adding boulders, log shelters and cedar tree revetments, the following fishery goals are expected to be achieved: 1) 300 brown trout greater than 13 inches in length per mile with 100 of those being 20-plus inches long; and 2) 1,500 rainbow trout per mile with 300 of those being 16-plus inches long.

The Micro Jig Method For Catching Trout

Howard, James Smith have proven tiny jig catches big numbers of fish

Howard Smith can't say much when his son, James, tells him he's going trout fishing and won't be at work the next day. The Howard L. Smith & Sons Construction Company will just have to do without one of the sons.

It was Howard who started this "fishing-before-work" ethic in the first place. He started bringing his son to fish in the White River below Beaver Dam when James was five years old.

"He couldn't cast, but he could reel them in," Howard said. "I guess that's why he's so obsessed with trout fishing. That's the main fishing he's been doing since he was a kid."

That obsession has grown into a business, a side business from the carpentry work. James Smith started the Northwest Guide Service in 1990.

When he needs another guide to help him, James calls on his dad.

If the fishing guide business paid as many bills as the house construction business, James and Howard Smith would both have a fishing rod, not a nail gun, in their hands fulltime. But the Beaver Tailwater section of the White River is only about eight miles long and the demand for fishing guides here is a tiny fraction of that on the White River below Bull Shoals Dam.

That's okay. The Smiths don't go to the White River to make money. They go because they love it. Howard grew up in western Washington County. His father taught him how to fish for smallmouth bass in the Illinois River and Barren Fork Creek. Now Howard has passed the tradition down to his son.

"I'm a stream fisherman," Howard said. "I like to wade, so trout fishing just kind of replaced my smallmouth fishing."

Now Howard and James Smith average over 100 fishing trips a year to the Beaver Tailwater. Most of those outings they make together, no guiding involved, just a father and son fishing trip.

"Our wives think we live up here because we spend more time here than we do at home," Howard said.

As a result, they know this section of the White River as well as anyone. And when they travel, on vacations or whatever, they look for other fishing methods to bring back to the White River. That's how they came upon the Micro jig, a tiny artificial lure made in Springfield, Missouri.

James (left) and Howard Smith prepare a shore lunch after a successful morning of trout fishing on the Beaver Tailwater.

One advantage in using a Micro jig is that a fish seldom swallows the lure. Most often, a trout will be hooked in the upper jaw area and is easily released.

Before that, Howard and James had mainly used live bait for catching trout. One year, while on vacation in Colorado, Howard talked to an angler using spinning gear, a clear plastic bubble float and a tiny fly. The man had caught a 4-pound trout on his combination of spinning and fly fishing gear. Then James and his brother, Kenneth, started fishing at Roaring River State Park in Missouri, where Micro jigs are a popular lure.

But Micro jigs are usually fished without a bobber at Roaring River, so Howard and James started tinkering with combining a float and jig.

"We tried using those clear plastic bobbers that you can fill with water," Howard said. "But they had so much resistance the trout would spit out the jig. We missed a lot of fish. We knew we needed a smaller bobber."

They began using a small teardrop-shaped Styrofoam bobber and held it in place on the line with a lead split shot above it and below it. That did the trick.

"The fish don't feel any resistance when they take that Micro jig," Howard said.

But the Micro jig is the key ingredient here. Gary Thomas and Turner Jones are the men behind the Micro jig. The two most popular sizes are the "full" Micro jig, weighing, 1/128th of

an ounce, and the "half" Micro jig, weighing 1/256th of an ounce. Most of the other jigs you'll read about that are associated with trout fishing and spinning gear weigh from 1/8th of an ounce to 1/100th on an ounce. The Micro jig is fly fishing-type tackle that is made for spinning gear, but, of course, it can be used on a fly rod as well.

Because of their size and the labor-intensive manufacturing process, Micro Jigs aren't cheap.

"The main thrust of our business is on the West Coast," Thomas said. "They sell for two dollars apiece out there. Yes, that seems like an outrageous price, but the jigs are handled eight times before they are sent out. All the lures are hand painted. We use a feather that no one else uses.

"We don't do any advertising. We think word of mouth is more effective. Once you learn to use Micro jigs, nothing else works quite as good."

Howard and James Smith discovered that for themselves. They use the 1/256th "half Micro" for trout.

"The jig represents the natural food in the river - a freshwater shrimp or a scud," Howard said. "With a little jigging action, the hair on the jig pulsates and looks so real to a trout."

There is one more key ingredient in this Micro Jig rig - 2-pound-test line.

"It's a combination of the three things," James said, "the jig, the bobber and the line. There is no use trying to catch them with 4-pound-test. You won't get any action on the jig. It's like tying it with lariat rope. The jig just hangs there."

James made a believer out of Hank Parker, the two-time BASS Masters Classic champion and TV outdoors show host, when it comes to 2-pound-test line. Parker came to northwest Arkansas for a charity benefit in 1991 and brought his TV crew along. They spent one morning with Smith and Kirk Dupps, one of the charity organizers, on the Beaver Tailwater.

Micro jig fishing for trout, as the Smiths do it, is a low-water technique. When the power generators are running, the jigs aren't effective. But low water in the Beaver Tailwaters gives the trout an advantage. They aren't easily fooled with big lures and heavy line.

> "We continue to learn something new about fishing Micro jigs. I don't know of anything that works better when the power generators aren't running."

And as the sun gets higher in the sky, the trout become even more wary.

That's why, even with a tiny lure and light line, Micro jig fishing is enhanced by a slight breeze. The ripple on the water seems to give the lure a subtle action that greatly increases its effectiveness.

"That day we were fishing with Hank Parker, the wind quit about 11 o'clock and fishing got tough," James said. "About 12:30 the wind picked up and Kirk and I started catching fish right and left. We had on 2-pound-test line and Hank was using 4-pound-test.

Micro jigs (lower left and lower middle) are closer in size to this No. 14 Beadhead Caddis (lower right) than they are to the traditional jigs shown here.

"Finally, Hank started getting a little frustrated. He said, 'James, have you got any more of that 2-pound test?' He caught an 18-inch rainbow on his first cast after he changed over."

After the fishing trip, Parker said, "I've learned a new technique with that Micro jig deal. I was pretty impressed with that."

The Micro Jig company at one time sold 6-foot and 7-foot Micro rods designed especially for use with the jigs. These rods are now hard to find. Any long, limber ultralight spinning rod will do.

Long rods are helpful in getting extra casting distance and because at times the bobber must be set 8 to 10 feet above the Micro jig, when fishing a deep hole.

"If the water is over 15 feet deep, you can forget the jig," James said. "You want to fish a Micro jig about one to two feet from the bottom."

Micro jigs come in several colors. But day-in and day-out the Smiths rely on two colors - beige (some call it "tan" or "ginger") and brown.

"We've been using Micro jigs for eight years now," James said. "Those are the two colors to use if you're going to catch trout in the Beaver Tailwater."

They usually start out the day with beige and will stick with it if there is some cloud cover. However, on a clear day, they'll switch to brown during the hours of bright sunshine.

With 2-pound-test line, having a spinning reel with a better than average drag system is a must. The Smiths have caught brown trout up to 6 pounds on their 2-pound-test Micro jig rigs.

There is little margin for error in the drag system when a big fish is on 2-pound test line and even a small trout will strip line from the reel when the drag is set correctly.

"We've worn out some reels," Howard said.

But it has been worth it. When the power generators are running and fishing is tough, the Smiths will drift down the river bouncing nightcrawlers off the bottom, but 99 percent of the time you'll find them throwing Micro jigs in low water and Countdown Rapalas when the power generators are running. Their live bait days have almost ended.

Which brings us to one final advantage of the Micro jig. Fishing with these jigs on a float is almost like typical bream fishing with a bobber and crickets - when the float goes

under, set the hook.

Unlike fishing with live bait, however, you'll hardly ever have to dig a Micro jig from deep in a trout's mouth. The jig hook will usually be stuck near the front of the trout's upper jaw. You barely have to touch the fish in order to practice catch-and-release.

When you play the fish to the boat or bank, simply grab the jig between your thumb and index finger or in a pair of hemostats, give a slight pull and the fish can swim off with none of its protective slime coating removed. That's important, because it's not unusual for the Smiths to catch-and-release 40 to 50 trout per day in the Beaver Tailwater.

James and Howard usually fish from a wide, flat-bottom aluminum johnboat. When the river level is low, they'll pull it ashore to fish certain areas from the bank.

Micro jigs are most effective when fished in slow moving water - either a foot or two below the bobber in an eddy near a riffle or 4 to 6 feet below the bobber in a deep pool.

"We continue to learn something new about fishing Micro jigs," Howard said. "I don't know of anything that works better when the power generators aren't running."

A spinning reel with a sensitive drag system is crucial when trying to land a trout on 2-pound-test line.

Eureka Springs Gardens Has Trout, Too

Blue Spring has been attracting visitors for thousands of years

Take one look from Inspiration Point, located high above the White River on Highway 62, and you'll know this is a special place in the Ozarks. The combination of high bluffs and clear water is what gives the Ozarks its majesty.

Let your eyes follow the river downstream and you'll see one side of a long White River peninsula. Near the middle of the peninsula, hidden by trees from Inspiration Point but highly visible through history, is Blue Spring, where 38 million gallons per day of 54-degree water flow from the ground, then into the White River.

Legend has it that a group of Spanish explorer Hernando DeSoto's men came here in 1541 and thought they had found "The Fountain of Youth" when they saw the cobalt blue water pouring from this 75-foot diameter spring. The Osage Indians of the Midwestern Plains called it "the great healing spring of Arkansas." Before that, other Native Americans simply called it "endless waters."

"Scuba divers have tried to go in the opening, but there was just too much water coming out," said Steve Chyrchel,

who owns this 250-acre peninsula now.

In the spring of 1993, Chyrchel began making special use of that water. It is the lifeblood of Eureka Springs Gardens, a 33-acre botanical garden built around Blue Spring.

"The location was a natural for botanical gardens because nature had already done much of the landscaping," Chyrchel said.

For the White River trout angler, this is a pleasant diversion. Azaleas, forsythia, roses, philodendron, peonies, wildflowers and ornamental grasses are just a few examples of what has been planted along the hillsides and pathways of this garden.

There are trout planted here, too. You can clearly see these rapidly growing rainbows as you toss them some "trout chow" from the wooden pavilion built over a long pool below Blue Spring.

You can't fish for them here, but you might catch a former Blue Spring resident trout in the Beaver Tailwater. Chyrchel, whose father bought this land in 1968, says Blue Spring's trout population was flooded into the White River several times before the botanical gar-

den was built, including one time when the smallest Blue Spring rainbow weighed about 10 pounds.

But you are not here to scout for trout. A visit to Eureka Springs Gardens is just another way to appreciate the White River, which gets much of its character from the hundreds of springs that feed it in the Ozarks. Sixty-three springs are located within the nearby town of Eureka Springs, which became a national tourist attraction in the late 1800s because of the healing powers credited to the water.

This is a place to gain a sense of the region's history. Chyrchel said the University of Arkansas conducted an archeological dig around Blue Spring that produced artifacts estimated to date back to 8,000 B.C.

In more recent history, Native Americans from the Osage and Cherokee tribes called this a neutral ground and would not fight here. Drawings on the rock bluffs nearby are said to chronicle Native American occupation from 1541 to 1881.

If you visit Blue Spring, you'll only be doing what's been natural for thousands of years.

Thirty-eight million gallons of 54-degree water flow from Blue Spring every day, adding to the character of White River.

Skip Halterman's love of fly fishing has led him to a career in the sport, as both an instructor and an inventor.

Halterman Simply Following His Bliss

"I thought, 'What do you want to do?' The answer was - fish."

The late Joseph Campbell, a teacher and mythology expert, had one simple message for all his students: "Follow your bliss. Find where it is, and don't be afraid to follow it."

Skip Halterman was pursuing a medical career when he saw the PBS television series of interviews with Campbell by Bill Moyers. Halterman had earned an undergraduate degree at Southwest Missouri State University before getting a master's degree in pathology from the Missouri School of Medicine at Columbia.

But Halterman wasn't finding much bliss in the field of medicine or anything else he tried. And he couldn't

get Campbell's message out of his head.

"I thought, 'What do you want to do?'" Halterman said. "The answer was - fish. I'm better qualified to fish than anything else. I've spent more time doing that than any other activity."

Halterman lived in Aurora, Missouri, until he was eight years old. Then his dad bought the Campbell Point Boat Dock on Table Rock Lake. His youth was one long fishing story.

"I think I was a fisherman from the day I was born," Halterman said. "But my grandfather was the main catalyst for it. We never missed a weekend from the time I was eight or nine until I was 16 years old."

Fly fishing was Halterman's particular interest in the sport. He started fly fishing for bluegill with popping bugs at the age of 15.

"I cut my teeth on bass fishing," Halterman said. "But to me, bass fishing (with casting and spinning tackle) is more of a science. Fly fishing is more of an art form. I'm fascinated by it. The principle has remained the same for hundreds of years. It is the same as it was when Izaak Walton wrote 'The Compleat Angler' (in 1653)."

With encouragement from his wife, Ruth, Halterman opened the White River School of Fly Fishing in October 1989. It is housed in the same building where Ruth's "A Sure Sign Company" is located, on Highway 23 in Eureka Springs.

"I realized there were no Midwestern fly fishing schools, and we have some great year-round fishing in this area," Halterman said.

But Halterman's decision to follow his bliss grew into something much bigger than just a fly fishing school. Halterman also has a background in hydrology. He is an outspoken environmentalist, who may well be the loudest voice of concern for the future of the White River and other Ozark streams. And Halterman is an inventor. His most successful creation is "Skip's Original Turn-On Strike Indicator," first marketed in 1992 and now being sold in fly fishing shops all over the world.

Just like the decision to dedicate his life to fishing, the idea for the strike indicator came from that "follow your bliss" philosophy.

"In April 1991, I was fishing the lower section of Roaring River (in Missouri)," Halterman said. "There are some wild fish there, and it's one of those one-fish, one-cast situations. You don't get many shots. There was a rainbow (trout) below an undercut bank. About the only way to fish it was with a strike indicator."

Halterman slipped one of the traditional "corky" strike indicators on his line, then tied on another fly. He didn't catch the fish. Rather than remove the fly from his line to remove the strike indicator, Halterman broke the indicator in two pieces and stuck them in his pocket. As he was driving back to Eureka Springs that day, he placed the pieces of the broken strike indicator on his dashboard.

"It was just one of those things that flew into my brain," Halterman said. "I put those pieces out there and I could see the whole thing. I was excited as hell when I got back to the shop."

He was so excited that he sat down at one of the band saws used in Ruth's sign-making business and made a prototype of what would be the Turn-On Strike Indicator.

Today, the strike indicator comes in several sizes of high-density polystyrene. The fluorescent yellow and orange indicators are highly visible. But the key feature is their ease of use. A rubber band linking two polystyrene pieces allows you to place and remove an indicator with ease and without removing the fly from your line.

Halterman's invention is somewhat of a variation on an old concept - the rubber-core sinker. But it is different, and Halterman's strike indicator is patented.

In addition to the strike indicator, Halterman has produced a fly fishing reel and written a book, "What Fly Should I Fish Today?" Halterman markets those items and others under the name "Skip's Specialties for the Angler."

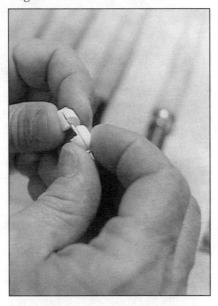

The idea for Skip's Turn-On Strike Indicator came to Halterman after a day of fly fishing at Roaring River.

Halterman continues to teach fly fishing and fly tying lessons at his school and he also continues to guide. But he hopes his future is with new products in the fly fishing business.

"My ambition is not to be a full blown manufacturing executive," Halterman said. "I want to continue to build new products. The fact is, when you are doing something you really, really love to do, ideas fly out so fast you can't do them all."

Skip Offers Tips For Fly Fishing Beaver Tailwater

Skip Halterman, owner of the the White River School of Fly Fishing in Eureka Springs, doesn't live on the White River, but he's so close he can hear the horn blow at Beaver Dam when power generation is about to begin. And he's close enough to take a fly fishing trip to the Beaver Tailwater whenever the urge hits him.

"This isn't the best fishing on the White River," Halterman said, "but it's a place where you know there will always be some fish."

Halterman says three basic patterns are best on the Beaver Tailwater - 1) Woolly Bugger, 2) Sparrow, 3) soft hackles, especially the Partridge and Quill.

"An olive-green, size 10 Woolly Bugger with some Krystal Flash is the standard," said Halterman. "It would be No. 1. But I don't fish Woolly Buggers as much as I do the two other flies.

"The Sparrow is best in sizes 12 to 14, and it should be weighted enough so that no split shot is needed. You can use it with or without a strike indicator.

"The soft hackles should be in sizes 16 to 20. I think the reason why they work so well is because they are so life-like in the water. Sometimes the fish won't take a dry fly, but they will hit something just under the surface."

Halterman particularly likes soft hackle flies, on any of the Ozark tailwaters. In fact, on a strictly personal fishing preference, the soft hackle is Halterman's favorite. He ties them light, so they won't sink more than an inch. When trout are reluctant to come to the surface, which is often, they will hit something fished in the film.

Halterman thinks trout will rise from depths of 8 to 10 feet to hit a soft hackle. When they do, they immediately go back down after taking the fly, resulting in a hard strike.

"You want to fish it in a way to

absorb the shock," Halterman said. "Don't point your rod at the fly when you strike. If you do that, you'll either snap off or the fish will miss it. Keep the rod straight across the stream. The fish will take the fly, spin and go. Once it makes the turn, it's easy to strike them and get a hookup in the corner of the jaw."

Halterman ties them in sizes 12 to 16, with the 16s usually reserved for smaller streams, like Roaring River.

> "Keep the rod straight across the stream (when fishing a soft hackle). The fish will take the fly, spin and go. Once it makes the turn, it's easy to strike them and get a hookup in the corner of the jaw."

There is a midge hatch almost 365 days a year in the Beaver Tailwater, according to Halterman. A midge imitation in the size 20 to 24 range is best.

There are occasional mayfly hatches here. Halterman has noticed in recent years that if the wind is right, a mayfly hatch in Beaver Lake blows over the dam into the tailwater.

Halterman doesn't enjoy nymph fishing here.

"I don't care anything about fishing nymphs in this water because it is so slow," Halterman said.

Scuds and sowbugs make up a valuable food source in the Beaver Tailwater and shouldn't be ignored by anglers who like to fish nymphs. However, you might find, like Halterman has, that soft hackle patterns, like the Partridge and Quill will provide just as many strikes and a lot more fun.

Partridge and Quill

Hook: Tiemco 100, sizes 12 to 16
Thread: Gray or black
Body: Peacock herl
Thorax: Hare's mask-type fur blend
Hackle: Gray partridge

Soft hackle patterns, distinguished by their lack of wing or tail, date back more than five centuries. They are versatile, imitating a variety of trout foods and accommodating a wide range of trout fishers, from the beginner to the veteran.

"Nothing is any easier to tie and looks buggier," Skip Halterman says.

Halterman prefers a 1X dry fly hook. If you use a heavier wire hook, it takes the fly down faster. Halterman fishes this pattern just under the surface, thus the fine, light hook.

The peacock herl must be stripped down to the quill. You are trying to imitate an insect body.

When the bare quill is wound around the hook, that's exactly what it looks like - a segmented insect body. Give it a heavy coating of cement to protect the fragile quill.

The thorax must be a tight, round ball, so it will hold the hackle fibers out and keep them from being plastered against the hook.

Halterman prefers lighter-colored partridge feathers. He makes two turns with the feather. Emphasis is on keeping the hackle sparse. The hackle length should extend to the back of the hook.

Simple Sow

Hook: Tiemco 2487, Orvis 1639 or Mustad AC 80200 BR, sizes 14 to 20
Thread: Gray 8/0
Body: Gray Antron or muskrat
Back: Peacock herl

Unlike Skip Halterman, who doesn't care for nymph fishing in the Beaver Tailwater, that's 95 percent of what Bill Tenison does. Tenison agrees with Halterman that the Woolly Bugger is No. 1 here. However, Tenison concentrates on nymphs like sowbugs, scuds (sizes 14 to 16), Pheasant Tails (12 to 16), Gold-Ribbed Hare's Ears (12 to 16) and Serendipities (16 to 20) when fishing the Beaver Tailwater.

And there is one nymph that Tenison tries first. It's sort of a sow-bug-scud combination called the Simple Sow.

"It's not flattened like a sowbug, and it's tied on a scud hook, so you get that silhouette," Tenison said. "It's so skinny, it doesn't look real pretty to us, but the fish like it."

Tenison manages Bancroft & Tabor clothing and gift store on Dickson Street in Fayetteville. Bancroft & Tabor is also a full-line Orvis dealership; one-fourth of the store is made up of fly-fishing equipment and supplies. Tenison is the resident fly fishing expert.

Typically, Tenison will fish a Simple Sow under a strike indicator on a dead drift. He'll have 6 feet of leader between the fly and the indicator and a split shot 12 to 18 inches above the fly.

The usual sizes are 14 and 16, but Tenison will tie Simple Sows as small as No. 20. He thinks its more of a midge imitation at that size. When trout are taking midge emergers, Tenison tries a size 18 or 20 Simple Sow. He leaves off the split shot, greases his leader and fishes the Simple Sow in the film.

Carolina Rigs, Crankbaits Give Anglers Versatility

When fishing any of the White River System tailwaters, you need to be prepared for both high-water and low-water conditions. Some anglers using spinning gear prefer high water, as the added current tends to place the trout near certain structure and the fish aren't as wary as they are during low water. The following methods are favored by these Beaver Tailwater anglers.

The Carolina Rig: John "J.R." Robie began managing Spider Creek Resort since 1989. Since then, he's taught many people how to trout fish in the Beaver Tailwater. Robie at one time was an avid bass tournament fisherman, so it's natural that he would prefer a Carolina rig for trout. The Carolina rig has been one of the most popular methods of catching bass on the pro circuit for several years.

"For somebody who has never trout fished before, this is the easiest method to teach them," Robie said.

To make a Carolina rig, thread a 1/4-ounce slip sinker, then a glass or plastic bead on your line, and tie the line to a barrel or snap swivel. The main line can be anything from 10- to 4-pound-test. Now take a 2- to 3-foot section of 2-pound-test line and attach one end of it to the other end of the swivel and the other end of it to a No. 12 hook.

Robie prefers a snap swivel because he carries a package of snelled 2-pound-test leaders attached to chemically-sharpened Gamakatsu hooks. If he gets hung up, it's easy to break off the leader and attach a new one. That's also another reason you want to use a heavier main line than your leader. In addition to the fact that trout aren't as wary of 2-pound-test leader, if you do get snagged and have to break off, the break will usually take place in the leader, therefore, you won't lose the slip sinker, bead and swivel.

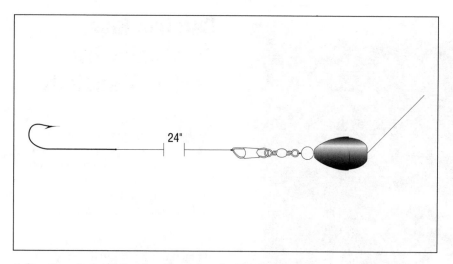

24"

A Carolina rig consists of a slip sinker, bead, snap swivel, leader and hook.

You can use any of the usual trout baits on a Carolina rig - red worms, nightcrawlers, waxworms, corn, salmon eggs and the various colors of Berkley Power Bait and Power Eggs.

Another key with this rig is to float the bait off the bottom. One of the easiest ways to do this is to thread a miniature marshmallow on the hook before putting on the bait. The marshmallow acts as a float and doesn't seem to scare off the fish.

This Carolina rig can be used in low-water and high-water conditions. Use a smaller slip sinker when the power generators aren't running.

When the generators are running, a Carolina rig can be used from the bank or a boat to fish eddies and deep holes, or it can be used from a boat as a drift-fishing rig.

By drifting downstream with the current and letting the slip sinker bounce along the bottom, you can put your bait near gravel bar dropoffs and other structure, where the trout are holding.

Crankbaits: Like the Carolina rig, crankbaits give the angler opportunities in high-water and low-water situations. Some of the more popular crankbaits for trout fishing include Rapalas, in both floating and "Countdown" or sinking styles, Rattlin' Rogues and the various styles of Norman and Rebel lures. Most of these represent minnows and other baitfish. (Long, thin crankbaits are also referred to as "stickbaits" or "jerkbaits.") Crawfish and grasshopper or cricket crankbait imitations will catch trout, too.

Generally, you want to fish a smaller lure in low-water conditions and a bigger lure in high-water conditions.

One of Robie's favorite methods for fishing high water and catching big trout is to use floating Rapalas in the No. 9 and No. 11 sizes. These slim-profile, minnow-type lures are 3 1/2- and 4 3/8-inches long, respectively.

Robie likes to fish eddies with these lures. He casts so his lure will be retrieved against the current. By twitching the lure forward, then letting it sit motionless and drift backward, Robie can keep working the lure in an eddy for as long as he wants without retrieving it and making another cast.

"I think any kind of a shad-like bait will work," Robie said. "The key is keeping it in the eddy. If there's a big brown in there, it will usually get mad at the bait after awhile and come hit it."

When using crankbaits like this, you can look for the same targets a bass angler would - logs, rocks, cut banks - anything that offers the trout protection from the current and a steady flow of food nearby.

Big brown trout feed almost like bass - finding an ambush spot out of the main current and waiting until a meal swims by. The longer you can keep your lure in these "strike zones" the better chance you'll have of catching a fish.

James and Howard Smith prefer a different method for fishing crankbaits in high water. When the power generators start, the Smiths put away their Micro Jigs, switch spools on their spinning reels to 4- or 6-pound-test line, then tie on Countdown Rapalas. But rather than a larger lure, they prefer the No. 5 and No. 7 sizes that are 2 and 2 3/4 inches long, respectively, in either silver-and-black or gold-and-black color patterns.

If they had to pick one Countdown Rapala, it would be the 2-inch silver-and-black model. It most closely resembles the threadfin shad that come from Beaver Lake through the turbines at the dam. Threadfin shad are a favorite food of all trout, but especially brown trout.

Knowing the river bed and keeping the boat in proper position are keys to drift-fishing Countdown Rapalas. Bumping any kind of wood structure, like a log or root wad, with a treble-hooked lure in fast current usually means that you won't get the lure back.

Howard and James concentrate on gravel bar dropoffs. Trout prefer dropoffs because they can stay out of the main current, but still make quick dashes into it to grab food that is drifting by. If there are no big rocks or wood structure at the top of the dropoff, a small crankbait can bounce over the top of the gravel without hanging up.

When the Smiths get to an area where they know there's a gravel bar dropoff, they'll motor 25 to 50 yards above it before cutting the motor and beginning a drift.

Then they'll cast Countdown Rapalas upstream about 25 feet and keep a tight line until they can feel the lure bumping bottom. After feeling a dozen or so bumps on the bottom, they begin a slow retrieve. Then the process is repeated - cast, bump, slow retrieve.

When a trout hits this lure in current, there is no hook-setting needed. Just keep a tight line and play the fish to the boat.

Walleye, White Bass Mingle With Trout

Fish from Table Rock Lake come to Beaver Tailwater during spawn

Walleye and white bass take some of the attention away from trout during the late winter and spring spawning runs. Both species come from Table Rock Lake and congregate in the White River below Beaver Dam.

Beginning in February, walleye in the 3- to 6-pound range are common. Most will be found from the Highway 62 bridge down to the town of Beaver, but some will be found all the way to Beaver Dam.

March is usually the peak month for walleye fishing, but, because of the cold water releases from Beaver Dam, water temperatures rise slowly in the spring and spawning activity tends to be spread out over several months.

The same is true for white bass. If spring rainfall is plentiful and extended periods of power generation keep water temperatures low, the white bass spawning run can extend into June. April and May are usually the peak months.

The best white bass fishing is found in the mouths of creeks in the Holiday Island area. Leatherwood Creek and Butler Creek are popular spots.

The overall size of white bass from Table Rock Lake is outstanding - 3-pound white bass are common.

White bass tackle tends to be simple - spinning gear, 6- or 8-pound-test line and plenty of jigs. White is the best jig color, but chartreuse, yellow and gray work well at times, too. The best sizes are 1/8th- and 1/16th-ounce.

Live-bait anglers prefer crawfish, usually the smaller the better.

Fly fishers can take advantage of the white bass run, too. Good fly choices include any type of shad- or minnow-imitating streamer in sizes 6 through 10.

Walleye anglers here tend to go with either live bait, like minnows and nightcrawlers, or deep-running crankbaits, like Rapalas, Rogues and Wally Divers.

James Smith holds a 4-pound walleye caught on a Countdown Rapala.

Stripers and hybrids: The high-water spring of 1990 was a bad one as far as the Beaver Tailwater trout fishery was concerned. The floodgates were opened at Beaver Dam for one of the few times in history, and they stayed open for 10 days.

This not only sent a stream bed-gouging current down the White River, but it also dumped striped bass and hybrid stripers from Beaver Lake into the tailwater.

Trout are a favorite food of stripers and hybrids. The Arkansas Game and Fish Commission made an effort to remove as many of these fish as possible. Using electrofishing equipment during the summer of 1990, trout biologist Jim Spotts documented the removal of almost 400 of these fish, which were mostly hybrids in the 8- to 12-pound range. Most were transferred via hatchery truck back to Beaver Lake.

Spotts took stomach samples of 25 hybrids and found that 30 percent contained trout remains.

Anglers caught several stripers and hybrids in the Beaver Tailwater over the next two years. During the summer of 1994, AGFC electrofishing samples removed stripers weighing 50 and 40 pounds from the Beaver Tailwater.

The Missouri Department of Conservation doesn't stock stripers or hybrids in Table Rock Lake. However, it is quite likely that a few survivors of that spill through the floodgates from Beaver Lake in 1990 are still lurking in the lower sections of the Beaver Tailwater and in Table Rock Lake.

In 1990, AGFC trout biologist Jim Spotts removed almost 400 hybrid striped bass and stripers.

Highlights Of Trip Down Beaver Tailwater

("Left" and "right" directions assume the angler is facing downstream.)

The Beaver Tailwater has the highest ratio of public access per river mile of tailwaters in the White River System. This is due mostly to the size of the U.S. Army Corps of Engineers-operated **Dam Site Park**. As you go down the river, almost the entire left-hand side from the dam to Spider Creek is part of Dam Site Park.

Just below the powerhouse on the north side of Beaver Dam, there is an overflow camping area and a large gravel parking lot. Along the river, a rip-rap covered point serves as popular fishing spot at all water levels.

The same road that leads to the gravel parking lot, also turns downstream and ends at a paved parking lot and boat launching ramp. The concrete boat ramp was extended in 1993, so launching is possible at low water levels on the wide gravel bar. The gravel bar extends a quarter-mile downstream. Boulders in the stream bed on the opposite bank provide good habitat and make this a popular place for bank- and wade-fishers.

Dam Site Park camping areas C and D provide public access down to **Crane Roost Bluff**. The area between the two camp sites features a fish-holding pool above another long gravel bar.

The catch-and-release area established in January 1995 begins in campsite C and extends one mile to 100 yards above Parker Bend.

At Crane Roost Bluff, the river starts to bend right; the left side becomes the steep bank, leading up to Crane Roost Bluff, and the gravel bars shift to the right bank. Near **Dam Site Park Camping Area D**, the left bank is lined with cane, and this is often referred to as the "**Cane Brake Hole.**" Bank-fishing is popular here, as this is the deepest hole in the first section of the Beaver Tailwater and holds good numbers of trout, especially at low water levels.

There is another, even deeper hole just downstream, sometimes called the "Horseshoe Hole." **Crane Roost Bluff** overlooks it on the left side, and the right bank is privately owned, making this area accessible only by boat.

Dam Site Park borders the river again at **Parker Bend** (also called **Parker Flat**), one of the most popular spots for waders and bank fishers on the Beaver Tailwater. Its features include a wide, flat area above a sharp bend in the river, then a riffle and deep pool as the river makes a northwesterly turn. The upper section usually includes some tree root wads and a small, mud and sand island on the right side. These features are remodeled at times by heavy water releases from Beaver Dam.

Dick's Creek enters the White River on the right side, just below the island. The left bank is a gravel bar. During high water, the sharp river bend forms a fish-holding eddy on the back side of the gravel bar.

Adding to the beauty at Parker Bend is **Wallace Bluff**, located on the opposite bank. It extends down the river to **Clayborn Creek**, which enters at the lower end of **Camping Area E**, on the opposite, or right-hand bank. There is good fishing both above and in a short riffle near the mouth of Clayborn Creek. An old concrete bridge piling on the left-hand side marks this spot.

A long, relatively straight pool marks the river down to Spider Creek. There is some good habitat here, mostly along the right-hand side, in the form of submerged boulders. At one time, Clayborn Creek formed a long, narrow island down the right bank. That is now only a slough, but it serves as a refuge point for trout during high flows and is accessible only by boat.

The Arkansas Game and Fish Commission built **Bertrand Ramp** access point in 1994, on the left bank. Just past it, Spider Creek enters the White River on the left. It is marked by a large, gravel parking lot that is part of the privately-owned access area at **Spider Creek Resort**. At high water, a large eddy forms at the mouth of Spider Creek. During low water, anglers can wade to an island just downstream. There are riffles at the head of the island and down the left-hand side. The main river channel goes right of the island.

The next 4 miles of the Beaver Tailwater are accessible only by boat. Privately-owned land lines both sides of the river. Except when Table Rock Lake is extremely low, the water depth here is more suited to boaters anyway. The concrete pilings from the **old Highway 62 bridge** rise from the river bed here.

The **Highway 62 bridge** is 4.5 miles downstream from the dam. **Riverview Resort** is located on the right side of the bridge. Deep water marks this section of the river.

Houseman Access is considered the end of the Beaver trout water, as far as the AGFC is concerned. The AGFC-built boat launching ramp here is also a trout stocking site, so you'll find trout several miles downstream, especially during winter months. **White River Oaks Bed and Breakfast** and **Ferguson's on the River** are located just downstream from Houseman Access.

Blue Spring flows into the White River on the opposite (right) bank. The mouth of Blue Spring holds good numbers of fish - everything from trout to bass - and is accessible only by boat. **Charlie's Cabins** resort is just downstream, on the left.

It's about 5 miles from here to the **town of Beaver** (pop. 81), which is located on the left bank at the Highway 187 bridge crossing. A city park on the river includes a public boat ramp and swimming area. Just before you get to Beaver, **Butler Creek** enters the White River on the left.

Past the town of Beaver, the right-hand bank is the resort community of **Holiday Island.**

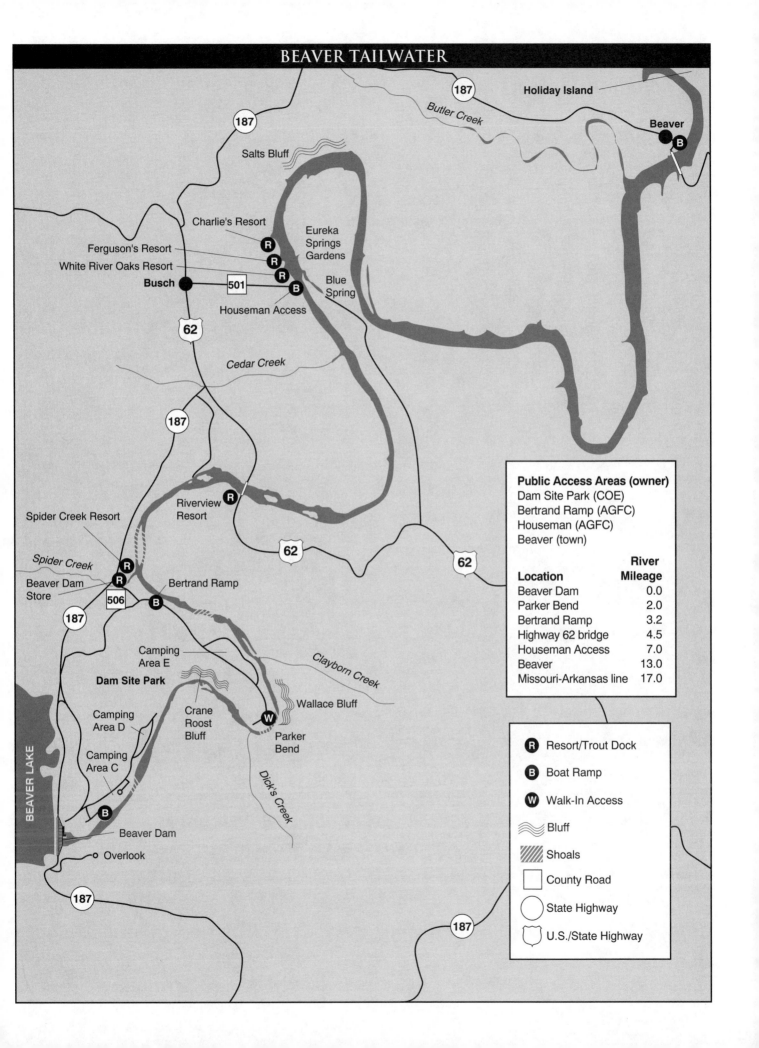

BEAVER TAILWATER

187

Holiday Island

Butler Creek

187

Beaver

B

Salts Bluff

Charlie's Resort

R

Eureka
Springs
Gardens

Ferguson's Resort

R

White River Oaks Resort

R

Blue
Spring

Busch

501

B

Houseman Access

62

Cedar Creek

187

Riverview
Resort

R

62

62

Spider Creek Resort

Spider Creek

R

Beaver Dam
Store

R

506

Bertrand Ramp

B

187

Camping
Area E

Dam Site Park

Clayborn Creek

Camping
Area D

Crane
Roost
Bluff

Wallace Bluff

Camping
Area C

W

Parker
Bend

B

Beaver Dam

Dick's Creek

BEAVER LAKE

Overlook

187

187

Public Access Areas (owner)
Dam Site Park (COE)
Bertrand Ramp (AGFC)
Houseman (AGFC)
Beaver (town)

Location	River Mileage
Beaver Dam	0.0
Parker Bend	2.0
Bertrand Ramp	3.2
Highway 62 bridge	4.5
Houseman Access	7.0
Beaver	13.0
Missouri-Arkansas line	17.0

R Resort/Trout Dock

B Boat Ramp

W Walk-In Access

≈ Bluff

Shoals

County Road

State Highway

U.S./State Highway

WHITE RIVER

TABLE ROCK TAILWATER

Lake Taneycomo - Trout Fishery On A Comeback

In terms of trout stocked per mile, no other fishery in the White River System comes close to that of Lake Taneycomo. In 1993, 760,000 trout were stocked in the 22 miles between Table Rock and Ozark Beach dams. The stocking numbers have been as high as 1.6 million in 1984.

This high volume program, made possible by the Missouri Department of Conservation's nearby Shepherd of the Hills Hatchery, has made for some easy fishing. That, generally, is the reputation here.

For many people, Lake Taneycomo trout fishing is just another Branson tourist experience - see a music show on "The Strip" that is Highway 76 Country Boulevard, take a boat ride and catch a trout on Lake Taneycomo. There's a Coney Island atmosphere to Lake Taneycomo near downtown Branson, where you're likely to see a mock battle with a pirate ship.

But to portray that as the Table Rock Tailwater trout fishing experi-

◀ **The Shepherd of the Hills Hatchery outlet just below Table Rock Dam is a popular place for anglers.**

Lake Taneycomo and Table Rock Dam, as seen from an overlook along Highway 165.

ence would be to sell this fishery way short. Despite the fact that Branson attracts over five million tourists a year, the upper and lower stretches of Lake Taneycomo still offer some soli-

tude. And the trout fishery is much like that of the others in the White River System. It is characterized by large numbers of stocker-size rainbow trout and a few trophy-size browns.

"It's easy fishing," said Missouri Department of Conservation fisheries research biologist Spencer E. Turner. "That's both the problem and the attraction. Taneycomo has the potential to produce a world record brown trout in the next 20 years, but there are not many rainbows over 12 to 14 inches right now. The question is, 'How do we keep them in there long enough to grow?'"

In many ways, the Table Rock Dam Tailwater is a peek at the future of the other trout fisheries in the White River System. As more and more people discover the Ozarks, the other tailwater trout fisheries are likely to experience the same ups and downs that are already part of history here.

"Why don't you just stock more trout?" That is the most common suggestion given to solve any and all problems in these White River System tailwaters. Because the trout fisheries are so dependent on hatchery stockings

TABLE ROCK TAILWATER AT A GLANCE

Location: Between Table Rock Dam and Ozark Beach Dam on the White River. The Missouri towns of Branson and Hollister are separated by Lake Taneycomo and connected by the Highway 65 bridge eight miles downstream from Table Rock Dam. The communities of Point Lookout, Rockaway Beach and Forsyth are also located on Lake Taneycomo.

Highway Miles to Table Rock Dam:

Little Rock, Ark.	177
Memphis, Tenn.	313
Tulsa, Okla.	250
St. Louis, Mo.	252
Kansas City, Mo.	206
Dallas, Texas	483
Shreveport, La.	382
Chicago, Ill.	562

Length: 22 miles, from Table Rock Dam to Ozark Beach Dam. Most of the trout fishing takes place in the first 10 miles, from Table Rock Dam to Branson. Although water surface temperatures in the lower section warm past the comfort zone for trout in the summer, the presence of Ozark Beach Dam prevents any upstream movements of warm water from Bull Shoals Lake. Therefore, a sub-surface stream of cool water moves through the lake and good numbers of trout will be found throughout the length of it.

Dams: Lake Taneycomo was formed with the completion of Powersite Dam in 1913. Now named Ozark Beach Dam, it was said to be the largest impoundment for production of electric power in the U.S. With the completion of Table Rock Dam in 1958, Lake Taneycomo became a coldwater fishery. Table Rock Dam has four hydroelectric power generation units. The project cost approximately $65.4 million. Lake Taneycomo is 2,080 acres, while Table Rock Lake is 43,100 acres (at the power pool level of 915 feet).

Trout stocking: Shepherd of the Hills Hatchery is located just below Table Rock Dam. It is the largest hatchery operated by the Missouri Conservation Department. Hatchery stockings of trout into Lake Taneycomo have ranged from 1.6 million in 1984 to 760,000 in 1994. (Studies are underway now to determine the optimum number of trout for the lake, based on fishing pressure and forage base.) Most of the trout released are 10-inch-plus rainbows. Only 10,000 brown trout per year are stocked. Steelhead were stocked as late as 1975, but not since then.

Power Generation: For present conditions, call 417-336-5083. For a 24-hour forecast, call the Southwestern Power Administration recorded message center at 918-581-6845 and press #13 for Table Rock Dam.

Trout Regulations: Daily limit is 5. Only 1 brown trout may be possessed, and it must be at least 20 inches long.

Scenic Views: Highway 165 goes south over Table Rock Dam, then east along the south side of Lake Taneycomo. There is an overlook on the south side of Table Rock Dam, just off Highway 165 in Table Rock State Park, and another overlook off Highway 165 just across Lake Taneycomo from Point Royale, about two miles downstream from the dam.

Historical Note: The first signs of the tourism boom that now draws over five million visitors a year to Branson can be traced back to Harold Bell Wright's novel "The Shepherd of the Hills." After the book was published in 1907, it became a bestseller and tourists began coming to the Ozarks to see the land and the people described in Wright's book.

rather than natural reproduction, that would seem to be a logical solution. But, as Lake Taneycomo has proven, maintaining a quality fishery while fishing pressure increases exponentially is a complex process.

Simply stocking more trout isn't the answer. In fact, the stocking rate in Lake Taneycomo has been reduced from that 1984 high of 1.6 million to 750,000, while studies are done to determine the optimum stocking rate.

Because it has a dam 22 miles downstream on its lower end, the Table Rock Tailwater doesn't have a wealth of wading and fly fishing opportunities. You are dealing with a lake here, not a river. That makes it unique among the five tailwaters in the White River System.

Although hydropower generation from the four units in Table Rock Dam causes rapid fluctuations in water flow, those effects decrease quickly as you move downstream. Ozark Beach Dam creates a stable waterway on most of Lake Taneycomo. Navigating shallow shoals isn't a significant factor in Lake Taneycomo fishing, so you'll see a wide variety of watercraft, everything from party barges to johnboats.

The first 3 1/4 miles, from Table Rock Dam to Fall Creek, are typical of the other White River System tailwaters. Table Rock State Park offers plenty of public access for waders and bank anglers.

Fly fishing is concentrated in this area. And there is a dedicated group of fly fishers here. You'll find them at all hours of the day and night, especially the night.

Nighttime fly fishing has several attractions. Power generation is usually limited to daytime hours, so water conditions are good. The nocturnal nature of brown trout makes this the best time to catch trophy-size browns. Few other anglers brave the darkness of night.

Finally, with the Table Rock Tailwater so close to Branson, a few hours of night fishing here is as convenient as taking in an evening movie or an early morning jog.

Rainbow trout make up the bulk of the trout stocked, but brown trout have grabbed all the headlines at Lake Taneycomo in recent years, just as they have in the other four White River System tailwaters. But the brown trout news is even bigger here because browns weren't stocked in Taneycomo until 1980.

(Browns got an added boost at Lake Taneycomo when the Missouri Department of Conservation instituted a 20-inch minimum length limit in 1985. The Table Rock Tailwater was the first in the White River System to have a length limit regulation.)

During low water flow periods, it is in this first stretch of Lake Taneycomo where you can do some daytime sight fishing for browns.

Shepherd of the Hills Hatchery makes this area even more attractive to brown trout. Brood stock browns aren't kept in the hatchery, but are gathered each fall during the spawning run as they congregate near the hatchery outlets.

As you move farther down the lake, past Table Rock State Park, commercial operations and private homes line the banks. This is both the good news and the bad news.

Lodging, bank fishing and boating opportunities are almost endless. If you want a lakeside cabin, a fishing boat or just a place to cast a line and prop a pole, you'll find it.

But it is all this development that worries environmentalists about the future of the lake. Some say that water clarity has diminished in recent years. Studies are underway to scientifically document any change.

Trout, therefore, may become even more important in the future of the Table Rock Tailwater. Because of their need for clean, cool water, trout are the "canary in the coal mine," acting as the barometer of Lake Taneycomo water quality.

That, ultimately, will be the key to the White River System - finding a balance to all the conflicting pulls found in real estate development and trout fishing. As the oldest man-made lake in the Ozarks, and the one that has seen the most changes, Lake Taneycomo may hold the answers.

Lake Taneycomo Trout Subject Of Tagging, Other Studies

From March 1991 through June 1994, the Missouri brown trout record was broken twice at Lake Taneycomo - first with Marty Babusa's 23-pound, 4-ounce lunker, then with Kevin Elfrink's 24-pound, 15-ounce brown. In between, Missouri Department of Conservation fisheries biologists electroshocked and released a 36-inch brown trout in Taneycomo.

These don't sound like stories from a fishery in decline. And, in fact, Lake Taneycomo may be on an upswing. But there is no doubt that this trout fishery has experienced some lean years in comparison to its early glory.

Just like on all of the White River Basin trout fisheries, overall size of rainbow trout has declined, mostly because of fishing pressure.

"In 1969, I could count six or seven stringers a day - five fish stringers - that weighed over 35 pounds," said Gordon Proctor, the Shepherd of the Hills Hatchery manager.

A new state record 16-pound, 12-ounce rainbow trout was caught in December 1984. (Roaring River State Park later produced a new record rainbow of 16-13.) It was shortly after this when a still-unexplained loss of scuds (also called freshwater shrimp), sent the fishery into a decline.

"The forage base took a real nose-dive about 1987," said Bill Anderson, an MDC fisheries management biologist. "It declined about 90 percent and we don't know why."

Possible causes for the scud decline include: poor water quality as a result of all the development taking place around the lake; an increase in the number of white suckers, which may compete with the trout for food; and overstocking trout.

MDC fisheries research biologist Mike Kruse began a five-year study on Taneycomo in 1992 that is expected to answer many questions about the trout fishery. One of the areas Kruse is looking at is growth rates, and early results showed that Taneycomo still

has trophy-growing potential. Kruse said a 1968 study determined that trout grew an average of 7/10ths of an inch per month in Taneycomo. Kruse marked and recaptured trout that grew anywhere from 4/10ths of an inch to one-inch per month during the spring of 1993.

One trout grew just over two inches in a 65-day period. But those numbers won't be scientifically significant until they are documented over the length of the study.

Anglers should watch for rainbow trout that have been tagged for use in this study. Rewards ranging from $5 to $100 are offered for the returned tags.

In addition to the positive signs in growth rates, there are also some signs that the scud population is rebounding, according to MDC biologists.

Of the invertebrates found in Lake Taneycomo, amphipods (scuds) are more important as a trout food source than isopods (sowbugs) because of their higher protein content.

The most commonly found member of the scud family in Lake Taneycomo is the gammarus. It is about twice the size of another scud found in the White River System, the hyalella.

"Gammarus are probably the perfect trout food," said Kruse. "The White River System is fortunate to have good production of gammarus."

These initial observations about scuds and growth rates will be proven or disproven by data collected in the next few years. (At least three other studies are looking at various aspects of the Lake Taneycomo trout fishery.)

After enough information has been gathered to document the status of scuds, other trout forage and the overall condition of the fishery at Taneycomo, the MDC may take a look at adding length limit regulations that could improve the size of the average rainbow trout in the lake.

Vincent Realizes Dream As Fishing Guide

Fine-tuning nightcrawler technique allows him to guarantee a limit

When he was growing up in Mead, Kansas, classroom windows had an adverse effect on Charlie Vincent's studies.

"I'd be sitting there in the schoolhouse, looking out the window," Vincent said. "And I'd just get up and walk out. That didn't go over too well with the teachers."

It was the outdoors that pulled Vincent from the classroom. The urge to hunt and fish was stronger than any other in his life.

That interest in the outdoors never waned. In 1986, Vincent started studying Lake Taneycomo trout every day. He and his wife, Dee, moved here from Garden City, Kansas, after Vincent retired as a night shift manager at an animal feed mill.

Charlie's retirement consisted of 339 working days in 1992 and 341 in 1993. But he's working as a fishing guide, and to Vincent that's just not work.

"I guarantee a limit of fish," Vincent said. "In seven years I've only had three trips where we didn't catch a limit, and all three were because of the weather."

Vincent's specialty is fishing with nightcrawlers. Long-time Lake Taneycomo angler Floyd Shook is said to have caught 183 trout weighing 6 pounds or more during 1980, the one year when he kept a tally.

"He looked like an old blue heron, the way he sat on the front of his boat with a rod in his hand," Vincent said. "He was strictly a nightcrawler fisherman. That's where I picked up the technique. I caught more trout after instructions from Floyd Shook than I ever did before."

Vincent uses what is sometimes called a "Taneycomo rig," - 6-pound-test line attached to a snap swivel that has a 12-inch dropper line connected to a quarter-ounce bell sinker, plus a 2 1/2- to 3-foot leader line connected to a No. 8 hook. This is the rig used by most Lake Taneycomo anglers for fish-

Nightcrawlers are Charlie Vincent's trout bait of choice. But he says that knowing where to fish at various current levels is more important than the bait.

ing everything from nightcrawlers to corn to Berkley Power Bait. It's similar to the other drift rigs used on these White River System tailwaters.

Vincent usually prefers 4-pound-test line on the leader, but will drop down to 2-pound-test when the fishing gets tough. And he knows some

anglers who claim they have coaxed unwilling trout to bite after dropping even further down, to 1-pound-test line.

One secret to Vincent's technique is tearing a worm in two pieces. He uses about half a nightcrawler, and only the top half. He pinches it in two about 1 to 1 1/2 inches below the band around the worm, then inserts the hook about a quarter-inch from the tip.

"If you use any more than that, the trout will just steal it," Vincent said. "A trout starts at the end and nibbles its way up. It won't take a whole night-crawler, like a bass will, with the exception of a big brown trout, which will take a big bait at once.

"Usually you've got to give trout time to eat a nightcrawler. That's where most people make a mistake. They try to set the hook too soon. You've got to give them time."

However, you don't want to give them too much time, or the trout will swallow the hook. Over the years, Vincent has developed a feel for when to start reeling. After digging through the bedding in a box of worms, he sets the rods down across the seats in his Tracker aluminum boat - one pole sticking out each side.

He is particular about his rods and reels. The drag system on a reel is the key element.

"When you get a big trout on, it's very important to have a good drag system," Vincent said. To demonstrate that, Vincent occasionally fishes for carp off the Branson Trout Dock. He has landed a 29-pounder on 4-pound-test line. The drag system on his reel (he prefers Shimano) did most of the work in a fight lasting almost an hour.

Vincent prefers a medium action rod at least 6 feet long with a light tip.

"If a fish is six pounds or bigger, you've got to have a rod that will stand up," Vincent said. "And you've got to have a tip light enough to see the bite."

Within a minute, one rod tip is vibrating, signaling that a trout is nibbling its way up a nightcrawler.

Vincent eases over to the rod and slowly picks up the handle while keeping the rod tip down, near the water. He gives the rod tip a smooth sweep, not a jerk, to set the hook, then starts reeling. A 14-inch trout is brought to the boat, hooked in the mouth.

"People want to make trout fishing harder than it really is," Vincent says, as he releases the fish.

The canvas hat on Vincent's head indicates that he is an advocate of

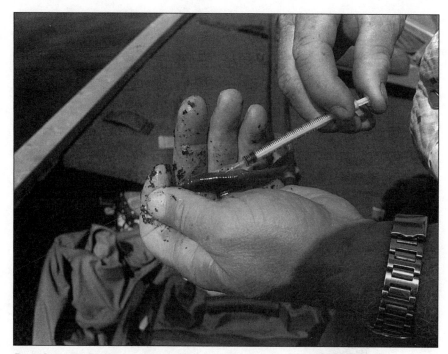

By using a syringe to pump air into a nightcrawler, Vincent keeps his bait floating off the bottom, where trout can see it better.

catch-and-release. The hat is circled with pins awarded for returning trophy-size fish to the water.

"Guides should be interested in trying to save as many fish as they can for their future business," he said.

To some, it might seem that Vincent is talking out both sides of his mouth - extolling the benefits of catch-and-release while at the same time guaranteeing a limit of trout to his customers and primarily fishing with bait.

It has been proven that trout caught on bait - nightcrawlers, corn, salmon eggs, Power Bait, etc., - are more likely to die when released than fish caught on artificial lures.

However, you don't have to spend much time with Vincent to know that he is truly concerned with the future of the resource. He has seen the average size of the rainbow trout caught in Taneycomo diminish over the years.

"I won't keep any fish over 20 inches," Vincent said. "And I won't keep any browns. If my customers catch one, I try to get them to release it."

And if you think money is Vincent's motivation in providing a guide service, you're wrong. He charges only $75 per day. That's less than many Lake Taneycomo marinas charge just

to rent a boat and motor.

"I enjoy seeing people catch fish," Vincent said. "No fish, no fun. I just really get a kick out of seeing people catch fish."

By taking his nightcrawler technique and finding ways it can be adapted to every type of water flow situation, Vincent is able to get a creel full of enjoyment from his sport.

"You've got to fish the water conditions," he said. "If the water conditions change seven times during the day, you've got to fish in seven locations, use the whole lake. You're thinking ahead of the fish."

When Vincent hears the siren announcing power generation is about to begin or increase, he knows exactly where he will go next and how long it will take for the water to rise and stabilize before the fishing will get good there. That comes from experience.

But someone with less experience can use a simple tool of Vincent's to find the right water to fish in. That tool is the quarter-ounce bell sinker on a Taneycomo rig. It's the only size weight that Vincent ever uses on this rig.

"A bigger sinker won't work," he said. "I'm a great believer in the current telling you where to fish. That sinker has got to be bumping the bottom. If you don't feel it bumping the bottom, the current is too fast. Then you've got to get behind an island or something where the current slows down enough for that quarter-ounce sinker to bump bottom.

"I want it to bump, not drag. You've got to feel the bottom. Using that quarter-ounce weight tells me where I should be fishing."

When Vincent finds a stretch of river to his liking, as far as current is concerned, he'll plow it like a farmer does a field. After one drift through with a nightcrawler floating just above the sinker bouncing on the bottom, he'll motor back upstream, move over slightly and begin the process again until he finds where the fish are holding.

Vincent also uses this same Taneycomo rig to fish strong current from an anchored boat. But he is careful to pick his spots.

(A word of caution about anchoring is necessary, according to Vincent. Anytime a boat is anchored in these White River System tailwaters, there is a chance that power generation will increase and the anchor could become stuck in the stream bed. This, in turn, can cause a boat to capsize and present a life-threatening situation. Don't anchor in the main river channel when the current is strong. Don't ever anchor a boat in one of the White River tailwaters without having a knife or another device that can cut the anchor loose in an emergency.)

Vincent looks for slow-moving water, behind an island or gravel bar, to drop anchor. This not only eliminates much of the danger involved in using an anchor, but also puts Vincent where the fish are.

Trout will hold in slower water, where they don't have to expend so much energy to take advantage of the food flowing by in the current.

Again, Vincent lets the current and the quarter-ounce sinker tell him where to fish. He makes a quartering cast downstream into the current, which pushes the Taneycomo rig behind the boat. As it moves toward

the slower water where Vincent is anchored, the current force diminishes and the quarter-ounce sinker will take hold on the bottom. This is usually where the trout will be holding, too.

Vincent carries a syringe that he uses to pump air into nightcrawlers. With two or three injections, the nightcrawler will float just above the bottom.

"You want to keep the nightcrawler right in the fish's face until he decides to take it," Vincent said.

Vincent has caught three rainbow trout from Taneycomo in the 13 1/2-pound range. His biggest brown is an 11-pounder and he says he's caught hundreds of them from 4 to 8 pounds.

"That's the reason I don't jig fish," Vincent said. "I believe more lunkers in this lake are caught on night-crawlers than any other lure.

"Even way back, when fishing was at its best here, guides were strong on nightcrawlers."

Vincent thinks anglers can be more successful releasing fish caught on nightcrawlers if they'll do two things - 1) learn that fine line between setting the hook too soon and too late; and 2) cut the line on a deeply-hooked fish rather than trying to dig the hook out.

"I've seen trout weighing six pounds that had three or four hooks in them," Vincent said. "It's a lot cheaper to replace a hook than it is to replace a fish."

Tests have proven this to be true, although a gut-hooked fish, no matter how well-handled, still has less than a 50-50 chance of surviving. But that is better than zero, a trout's chances when you try to remove the hook from its gut.

Vincent keeps a couple sets of long-nose pliers in the boat. These, too, can help save a fish that is going to be released, as they allow quick removal of a hook.

On this day, Vincent released every fish caught. It seemed he could have caught 100 if that's what he wanted to do.

Charlie Vincent has learned his trout fishing lessons well since beginning his studies at Lake Taneycomo.

Vincent Varies Tactics As He Moves Down Lake

Charlie Vincent lives at Rockaway Beach, on the lower section of Lake Taneycomo. That's where he first learned to catch trout here.

Later, when he started working out of the Branson Trout Dock, he concentrated his angling on the upper section of the lake. As a result, Vincent knows how to catch trout from the entire 22 miles of Lake Taneycomo.

The following are some tips from Vincent on fishing techniques in different areas:

■ Nightcrawlers are all Vincent uses for bait when he's fishing the first 3 1/4 miles of the lake, from the dam to Fall Creek.

But between Fall Creek and Short Creek current and water color differences cause Vincent to change baits. He prefers Berkley Power Eggs from here down. Vincent fishes with two Power Eggs - one orange and one chartreuse - on a No. 8 hook.

"A woman taught me how to do that," Vincent said. "I was guiding her on a day when fishing was real tough. She said, 'If I'm going to sit out here and catch nothing, I at least want to have something pretty on my hook. Put two different colors on there.'

"She started catching fish one after another. From that day on, I've always used two colors."

■ The "Lookout Hole" is the area below a scenic overlook of Taneycomo from Highway 165. As you go downstream, three large rocks are located on the right bank. These are prime fish-holding structures during high water. The rocks are visible during low water.

■ After you pass Short Creek, which enters from the right, the bank along the left side is lined with trees until you get to Lilley's Landing. "If you're going to catch a brown trout on a crankbait, that's the place to do it," Vincent said.

■ Boat docks line the left side of the lake from Lilley's Landing to Cooper Creek. This is a good area to drift fish using Vincent's "plowing a field" method of thoroughly covering the water from bank to bank with several drift runs. "I guarantee you one of those drifts through this part will pay off," Vincent said.

■ One mile below Cooper Creek, the river channel side is on the left and there are lots of downed trees. "It's rougher than hell to fish, but there are a lot of good ones in there," Vincent said.

■ Just over eight miles down Lake Taneycomo, the Highway 65 bridge is the first of three (one is a railroad bridge) that connect Branson and Hollister. The bridges attract trout, according to Vincent. Some big brown trout have been caught near the bridge supports.

■ Roark Creek enters Lake Taneycomo in Branson. The warm water from this stream at times is an attraction for brown trout, according to Vincent. And because the water is deep, too - as deep as 20 feet - big fish can lay here relatively undisturbed. Trolling with crankbaits, like Shad Raps and Countdown Rapalas, is popular in this area.

■ Before you get to Bull Creek, which enters Taneycomo on the left side, just above Rockaway Beach, there are a couple of islands on the the left side. When Vincent first started fishing Taneycomo, he heard about good fishing at "the corn field," but he couldn't ever find a corn field. Later he found out the area around the islands is called "the corn field" because so much corn is used in trout fishing here. It continues to be one of the most popular methods of fishing in this area, along with trolling.

■ Most people think the area below Table Rock Dam is where all the lunker brown trout hang out. However, a 22-pounder was caught near Rockaway Beach during the summer of 1992, and Vincent thinks a state record could come from the deep water in the lower end of the lake.

"Some troller using a big lure will catch it," Vincent said. "You see some big fish on your depthfinder here. One of them could be a record brown."

Marty Babusa takes a hunter's approach when going after big trout in Lake Taneycomo. He wears camouflage clothing and quietly stalks his prey.

Babusa Prefers Trophy Fishing

The fact that Marty Babusa held the Missouri brown trout record (23 lbs., 4 oz.) is no accident.

"I pretty much trophy fish," Babusa said. "I've found that if you start messing with little fish, you lose your chance at a big fish.

"There are guys who fish here a lot and catch a lot more fish than I will. But I'll be walking the banks, watching the water for a big fish."

Babusa's other big fish from Taneycomo include a 9 1/2-pound brown trout and a 9-pound rainbow. He primarily uses spinning and fly fishing tackle, although his record fish came on baitcasting gear.

Babusa likes to wade fish, when water conditions are right for it, but he has methods for fishing Lake Taneycomo at all water levels.

"It doesn't matter to me what the water does," he said. "The best thing is if it's constant. On days when it is rising and falling it seems to disturb the fish."

And Babusa is careful not to disturb the fish. He takes a hunter's approach, wearing camouflage clothing and quietly stalking his prey. Babusa says he once observed a Lake Taneycomo angler who moved just like a great blue heron - almost in slow motion, with long periods of no movement at all. And he learned from that.

"As long as you look like you belong there, the fish aren't going to be spooked," Babusa said.

For that reason, he has started using a 9 1/2 foot spinning rod, which has enough backbone for hook setting and long casts, but also allows him to flip and pitch a lure short distances with little rod movement.

He normally uses 8-pound-test line. His favorite lure on spinning tackle is a 3 1/2-inch black-and-silver Rapala. At night he'll go to a bigger lure, up to 6 inches long.

Babusa prefers a slow retrieve. The long rod helps him position the lure in various "lanes" where he has noticed big fish moving. He will stop the lure and let it flutter in these spots for several seconds, or move his rod tip downstream a few feet before beginning his retrieve again.

Babusa employs the same techniques when fly fishing. He uses a 9 1/2-foot, 7-weight rod, which aids him in keeping a fly in a feeding lane and in making roll casts. A marabou streamer is his favorite pattern.

"Even if you can't see the fish, you never know when one could grab the lure or fly," Babusa said. "You want to keep the lure in a potentially productive area as long as you can."

Hours Of Study Paid Off For Babusa

Muddler Minnow, spinning gear, patience finally led to big catch

Marty Babusa first saw the fish in January 1991. When Babusa isn't working, he's at Table Rock State Park, studying the trout in Lake Taneycomo.

"When I'm down here, I spend a lot of time walking the bank, watching, trying to spot fish," Babusa said. "One day I happened to be walking along, and I saw this huge trout circle right in front of me. I thought it must have been a yard long.

"A day or two later, I hooked it on a light marabou jig. It took it into the current and broke off before I knew it. I thought I'd keep fishing for it, as long as it was coming in there."

Babusa moved to the Branson area from Kansas City in 1980. He says he has been seriously into fishing for many years. The move here helped fuel that interest, as Babusa can work and still get some fishing time in each day at the nearby Table Rock Dam Tailwater.

Babusa is primarily a trout fisherman now. But he does like to bass fish, too. He especially enjoys the technique of flipping - where a lure is dropped in the middle of thick cover on heavy line.

Babusa says he studies all types of fishing. When he's reading a magazine article about muskie fishing in Canada he tries to figure out some way those techniques could be used on trout in the Ozarks.

After he saw that big trout in Taneycomo, Babusa started doing some research on big trout and what they like to eat. Earlier, he had bought a 3-inch white Muddler Minnow from a bargain basket at Bass Pro Shop in Springfield. Babusa knew that brown trout like to eat shad and minnows and a big lure is often attractive to a big fish.

"I fished for that fish for a month and a half," Babusa said. "I couldn't seem to get anything in front of it. You only had a couple of seconds each time."

Marty Babusa stalked this 23-pound, 4-ounce brown trout for almost two months before he landed it.

Photo courtesy Missouri Department of Conservation

Mike Ramsay is one of the few people who fishes the Table Rock Dam Tailwater more than Babusa. Ramsay is the custom fly tyer at "The Right Angle," a specialty fishing shop located in Branson's Engler Block. Ramsay fly fishes for trout here twice a day - morning and evening - and he sometimes comes back in the middle of the night, too.

Ramsay was the only other angler who knew about the big brown trout Babusa had been watching. On March 20, 1991, Ramsay hooked a big fish on a size 12 scud pattern that he created. Ramsay was using an 8 1/2-foot fly rod and 5-weight line with 4-pound test tippet.

"One-hundred-and-seventy-five yards of line and backing, he took all of it," Ramsay said of the fish. "I thought I was was going to lose everything, and I at least wanted to get my

fly line back, so I put some pressure on him. I couldn't believe it, but I was able to turn him and get some line back."

Ramsay had the fish on for 20 minutes.

"It was like having a bulldog on the end of your line," he said. "You don't just get excited. Your heart goes BOOM, BOOM, BOOM."

Ramsay was beginning to feel like he had a chance of landing the big brown trout when the hook slipped out of the fish's mouth.

"I just stood there for five minutes," Ramsay said. "I heard nothing but the birds singing and the water running. I was about ready to cry."

Since they see each other so often at Lake Taneycomo, Ramsay and Babusa have come to know each other well. They agree that Ramsay probably hooked the big brown they'd both been observing off and on for over a month.

But after Ramsay hooked it, Babusa lost track of the fish for several days.

"I had just about given up on seeing it again," Babusa said.

If he did see it again, he was going to be prepared. After that first experience when the fish broke off so easily, Babusa, relying on his "flipping" experience, spooled 12-pound-test line on a baitcasting reel. Most Lake Taneycomo trout anglers use 2-pound-test line on spinning gear, so the fish won't be spooked by heavy line.

"It's not always necessary to use light line, especially if you concentrate on lure presentation," Babusa said. "It's the same theory as flipping for bass - they see the lure and react. Plus, I've seen so many fish lost because people don't have heavy enough line to control the fish."

On March 29, 1991, Babusa went fishing at Table Rock State Park. It had been a cool, clear day, but it was 6 p.m. and almost dark. Babusa had tied on the 3-inch Muddler Minnow.

He had noticed that the big brown

would cruise through a particular spot, right along the bottom. Three Shepherd of the Hills Hatchery outlets line the north bank below Table Rock Dam. The outlets create a flow of highly-oxygenated water that is attractive to trout.

Babusa weighted the Muddler Minnow, normally used on fly fishing tackle, with enough split shot to cast it with his heavy baitcasting gear. He wanted to put it right in the middle of the lane where he'd seen the fish cruising before.

"I saw the fish approaching," Babusa said. "I just kind of flipped the fly out there where I knew he'd come through. He grabbed hold of it about five feet from my feet."

All four power generators were running at Table Rock Dam. Babusa was afraid the fish would go downstream with the current and wrap his line around a tree. But the big brown trout went upstream instead. Combined with the 12-pound line, that gave Babusa the leverage he needed to land the fish, but it still put up a 20-minute battle.

At that time, the Missouri brown trout record was 16 pounds, 10 ounces. Babusa was confident he'd caught a new state record fish.

"I figured it weighed 18 or 19 pounds," Babusa said. "I went to a tackle shop near here. It was closed, but they opened up and weighed the fish for me. It was 23 1/2 pounds there. I found Gordon (Proctor) and we took took it to the hatchery to have it officially weighed."

Officially, the fish weighed 23 pounds, 4 ounces. The first time Babusa saw the brown trout he'd said to himself that it must be a yard long. He didn't miss it much. The fish measured 36 1/2 inches in length. Its girth was 21 1/2 inches. The mount of Babusa's state record fish is on the wall at Backcountry Outfitters, where Babusa works.

After setting a new state record, Babusa decided to start a guide service for trophy trout fishing below Table Rock Dam. Things haven't changed much for Babusa. He continues to fish the Table Rock Dam Tailwaters, keep-

Brown Trout Mark Fell Again When Elfrink Landed Lunker

Kevin and Lisa Elfrink enjoy visiting Branson and Lake Taneycomo a couple of times a year. They live in Jackson, Missouri, about a six-hour drive away.

One of their Taneycomo trips was set for June 1994. Earlier that year, Kevin had spent 10 weeks in Cincinnati on a business project. While killing some time there, thinking about fishing, he bought a package of Bass Assassin soft plastic "Shad Assassin" jerkbaits.

When Kevin and Lisa launched their boat at Lake Taneycomo at 7 a.m. June 27, Kevin finally had a chance to use the new lures that had been unopened in his tackle box for two months. Thirty minutes later, Elfrink caught a new Missouri record brown trout.

"We started fishing around mile marker 16 or 17," Elfrink said. "On the north bank, there is a lot of fallen timber in the edge of the water. I was throwing right to the edge of the shore and working the bait back through the lay downs.

"There was about 20-foot of water. Fish tend to follow that lure. It was just outside the fringe of the cover when the fish came up and hit it."

Elfrink was using 8-pound-test line on a Shimano Bantam Mag baitcasting reel. The big brown trout made three short runs, then rolled over. Elfrink estimates it took only about five minutes to fight the fish.

When he got it to the boat, Elfrink knew the fish was the biggest he'd ever caught. He enjoys fishing for a variety of freshwater species. A 20-pound striper had been his previous personal best.

"It never crossed my mind that I might have a new state record," Elfrink said.

The Elfrinks motored up to Lilley's Landing Resort, where they were staying. Resort owner Phil Lilley, a veteran angler, took one look at the fish and called a Missouri Department of Conservation agent.

They took the fish to a Branson grocery store, where it officially weighed 24 pounds, 15 ounces. It measured 35 1/2 inches long and had a 24-inch girth.

That Elfrink caught the fish on a soft plastic jerkbait is just another example of how black bass and brown trout fishing tactics can be similar. Hard plastic jerkbaits, like Smithwick Rattlin' Rogues, have produced several big brown trout catches in recent years.

Elfrink's lure had a black back and pearl belly. A Shad Assassin is similar to a Slug-Go, which was one of the hottest new lures on the professional bass fishing circuit in the early 1990s.

The success of the jerkbait, both in hard and soft plastic, points to the fact trout look for bigger sources of food as they become bigger. Fish, in the form of minnows or shad or other trout, provide that bigger food source. And jerkbaits are a good imitation.

Just ask Kevin Elfrink.

ing an eye out for big fish, whether he's with a guide party or not.

In fact, another fish story indicates just how little things have changed for Babusa. The winter after he caught the state record brown brought him a sense of deja vu.

"I was fishing another area and almost the exact thing happened," Babusa said. "I saw a huge fish and thought it must be a yard long. But this one was a rainbow. I hooked it on a little black jig and had it on for 10 minutes. It made a long run downstream. I put a little bit of pressure on and the hook bent."

That just gave Babusa another reason to keep fishing for trophy-size trout at Lake Taneycomo.

Mike Ramsay, left, and Chuck Landry prefer fly fishing below Table Rock Dam before the sun lifts the fog from the water.

Ramsay Chooses Cover Of Darkness

Peace, quiet and chance to catch a big fish lure Branson fly fisherman

You could say that Mike Ramsay enjoys the night life at Lake Taneycomo. But Ramsay's fun has nothing to do with the buzz of activity in Branson. Ramsay prefers the cover of darkness for fly fishing below Table Rock Dam.

"I absolutely love fly fishing, and it means more to me at night," Ramsay said. "I like to fish at night because it's a change of pace from the hectic life in Branson. There's a lot of peace and quiet here at night. Also, a lot of the larger fish are active then."

Ramsay is somewhat of a newcomer to fly fishing, having started in 1987. But when it bit him, the fly fishing bug bit him hard. Ramsay has crammed as much fly-fishing experience as possible into the past few years.

"I had a fly rod a long time, but I was scared to bring it out," Ramsay said. "I was scared to ask questions. Then I made the mistake of teaching myself the first year. I was one of the worst instructors out there. Finally, I started asking questions. I asked a lot of silly questions, and I got a lot of great answers. I'm grateful."

That introduction to fly fishing is one of the reasons Ramsay is so accessible now to other anglers learning the sport. He remembers well the awkwardness a fly rod can create in a beginning fly fisher's hands. Ramsay is sort of the unofficial fly fishing coach of the Table Rock Tailwater - always willing to share advice and flies.

Ramsay carries more than the usual selection of flies. In 1991 he became the custom fly tyer at Right Angle, a custom rod and tackle shop in Branson's Engler Block. He also ties hundreds of patterns on a commercial basis for other fly shops in the Ozarks.

However, if he had to be limited to two fly patterns at Lake Taneycomo, Ramsay could handle that. His choice for daytime fishing is a scud in sizes 10 through 16. Ramsay's favorite pattern at night is a Woolly Bugger. He ties them big - from size 12 all the way up to size 4 - and in every color from black to white.

Ramsay gets serious when the subject turns to night fishing and the quest for trophy-size trout. His attitude is "no compromises."

"We're not playing games here," Ramsay said. "We're out here to catch fish. All I'm after is one big fish."

Ramsay landed a 20-pound brown trout in the White River below Cotter in June 1992, and, as mentioned in the story about Marty Babusa's 23-pound brown trout, Ramsay may have had it on his line before Babusa caught it. In a five-night period in the winter of 1993, Ramsay caught a brown trout each night that weighed between 8 and 14 pounds. On October 12, 1994, at 9:30 p.m., Ramsay landed a 19-pound brown from Lake Taneycomo.

"A dark brown Woolly Bugger with dark brown grizzly hackle is No. 1 in the fall," Ramsay said. "White is good when the shad start coming through the turbines. Not too many people fish white. I don't know why they don't. I've never seen a fish yet that wouldn't hit a white fly."

Ramsay thinks the best all-around Woolly Bugger for night fishing below Table Rock is a size 6 solid black with some pearl-colored Krystal Flash. But he never stays long with one color .

"I alternate from light to dark, and I work in toward the middle, green to brown," Ramsay said. "I change bugs every 10 minutes. Once you key in on a color pattern, stay with it."

Ramsay ties heavily weighted Woolly Buggers for night fishing. A size 6 will have 24 wraps of .020 lead.

He fishes them in a typical across-and-down pattern. As the fly starts to swing, Ramsay gives it small strips, about 3 inches long, then makes 10 to 15 similar strips at the bottom of the swing.

"Sometimes they'll take it real softly," Ramsay said. "Your line will be just heavy all of the sudden. When in doubt, set the hook. Other times, they'll tap it, then take it.

"One of the hardest things to do is allow the fish to take the fly without setting the hook after that first tap. You've got to let them take it and turn."

Ramsay could limit himself to Woolly Buggers only at night, if he had to, but he doesn't. He enjoys experimenting with several other patterns.

They include bass flies, like the Shinabou Shiner, big moth patterns up to size 2, Kauffman Stimulators, Royal Wulffs, White Wulffs and some salmon patterns.

"I've found out that rainbows will hit a lot of salmon flies," said Ramsay. And a No. 4 Ramsay variation of a salmon pattern is what coaxed the 19-pound brown in October 1994.

Night fishing requires and allows for a stronger tippet. Ramsay uses 6- to 12-pound-test on an 8-foot leader.

Ramsay's favorite time of the year to fish Taneycomo is fall, when the brown trout spawning run begins. He thinks September is a particularly good month to catch a big brown trout because the fish are moving upstream to spawn, but haven't actually begun the process yet.

Finally, one other tip on night fishing - don't blow your cover. Ramsay uses a small flashlight when changing flies. He is always careful to turn his back to the water before turning it on.

Ramsay says the top fly pattern for night fishing in the Table Rock Tailwater is a Woolly Bugger. He ties them in a variety of colors, but black is best overall.

Scud

Hook: Tiemco 2457, sizes 10-16
Thread: 3/0 red or light orange
Body: Two parts gray craft yarn to one part camel yarn, blended, plus, three-inch piece of pearl Flashabou

Scuds Could Be Perfect Food For Ozark Trout

Around Lake Taneycomo, they are called freshwater shrimp. And they do look like a miniature version of a saltwater shrimp.

But scud (order *amphipoda*) is the more accurate common name for this tiny freshwater crustacean, as the true freshwater shrimp isn't found in these waters.

No matter what you call it, you better know how to imitate it if you want to catch trout in the Ozark tailwaters, especially below Table Rock Dam.

Most fly fishers, like Mike Ramsay, know this and carry several sizes and color patterns of scuds.

But scud imitations aren't limited to fly fishers. Possibly the most popular lure on Lake Taneycomo is a marabou jig. The 1/100th-ounce jig, in particular, has been a favorite here for many years. It is fished under a bobber on 2-pound-test line. When a slight breeze puts a ripple on the water, bouncing the bobber, which in turn shakes the jig, this becomes a deadly trout-catching technique.

And all it's doing is imitating a scud. Unlike sowbugs, scuds can propel themselves through the water. A jig jiggling in the breeze closely imitates this motion.

There are dozens of scud species in North America. One in particular - *gammarus limnaeus* - is most common in Lake Taneycomo. It is one of the bigger scud species. Thus the 1/100th-ounce jig is a reasonable facsimile.

Scuds, like crawfish and other members of the crustacea family, molt and shed their exoskeleton. Trout seem to be aware of this and show a preference for freshly molted scuds, just like they do softshell crawfish.

That's why color can be so important in scud imitations. The orange and red under-wrapped thread is a key element in Ramsay's scud pattern. The color shows through the translucent body material, especially when it's wet.

Although Lake Taneycomo's scud population took a nose-dive in the late 1980s, it has stabilized somewhat and scuds remain a preferred trout food. Trout seem to key on the fact that scuds are a better source of protein than sowbugs.

Mike Ramsay likes to tie scuds relatively big and flashy for Lake Taneycomo.

Ramsay covers a Tiemco 2457 scud hook with either red or orange thread. Halfway down the hook shank he ties in a 3-inch piece of pearl Flashabou.

For dubbing, Ramsay uses various colors of synthetic craft yarn. His "shrimp mix" consists of two parts No. 38 gray and one part No. 47 camel cut in 5/8th-inch pieces and spun in a blender. He takes a pinch of the material, rolls it in the palm of his hand, then attaches it to the back of the hook shank with two soft loops.

"This is the crucial part," Ramsay said. "Grasp the Flashabou, thread and dubbing and twist it and grab it, twist it and grab it until you've got a tight noodle. Be careful not to pull too hard or you'll separate the the dubbing material."

Ramsay then wraps the combination of materials up the hook shank. He doesn't add a shell back, but does pick out some of the dubbing on the underside of the fly to give it a "buggy" look.

"This is my all-time favorite," Ramsay said. "It has proved itself time and time again."

Shepherd Of The Hills Hatching Trout

State-operated hatchery provides big numbers of trout for Taneycomo

When trout fishing gets a little slow on one of the White River System tailwaters, it's common to hear anglers direct their complaints toward a hatchery.

"They need to start stocking more fish in here," they'll say. "Fishing here just isn't what it used to be."

Gordon Proctor, the manager at the Shepherd of the Hills Hatchery on Lake Taneycomo, has worked for the Missouri Department of Conservation since 1962. He knows, as well as anyone, the complexity of managing a trout fishery like Lake Taneycomo, which has little natural reproduction of trout but increasing pressure from anglers.

Proctor remembers a time, in the late 1960s, when he could walk along the banks of Lake Taneycomo and see several five-trout limits weighing over 35 pounds. Yes, that's an average of better than 7 pounds per trout, and most were rainbows.

"There are not very many large fish coming in now," Proctor said. "You'll see one every once in a while."

Spencer Turner has worked over two decades for the Missouri Department of Conservation, most of them with trout-related studies.

"The question is, how do we keep the trout in the lake long enough to grow?," Turner said. "Is there potential? Sure there is. But it's a balancing act. From mom and pop on vacation to the trophy hunter, you have to deal with all aspects."

Shepherd of the Hills Hatchery mainly deals with the aspect of supplying 10-inch-plus trout for Lake Taneycomo. It also supplies some trout for other Missouri fisheries and trout eggs for three other Missouri hatcheries. But 90 percent of the production poundage from Shepherd of the Hills Hatchery goes into Lake Taneycomo.

The hatchery produces 350,000 to 400,000 pounds of trout each year. That translates into about 760,000

After trout are grown to 10-inches-plus, some are transferred from the raceways into a hatchery truck, then a stocking barge in Lake Taneycomo.

trout for Taneycomo.

"We used to say we stocked a million fish a year," Proctor said. "It's been as high as 1.6 million in 1984 and 1985."

Stocking will remain at about three-quarters of a million until several studies are completed. They will indicate the ideal number of trout to be stocked, based on food in the lake and fishing pressure.

Near the hatchery, fish are stocked in the lake from three outlets within Table Rock State Park. These outlets are open "streams." Fishing isn't allowed in them. Stocking in other parts of the lake is done with a barge.

The huge majority of trout stocked in Taneycomo are rainbows. In the past, both steelhead and cokene have been put in - cokene stocking ended in about 1969 and steelhead were stocked as late as 1975.

Rainbow trout brood stock are kept in the hatchery and can be viewed at the Shepherd of the Hills visitor center, which is open all year. Of the six hatcheries that supply trout for the White River System, Shepherd of the Hills is the only one that continues to raise trout from brood stock. All the others now get fingerlings or eggs from other hatcheries.

Some of the rainbow trout here are Missouri Strain. These fall spawners are descendants of the California McCloud Strain, first brought to Missouri in 1880.

"Trout fishermen pay for the program. They have a right to tell us what they prefer."

Only 10,000 brown trout per year are stocked in Taneycomo. No brown trout brood stock is kept in the hatchery. The brood stock are collected each fall when the browns make their annual spawning run and return to a site near the hatchery outlets.

The egg-to-stocking itinerary for rainbow trout at Shepherd of the Hills Hatchery is as follows:

- twice a year, during fall and spring spawns, eggs are taken from female rainbows;

- milt, or sperm, is taken from the male trout and used to fertilize the eggs;

- fertilized eggs are taken to the hatchery building and placed in jars, where they receive a constant flow of cold water;

- in two weeks, eyes develop and in one month the trout eggs will hatch;

- small trout are fed commercially processed trout food until the age of 15 months, when they are stocked as 10-inch fish.

The Shepherd of the Hills Hatchery is supplied with 14 million gallons of water per day through an 18-inch pipeline from Table Rock Lake. This is supplemented with water from two wells. Temperature of the Table Rock Lake water varies from 40 to 57 degrees; well water is about 60 degrees. Water temperature control is achieved by mixing the water from the three sources and through chilling in the hatchery.

Trout production is staggered over several months by manipulating water temperatures in the hatchery and the raceways - groups of trout are raised at temperatures from 45 to 56 degrees.

Proctor said trout stocking used to be the same each month, year-round, but it is now based on fishing pressure. Thus, more trout are stocked in the spring and summer months when more people are fishing.

Should more trout be stocked in Lake Taneycomo in response to increased fishing pressure, or should catch-and-release and lower creel limits be emphasized so the trout will have a longer period to grow in the lake?

Proctor notes that anglers need to remember there are limits to what the hatchery can produce. And there are limits to what the lake can sustain in terms of total poundage of fish. When those limits are reached a choice must be made - do you want bigger fish and fewer numbers, or smaller fish and greater numbers. On-going studies will help determine that figure, but trout anglers will have input as to minimum length limits, catch-and-release zones and creel limits for the future.

"Trout fishermen pay for the program," Proctor said. "They have a right to tell us what they prefer."

But keep in mind, the hatchery isn't the final answer when trout fishing gets tough on Lake Taneycomo. The final answer is in the hands of the trout angler.

The Shepherd of the Hills visitor center is open seven days a week, 9 a.m. until 5 p.m., from mid-March to mid-November. During winter months, the visitor center is open Saturday and Sunday only.

Owen's Presence Made Branson Float Trip Capital

Before Branson became famous for its country music shows, it was known as the float-fishing capital of the Ozarks. And from 1935 until 1958, Jim Owen was the king. Owen could put 35 wooden johnboats on the river at any one time.

Thomas Hart Benton, who was born in Neosho, Missouri, made a sketch entitled "Down the River" (or "The Young Fisherman") in 1939 as a result of a Jim Owen's float trip on the White River.

The cover of Life magazine featured one of Owen's float trips down the White River in 1941. (An 18-mile float trip from Forsyth to Moore's Ferry cost $22.50 for two people.)

Owen was a true Ozark character. He was a big man with an unwavering enthusiasm for the area. He owned a drug store, open-air bowling alley and sporting goods store in Branson, where he also served as mayor. Owen sold real estate and raised hunting dogs, too.

He was a friend of "Beverly Hillbillies" television show creator-producer Paul Henning, and Owen was a guest star in several episodes of the show.

But it was the float fishing service down the White River that established Owen's reputation. The White River was known then as one of the finest smallmouth bass fishing streams in the United States.

When construction of Bull Shoals Dam was completed in 1951 and Table Rock Dam's completion followed 10 years later, those long float trips down the White River for smallmouth bass had ended.

Owen died in 1972 at the age of 68. An exhibit marking his contribution to the Ozarks is part of the Ralph Foster Museum on the College of the Ozarks campus. The school is located in Point Lookout, which overlooks Lake Taneycomo just southwest of Hollister.

Photo courtesy of Presley Family

Three generations of the Presley family: (left to right) Scott, John, Steve, Eric, Gary (Herkimer), Greg, Nick and Lloyd.

Lloyd Presley Has Seen It All In Branson

Work as fishing guide helped pay the bills when theater first opened

If you want to know the success story of Branson, Missouri, - from country music to trout fishing - ask Lloyd Presley, because that's his story, too. Lloyd Presley worked as a parttime fishing guide and parttime musician when the Presley family opened a theater on Highway 76 in 1967. In some ways, nothing has changed. In other ways, everything has changed.

When Presley celebrated his 70th birthday on August 30, 1994, music and fishing still played big parts in his life, just like they always had.

Presley was born in a small town near Springfield, Missouri, the son of a Pentecostal minister. Everyone in the family made a musical contribution to Sunday services.

Lloyd's interest in music led to his forming a band, the Ozark Playboys,

that toured throughout southwest Missouri. In 1942, Lloyd married Bessie Mae Garrison of Alpena, Arkansas. By the 1960s, Lloyd and Bessie Mae had a family band - oldest son Gary played guitar, daughters Janice and Deanna sang, and youngest son Steve played drums.

When the Presleys decided to bring their act to Branson, they bought 10 acres on Highway 76 for $15,000 and built a "theater" that held 363 folding chairs.

"If this doesn't work," Lloyd said at the time, "we can convert this building into a place to store boats."

That was no joke. One night the Presley Family Mountain Music Jubilee Theater held a grand total of 13 paying customers. Everybody in the Presley family worked a second job in order to

pay the bills. Lloyd was spending most of his mornings in a boat then - guiding on Lake Taneycomo. Being a fishing guide came naturally, since Lloyd had grown up near the Sac River.

"Being raised right up on the creek bank, I'd always fished a lot," Lloyd said. "When we came on down to Branson and built the theater, I had fishing in my blood, so I didn't give that up."

Those were the days when big rainbow trout were plentiful in Lake Taneycomo.

"We were using ultralight tackle," Lloyd said. "It was kind of new then. The bass fishermen thought you were crazy if you were using 2- and 4-pound-test line. I've caught trout up to 7 pounds on 2- and 4-pound-test. You have to set your drag right, and it will

Branson Bulging With Entertainment

Branson might be the easiest place for a trout angler to talk a nonangling spouse and family into taking a vacation. It's estimated that over five million visitors a year are coming to this southwest Missouri town, which still lists its population as 3,609. It is the No. 2 driving destination in the U.S., trailing only Orlando, Florida.

Branson has been proclaimed "the new capital of country music." Country stars like Mel Tillis, Roy Clark, Loretta Lynn, Shoji Tabuchi, Ray Stevens, Box Car Willie and Christy Lane have theaters here.

But Branson isn't just country music - it's entertainment, period. Wayne Newton, Andy Williams, John Davidson and the Osmond family have theaters here, too.

There are over 30 entertainment theaters in Branson, which now claims to have more theater seats (50,000-plus) than Broadway.

Entertainers like Newton have previously been associated with Las Vegas. Newton now splits his time between Las Vegas and Branson. But while gambling is the primary entertainment attraction in Las Vegas, the emphasis is on family-style fun in Branson.

The Branson boom hasn't come without its problems. Construction is apparent everywhere. Traffic along "The Strip" (Highway 76) is bumper-to-bumper during the peak of the main tourist season, which runs from May through October.

Increases in soil erosion, from all the development, and treated sewage and septic systems, have had adverse effects on Lake Taneycomo water quality. The extent of those effects is a subject of much debate among local trout anglers and the subject of several studies designed to address the problem.

However, the facts remain that Lake Taneycomo produced a new state record brown trout in 1991 and again in 1994, and the lake gets stocked with about 760,000 trout per year. Its reputation as Missouri's most popular trout fishery hasn't been harmed. And although the downtown Branson area of Lake Taneycomo is hardly a tranquil setting, there are still places to escape from the crowd, especially on the upper and lower sections of the lake.

While Branson's booming success is fairly recent, the emphasis on tourism and entertainment is not. In fact, the birth of Ozarks tourism can be traced back to 1907, when Harold Bell Wright's "Shepherd of the Hills" was published.

After the book was advertised in the Saturday Evening Post magazine and the Sears & Roebuck catalog, it became an instant bestseller. Bell is the first American author to write a book that sold over one million copies, according to information at the Harold Bell Wright Museum and Theater.

Tourists came here to meet the main characters in Bell's portrait of Ozark life. The stage version of Bell's book still draws crowds of up to 2,500.

Silver Dollar City, an 1880s theme park, amusement park and crafts fair, had its beginnings in that early 1900s trickle of tourists attracted to the area by Wright's book.

Marvel Cave opened to commercial tours in 1892. Visitor's climbed down wooden ladders to see the cave's Cathedral Room. Hugo and Mary Herschend came to Branson on vacations from Chicago in the 1940s. After a tour of the cave, they became fascinated with it and moved here to assume the lease on Marvel Cave.

Silver Dollar City began as simply something to do for people waiting to tour the cave. The Herschend family developed it into an entertainment complex that, next to the live entertainment, is the biggest tourist attraction in the area.

Without a doubt, there is no lack of entertainment opportunities for trout anglers and nonanglers in the Branson area.

take you about 30 minutes. But Taneycomo is pretty open, gravel bottom and clear water, so you can do it."

Lake Taneycomo was the first place in the White River System where trout fishing with jigs became popular. A small jig provided a good imitation of the scuds, sometimes called freshwater shrimp, in the lake.

"Taneycomo was full of those little brown shrimp," Presley said. "We used 1/16th- or 1/32nd-ounce brown jigs. They looked a lot like the shrimp."

Table Rock Dam wasn't completed until 1958. Presley learned to catch smallmouth bass on the White and James rivers long before there were any trout in Taneycomo. The tradition of Ozark float trips runs deep in the Presley family.

"I'll never forget how Gary or Steve would hang off the back of the johnboat and swim while we were plugging in the front," Lloyd said. "They were kind of brought up in float fishing."

Just like they were in music. It's the music that has carried the Presley family to wealth and fame. Their theater now seats 2,000 for the six-days-a-week shows. Instead of just plain ol' Highway 76, the road in front of Presleys' Jubilee Theater is now known as 76 Country Boulevard and Branson is called "The Music Show Capital of the World."

The Presley' success was the subject of a CBS television "How'd They Do That?" segment in 1994.

"I believe the Presleys can absolutely take credit for what Branson is becoming and has become," said Wayne Newton, who opened his own Branson theater in 1993. "They were the first ones to say, 'If there's any way we can help, just ask.' They are the epitome of the perfect neighbor.'"

From 13 paying customers to a 2,000-seat sold out show, from the first theater in the tiny Ozark town of Branson to a major player in "The Music Show Capital of the World," Lloyd Presley has seen more than his share of changes. Throughout those changes have been the constants of family, music and fishing.

"If I never fish another day, I've done my share," Presley said.

A variety of lures can be used to imitate the threadfin shad that trout are gorging on, but a white jig works as well as any.

Shad Kill Brings New Life To Trout

Lilley enjoys "matching the hatch" of threadfin shad with a white jig

An abundance of threadfin shad in the lakes above the dams is a trait of the White River System. These small fish (usually about 1 1/2 inches long) are vulnerable to cold temperatures, and winter usually brings big shad kills to the lakes.

Many of the dead and dying shad will go through the dam turbines into the tailwaters below, where they become a favorite trout food. Threadfin shad kills spur a feeding frenzy that translates into rapid growth rates for White River System trout.

Shad kills can also mean increased opportunities for anglers. Phil Lilley, owner of Lilley's Landing Resort on Lake Taneycomo, enjoys fly fishing. But when power generators are running and water levels are high, Lilley quickly exchanges his fly fishing gear for spinning tackle.

"I really enjoy fishing with a 1/16th-ounce white jig," said Lilley, who moved here in 1983. "You've got an advantage if you know where the gravel bars are because that's where the fish will be holding."

By studying the area below Table Rock Dam when the power generators are off, you can learn the layout of the gravel bars.

When the generators are running and current is swift, it's important to get the lure down where the trout are holding in the dropoffs. Lilley will vary the jig size he uses according to the current, going up in size to 1/8th sometimes or down to 1/32nd on others, but 1/16th is the norm.

"Throw it out and jig it back, just like you would if you were white bass fishing," Lilley said. "When it comes over the gravel bars, they'll nail it."

Small crankbaits, like Rapalas, in shad patterns will also work well in these situations.

There is one downside to a shad kill. Sometimes it can be so massive that it's difficult to find a trout that hasn't got a belly full of shad. Drifting a shad-imitating lure past these fish doesn't always produce.

"The shad kill ran from mid December until the second week in April (in 1992-93)," Lilley said. "That's an extra long time. Shad imitations didn't work quite as well after awhile because the trout just gorged on them. There were shad all the way down the lake to Rockaway Beach.

"But that's also the reason why the fishing was better (in 1993) than it has been in the last 10 years. Growth rates were unbelievable."

As far as other spin fishing techniques, Lilley estimates that Berkley Power Bait, in one form or another, is probably the most-used trout bait on Taneycomo now, with corn ranking a close second, followed by nightcrawlers - all fished on a "Taneycomo rig" that is drifted with the current or still-fished in no or low current situations.

City of Branson Campground is located just below the Highway 65 bridge, which connects Branson and Hollister.

Highlights Of A Trip Down Lake Taneycomo

("Left" and "right" directions assume the angler is facing downstream.)

Finding your way around the Table Rock Tailwater, i.e. Lake Taneycomo, is made easier by a series of locator markers along the banks. The marker system starts at Ozark Beach Dam, marker No. 1 is near Pickle Cove, and continues up the lake, marker No. 22 is in Table Rock State Park.

The locator marker system is maintained by Empire District Electric Company, which manages Ozark Beach Dam and the hydropower plant there. Marker numbers are used in the following description of Lake Taneycomo highlights and they are shown on the map that follows.

Lake Taneycomo can be divided into four main areas, plus one. That extra section, which shouldn't be ignored by anglers, in fall through spring months especially, is below Ozark Beach Dam. But, first things first:

1) Table Rock Dam to Fall Creek, a distance of about 3 1/4 miles. This first section below Table Rock Dam offers typical White River tailwaters fishing when the power generators aren't running, with the first mile being the best. Because of the three outlets from the Shepherd of the Hills Hatchery, this can be some very productive water. The nutrient rich, highly oxygenated water from the hatchery attracts fish. Marty Babusa's state record 23-pound, 4-ounce brown trout came from the area below the dam in 1991. The hatchery doesn't keep brown trout brood stock, but collects them each year from the brown trout in the lake, which swim back upstream to their place of birth. So, obviously, if you want to catch a big brown trout, this is a prime spot.

There is a public boat launching ramp in Table Rock State Park. The park, which includes land on both sides of the river and extends just over one mile downstream, contains a big share of the public land on Lake Taneycomo. Like in the other White River System trout fisheries, a boat is beneficial even in this upper stretch because it can get you to some other fly fishing areas that you'd have to cross private land to reach otherwise.

This is also a good area for drift-fishing during power generation.

2) Fall Creek to Highway 65 bridge, a distance of about five miles. The first private boat dock going downstream from the dam is Fall Creek Dock, located on the left bank, just downstream from where Fall Creek enters Taneycomo, just past marker No. 20. The river makes a sharp bend to the right and Short Creek enters Taneycomo from the right bank.

There are gravel bars below Fall Creek and above Short Creek that boaters should watch for in low-water situations, but for the most part you are in a lake-like environment from here to Ozark Beach Dam. During power generation, the dropoffs below those gravel bars will hold good numbers of trout.

There are still some good fly fishing opportunities here, and this is an excellent area for jig fishing with spinning gear.

It's in this area, around marker Nos. 16 and 17, where Kevin Elfrink caught his 25-pound, 15-ounce state record brown trout.

There is no public access. Boaters must come down from the public ramp at Table Rock State Park or up from the ramps in Branson.

3) Highway 65 bridge to Bee Creek, a distance of just under four miles. This is easily the most-used section of Lake Taneycomo. Three bridges, the City of Branson Campground, numerous resorts and two city limits - Branson and Hollister, are located within this short stretch of Taneycomo.

The effects of power generation from Table Rock Dam are hardly noticed. Bait fishing is by far the method of choice here. Most anglers anchor and fish the deep holes. Trolling with artificial lures is also effective.

4) Bee Creek to Ozark Beach Dam, a distance of 11 miles. If you've seen the White River in Arkansas between the lock-and-dams above Batesville, this area will remind you of that. The river is wide and slow moving, and there is a definite sense of getting away from the bustle of Branson. Trolling is one of the top methods of

trout fishing in this area. There are a couple of islands just below marker No. 9. Bull Creek, a major tributary, enters from the left side just above the town of Rockaway Beach, opposite of marker No. 8.

The mouth of Bull Creek is so wide that it can cause confusion for boaters coming from the lower part of the lake, as it looks like it could be the main White River channel. There is public access at Rockaway Beach Park.

A mile past Rockaway Beach, Lake Taneycomo makes a sharp bend to the right. In the middle of this bend on the lefthand side is Cedar Point, a high bluff. Below it is some of the deepest water (about 45 feet) in Taneycomo.

With the cold current from Table Rock Dam running under the surface and warm tributaries and coves along both banks, this area is popular with black bass and crappie anglers as well as trout anglers. Just like in the section upstream, still-fishing with bait and trolling with artificials are the most popular methods.

Near the dam, there is public access at the Empire District Electric Company Park, which includes two boat ramps.

5) Below Ozark Beach Dam. Although technically this isn't part of Lake Taneycomo, it has a bunch of Lake Taneycomo trout in it, as fish can easily survive a spill over the 50-foot high Ozark Beach Dam. Plus, some trout stocked in Bull Shoals Lake may make their way up river to this area.

On March 27, 1994, Arkansas resident Mike Dees caught a 27-pound, 4-ounce brown trout in Bull Shoals Lake near Lead Hill Boat Dock. MDC biologists believe the fish came from Taneycomo.

Dees used a Rattlin' Rogue to catch his big brown. Rogues and Rapalas are good choices here, as well as live baits like shiners and nightcrawlers.

Walleye are an added bonus in this area. A Missouri state record walleye of 21 pounds, 5 ounces was caught on a nightcrawler here in 1988.

When rainfall and power generation are light, this area can offer some good wading and fly fishing.

Powersite Dam Signalled Start Of Tourism Boom

Although it formed a pond in comparison to the huge U.S. Army Corps of Engineers lakes that were to follow, Powersite Dam in Missouri foreshadowed future development in the Ozarks.

In 1911 Congress granted approval for Powersite Dam and by 1913 it was reality - the first dam on the White River. The dam is 1,300 feet long and forms 2,080-acre Lake Taneycomo, named for Taney County, Missouri. At that time it was reported to be the largest impoundment in the U.S. for the production of electricity.

That was big news, coming only 26 years after Thomas Edison's Pearl Street Station in New York City had become the first central power station in the world.

But Powersite Dam (now named Ozark Beach Dam) was just as important for its influence on tourism. Lakes, like trout, aren't native to the Ozarks. The abundance of rivers and streams that carved their way through the geological plateau known as the Ozarks found no natural lakes or obstructions in their paths. Thus, Lake Taneycomo was unique to the area and quickly turned nearby towns like Rockaway Beach, Missouri, into tourist attractions.

Lake Taneycomo did not, however, signal the beginning of tailwater trout fishing in the Ozarks. The lake is relatively shallow and water flows over the top of the 50-foot high spillway, so the water below Powersite Dam is about the same temperature as that in the lake. Before Table Rock Dam was built, the White River here remained a warmwater fishery. Not until cold water started flowing from Table Rock Dam did trout fishing become a possibility in Lake Taneycomo.

Table Rock Dam's location 22 miles upstream from Powersite Dam provides a comparison of hydropower production advancements in the first half of the 20th century.

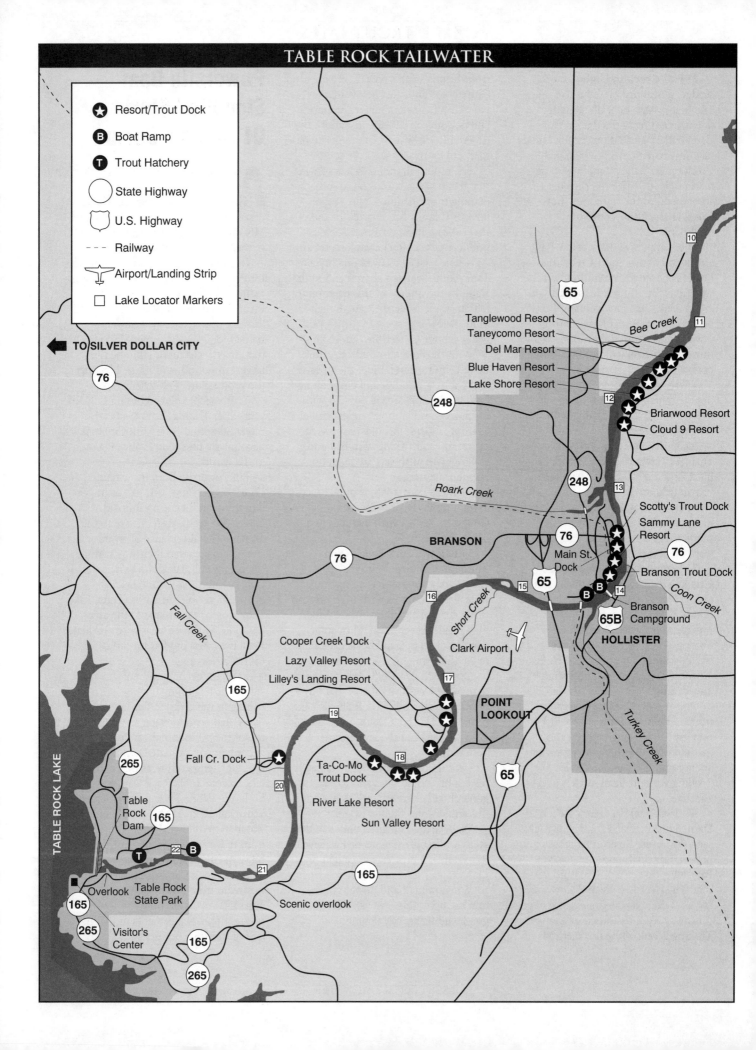

TABLE ROCK TAILWATER

Legend

⭐ Resort/Trout Dock
Ⓑ Boat Ramp
Ⓣ Trout Hatchery
◯ State Highway
⬭ U.S. Highway
- - - Railway
✈ Airport/Landing Strip
☐ Lake Locator Markers

← **TO SILVER DOLLAR CITY**

76

65

10

11

Tanglewood Resort
Taneycomo Resort
Del Mar Resort
Blue Haven Resort
Lake Shore Resort

Bee Creek

248

12

Briarwood Resort
Cloud 9 Resort

248

Roark Creek

13

BRANSON

Scotty's Trout Dock
Sammy Lane Resort

76

76

76

Main St. Dock

65

Branson Trout Dock

14

Branson Campground

65B

HOLLISTER

16

15

Fall Creek

Short Creek

Clark Airport

Coon Creek

Cooper Creek Dock
Lazy Valley Resort
Lilley's Landing Resort

17

POINT LOOKOUT

165

19

Fall Cr. Dock

Ta-Co-Mo Trout Dock

18

65

Turkey Creek

River Lake Resort

Sun Valley Resort

265

20

TABLE ROCK LAKE

Table Rock Dam

165

Ⓣ 22 Ⓑ

265

Overlook

Table Rock State Park

21

Scenic overlook

165

165

Visitor's Center

265

165

265

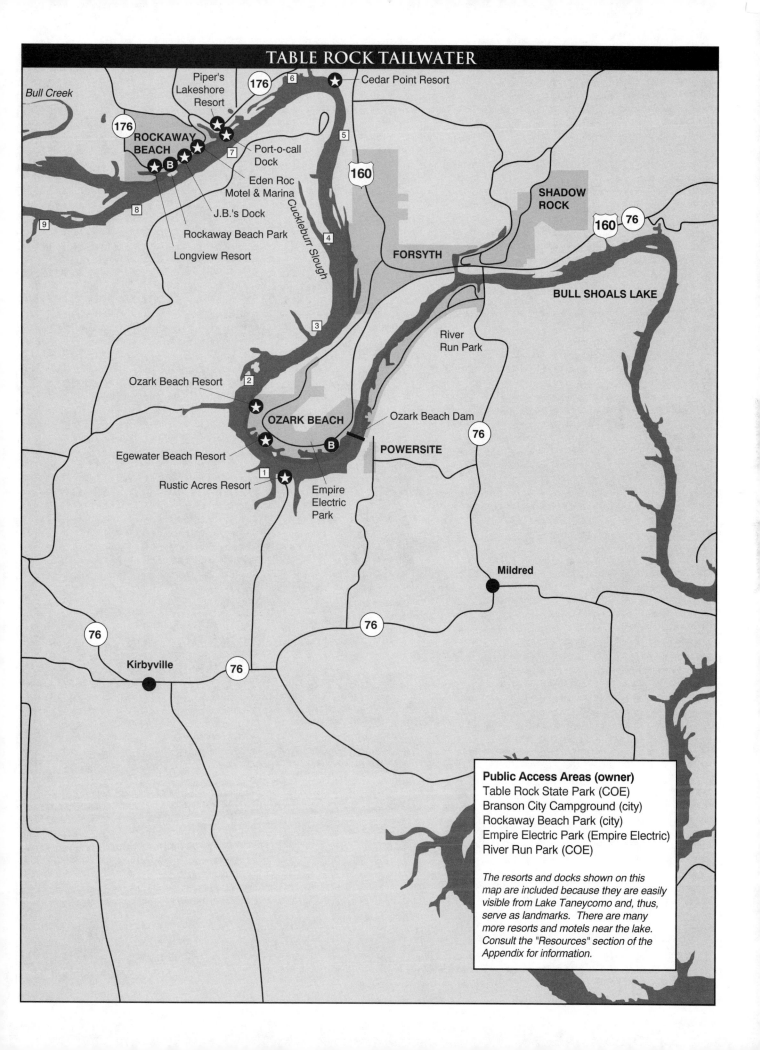

TABLE ROCK TAILWATER

Bull Creek

176

ROCKAWAY BEACH

176

6

Cedar Point Resort

Piper's Lakeshore Resort

5

Port-o-call Dock

7

160

Eden Roc Motel & Marina

J.B.'s Dock

8

Rockaway Beach Park

9

Longview Resort

Cuckleburr Slough

4

SHADOW ROCK

160 **76**

FORSYTH

BULL SHOALS LAKE

3

River Run Park

2

Ozark Beach Resort

Ozark Beach Dam

OZARK BEACH

B

76

POWERSITE

Egewater Beach Resort

Empire Electric Park

1

Rustic Acres Resort

Mildred

76

76

76

Kirbyville

76

Public Access Areas (owner)
Table Rock State Park (COE)
Branson City Campground (city)
Rockaway Beach Park (city)
Empire Electric Park (Empire Electric)
River Run Park (COE)

The resorts and docks shown on this map are included because they are easily visible from Lake Taneycomo and, thus, serve as landmarks. There are many more resorts and motels near the lake. Consult the "Resources" section of the Appendix for information.

WHITE RIVER

BULL SHOALS TAILWATER

Ozark Traditions Of Floating, Fishing Remain Strong

You will hear the expression on the Beaver and Table Rock tailwaters of the White River. An angler will ask, "How is the fishing on the White River?," or say, "I like to get over to the White River whenever I can," or mention a big brown trout caught "on the White River."

If you're new to the area, this might sound puzzling. "Doesn't he know he's on the White River now?" you think.

But after you've been around Ozark trout fishing for any length of time, you come to know that "White River" means the Bull Shoals Tailwater - 101 miles of trout water from Bull Shoals Dam to Lock & Dam No. 3 below Guion.

This is as close as you get to what the White River might have looked like when Henry Rowe Schoolcraft floated down it in 1819 and called it "one of the most beautiful and enchanting rivers which discharge their waters into the Mississippi."

Of course, three big U.S. Army

◀ **Float fishing for trout extends 101 miles below Bull Shoals Dam to Lock & Dam No. 3 below Guion.**

Over one million rainbow trout are stocked in the Bull Shoals Tailwater each year. Most are 9 inches long.

Corps of Engineers dams have been built on the White River since then and the water flowing from them is cold. Smallmouth bass habitat has been changed to trout water.

But the Bull Shoals Tailwater retains the classic float stream characteristics that made it famous before the dams were built - a long stretch of clear

water bordered alternately by bluffs and gravel bars. The overnight camping trip is still common on the Bull Shoals Tailwater. The other White River System tailwaters are too short to need a commissary boat and crew moving ahead of the anglers and setting up camp downstream.

And when it comes to trout fishing, the Bull Shoals Tailwater is unsurpassed. It has approximately 188 brown trout per mile in excess of 5 pounds, according to data from 1993 and 1994 Arkansas Game and Fish Commission population estimates compiled by trout biologist John Stark.

"As far as I can determine, this officially makes the Bull Shoals Tailwater the best brown trout stream in the world," Stark said.

That doesn't come as a surprise to long-time White River anglers, like world-renowned fly fishing expert Dave Whitlock, who has fished here since 1956.

"I've never seen water anywhere I've ever gone that has the richness of this water, as far as the quality of the fish it grows and how fast it grows them," Whitlock said.

BULL SHOALS TAILWATER AT A GLANCE

Location: On river mile 418.6 of the White River, Bull Shoals Dam is about 12 miles west of Mountain Home, Arkansas, on Highway 178.

Road Mileage to Bull Shoals Dam:

Little Rock, Ark.	170
Tulsa, Okla.	239
Shreveport, La.	411
Memphis, Tenn.	205
Kansas City, Mo.	260
St. Louis, Mo.	267
Dallas, Texas	468
Chicago, Ill.	590
Wichita, Kan.	343

Length of Trout Waters: Because Bull Shoals Dam has eight hydroelectric power generators and because the Bull Shoals Tailwater receives another charge of cold water from Norfork Dam 44 miles downstream, the trout habitat extends approximately to Lock & Dam No. 3 below Guion, Arkansas, - a distance of 101 river miles.

Dam: Commercial power generation began in 1952. The overall project wasn't completed until December 1963 when the last two generating units were installed. Cost of the project was $85.9 million. The dam forms a 45,440 lake at the power pool level of 654 feet above sea level. However, Bull Shoals has by far the largest flood control pool of the White River System dams. It becomes a 71,240-acre lake at the top of the flood control pool - 695 feet above sea level.

Trout Stocking: In 1952, a total of 16,156 rainbow trout and 1,800 brown trout, all 6 to 8 inches long, were experimentally stocked from Bull Shoals Dam to the confluence with the North Fork River. The 1994 stocking schedule called for 865,000 9-inch rainbow trout, 360,000 12-inch rainbow trout, 100,000 brown trout and 150,000 cutthroat trout for a total of 1.475 million trout.

Fishing Regulations: Daily limit is 6 trout, including not more than 2 browns or cutthroats. Brown trout daily limit is 2 with a 16-inch minimum size limit. Cutthroat trout limit is 2 with a 16-inch minimum.

Catch-and-Release Zones: From Nov. 1 through Jan. 31 (during the brown trout spawning season), brown trout caught from Bull Shoals Dam to the downstream boundary of Bull Shoals State Park must be released. Tackle within this zone is restricted to artificial lures or flies with a single, barbless hook.
(As of January 1995) Catch-and-release fishing only with barbless-hook artificial lures from 1) Bull Shoals Dam to 100 feet above Rivercliff Trout Dock (1.0 mile), and 2) Jenkins Creek to the powerline at lower Rim Shoals island (1.5 miles).

Scenic Views: There are dozens, but a good start would include: 1) Bull Shoals State Park, which provides an overlook near the dam; and 2) an overlook off Highway 412 west of Cotter, which includes a view the rainbow-arched bridge.

Power Generation Information: Call U.S. Army Corps of Engineers Bull Shoals Dam powerhouse at 501-431-5311 for a recorded message of current conditions. For a 24-hour forecast, call the Southwest Power Administration recorded message center at 918-581-6845 and press #14 for Bull Shoals Dam.

Historical Note: The exact origin of the name "Bull Shoals" is unclear, but the shoals where the dam now sits had that name when Henry Rowe Schoolcraft visited in 1819. He wrote: "Here the river has a fall of 15 or 20 feet in the distance of half-a-mile and stands full of rugged calcareous rocks, among which the water forms and rushes with astonishing velocity and incessant noise."

One look at the progression of Arkansas' state record trout confirms that. In the first year records were kept, 1959, the rainbow trout mark was broken four times - going from 11 lbs., 3 oz., to 15 lbs., 3 oz. All were caught in the White River below Bull Shoals Dam. Rainbow trout weren't stocked here until 1952.

The "twin lakes" area around Bull Shoals and Norfork has become a popular retirement and tourist area since the dams were built. Although new developments are common now, the Bull Shoals Tailwater still has a sense of remoteness about it. Commercial operations are concentrated in the first 18 miles, from the dam to Cotter. There are long stretches, especially from Norfork to Guion, that show few signs of development.

Ironically, Bull Shoals Dam itself helps maintain a sense of wildness here. With eight hydroelectric power generators, it has twice as many as any other White River System dam. When all eight generators are running, the Bull Shoals Tailwater becomes a swift, powerful, dangerous river. The combination of strong current and cold water proves deadly almost every year for inattentive waders and inexperienced boaters. And all that swift water keeps some people away out of fear.

At its lowest level, when no generators are running at the dam, the Bull Shoals Tailwater again presents problems for the inexperienced boater. Certain sections, like Wildcat Shoals, become almost impassable.

The high-water dangers, the low-water hassles and a world-wide reputation for excellent trout fishing create a high demand for guides. Cotter, Arkansas, bills itself as the "Trout Capital of the World." While that could be debated, the Bull Shoals Tailwater is no doubt the fishing guide capital of the Ozarks. It's estimated that well over 200 fishing guides regularly work the Bull Shoals Tailwater, most on a parttime basis, but at least 100 call it their fulltime job.

Because of the competitiveness between commercial operations and the guides themselves, the art and science of catching trout has developed here like nowhere else in the White River System.

No matter how you want to fish for trout - from dropping softshell crawfish in front of trophy-size brown trout to fly casting size 24 midges for surface-feeding rainbow trout - you can find a guide who specializes in it on the Bull Shoals Tailwater.

The better guides, most of the ones that work at it fulltime, speak of the White River with pride and enjoy showing it off. And, if they've been here any length of time, they've seen the rise and fall of the trophy-size rainbow trout population in the river.

Five-pound rainbows have gone from common to rare. But they've been replaced by 5-pound brown trout. There seems to be an attitude of protecting the larger brown trout that wasn't here in the days of the big rainbows.

"It made a lot of the old-timers mad if you released a fish," said Carl Jones, who started guiding in 1963, following in his father's footsteps. "They were out here meat-fishing and that's all they knew. People are getting more conscious about releasing fish now."

A general raising of the conservation consciousness has the potential to pay bigger dividends on the Bull Shoals Tailwater than anywhere else in the White River System. Its size and relative lack of development are the key factors in that equation.

But if you've seen the Bull Shoals Tailwater when no water is flowing from the dam, and what a trickle it becomes, you can imagine the positive effects minimum flow requirements could have on the fishery.

And if you've seen the long stretches of loose gravel and lack of vegetation in some parts of the river, you can imagine what some habitat rehabilitation would do.

Bull Shoals Dam has already become the testing ground for turbine modifications designed to raise low dissolved oxygen levels that occur in water released from the dams each fall.

Ultimately, the Bull Shoals Tailwater will be the standard for man's success or failure of the White River System trout fisheries.

Outfitter's Catch-And-Release Program Paying Big Dividends

Almost every business in the White and North Fork rivers area should be pleased with the idea of encouraging catch-and-release fishing, according to Ron Branaman at Gaston's Resort. As the two rivers have grown into trophy brown trout fisheries, resorts have grown into 12-month businesses.

"Without those big brown trout, we'd be painting cottages all winter like we used to," Branaman said. "When I started working here (in 1977), a lot of resorts shut their doors by November 1. Now it's not unusual for us to be full on weekends in December, January and February. Those people are here because of the trophy brown trout fishing."

In the fall of 1983, the White and North Fork Rivers Outfitters Association started a Trophy Trout Release Program. They defined "trophy" as brown trout weighing at least 4 pounds, and rainbow and cutthroat trout weighing at least 3 pounds. The angler who releases a trout meeting the requirements fills out a brief application form and receives a pin and a certificate.

"The first couple of years, people were real picky about getting verification," Branaman said. "Now about 90 percent of the fish are released at the water.

"We don't have to see the fish or a picture of the fish. We want them to be released as quickly as possible."

For that reason, trophy fish don't have to meet the weight requirement anymore either. Brown trout measuring 20 inches long and rainbows and cutthroats 16 inches in length qualify for trophy release. Both measurements are liberal adjustments on 4- and 3-pound requirements.

"I think the name of the game is keeping quality fish in the river," Branaman said.

The White and North Fork Rivers Outfitters Association has proclaimed this the most productive release program in the U.S. The program has averaged recording 1,500 trophy releases per year since its beginning. In 1994, a 19-pound brown trout was among those released.

"The program has made this river a helluva lot better and made everyone's business a helluva lot better," Branaman said.

"I think it has helped the whole area, not just the resorts, but the grocery stores and everywhere else people go when they visit here."

Many businesses have recognized this and help sponsor the Trophy Trout Release Program. It's helping other, not-so-local businesses, too. Atlas, Berkley, Mepps and Uncle Josh are among the major bait and lure companies that sponsor the program.

Sponsorship is important. The pins, which are varied somewhat on an annual basis, wholesale for $1.67. Printing certificates and mailing costs are added to that.

To help keep costs down, an angler is given only one pin per year. Certificates are granted for other trophy releases during a calendar year, but if you want another pin, you have to buy it for $3.

Branaman stresses, however, that you can't buy a pin without catching and releasing a trophy fish. "The highest degree of sportsmanship," as the Trophy Trout Release certificate states, must be earned.

Catch-and-release trout fishing has been slow coming to the Ozarks. The outfitters' voluntary program may have helped pave the way for the official arrival of catch-and-release.

In August 1994, the Arkansas Game and Fish Commission approved year-round catch-and-release-only areas in the Bull Shoals and Norfork tailwaters, as well as the Beaver and Greers Ferry tailwaters, effective Jan. 1, 1995.

Jerry McKinnis, left, and Forrest Wood have taken many fishing trips together since meeting on the White River.

Fishing Led Wood, McKinnis To Success

They met when Wood guided McKinnis on first White River float trip

In 1957, Jerry McKinnis was a much better baseball player than fisherman. After high school in a St. Louis suburb, he spent four years in the St. Louis Cardinals' minor league organization.

At the same time, Forrest Wood knew a lot more about paddling a boat than building one. A day of paddling a client down the White River in a wooden johnboat earned a guide eight bucks. And that's how Wood was making a living.

McKinnis' only trout fishing experience was at Montauk State Park, one of the put-and-take fishing parks operated by the Missouri Department of Conservation. He was glancing through an outdoors magazine one day when he read about a White River float fishing trip.

"I found out I could go on a float trip for $20, which included everything, so I started saving quarters in a fruit jar," McKinnis recalled.

On McKinnis' first White River float trip, Forrest Wood was his guide. "I remember how close Forrest and I got," he said. "I went to his house for supper that night. He and I have been friends ever since."

McKinnis also fell in love on that trip to Arkansas - with the Ozarks and the White River. "That was it for me," McKinnis said. "I had to go back to St. Louis, but, mentally, I never left."

McKinnis was in his early 20s when he left baseball in 1958. He bought a piece of property at the confluence of Crooked Creek and the White River. He was going to start his own float fishing service there. But before he could get started, G.O. Tilley left the trout dock at Bull Shoals State Park

and McKinnis started running it. Forrest Wood was still guiding on the river, too. As much as they loved that association with the river, guiding wasn't putting many beans on the table.

"I was starving to death," McKinnis said. "Forrest was struggling, too. Struggling big time. We were both trying our damnedest to figure out how to make a living."

McKinnis remembers a conversation that took place between the two guides. They were standing on the river bank near Cotter after a float trip. McKinnis had decided he was going to invest in a marina at Beaver Lake in northwest Arkansas. Wood said he was thinking about manufacturing fiberglass phone booths. Both men followed up on those intentions as a means of getting where they are today. But neither could have dreamed the scenarios that led them to success.

McKinnis got into the boat dock business at Lake Maumelle, near Little Rock. The late Bud Campbell was the top television sports anchor in Little Rock then. McKinnis took a big stringer of Lake Maumelle bass by the station one day, and Campbell aired the footage.

"Those were the days when we thought it was neat to hold up a big stringer of fish," McKinnis said. "It isn't so neat anymore."

That was 1963, and Campbell asked McKinnis to do a weekly fishing report for the station. It was called "The Fishin' Hole." Now, "The Fishin' Hole" anchors ESPN's Saturday morning lineup of outdoors shows. It is the longest-running, most popular TV fishing show in the country. It has allowed McKinnis to make a comfortable living while fishing all over the world.

Wood stayed in the float trip business for awhile, taking over the Bull Shoals Trout Dock after McKinnis left. He kept many of his guides employed through the winter months with a house construction business. In 1968 Wood got into fiberglass manufacturing, but he made six fishing boats - no phone booths.

The first Ranger boat cost about $300. Four years later, Ranger Boats in Flippin made 2,400 boats. After a brief setback when fire destroyed the plant, Ranger regrouped and peaked at 25 boats per day and 600 employees in a town that lists only 1,072 residents.

Forrest Wood is considered the father of the bass boat, the sleek fiberglass rigs that are standard equipment for any bass tournament angler. Industry representatives say if Wood didn't come up with the original idea (and he may have), he at least was the first one to promote it beyond its traditional boundaries.

It's easy to trace some standard features on today's bass boat, like livewells and comfortable seats, back to White River johnboats, according to Wood. "The first bass boat was sort of a glorified johnboat," Wood said.

And it's easy to trace the success of Ranger Boats back to managing a successful float trip operation.

"Because we were fishermen, we knew what people wanted," Wood said. "And because of our experience in the float trip business, we knew the value of promotion."

McKinnis and Wood haven't let success take them away from the White River. Wood and his wife, Nina, still take float trips down the river, along which they now own about 6,000 acres. McKinnis, who sold his original purchase of White River land to Wood, recently bought 150 acres just down river from his first holding and plans to eventually retire here.

"I always tell people that Forrest and I own 26 miles of White River frontage," McKinnis said. "I own half-a-mile and Forrest owns twenty-five-and-a-half."

> ## "After the dams were built, they stayed mad for the next five years because their smallmouth were gone."

Both can laugh about the good old days, when the trout were bigger than their bank accounts. Wood tells a story about guiding TV personality Harold Ensley on a trip in which Ensley had a six-trout-limit of rainbows weighing 52 pounds. McKinnis likes to tell a story about how Wood, while waiting to get his johnboat into the boat washing rack at the dock, put his one remaining salmon egg on a hook and caught a 15-pound trout. Similar stories were common in the late '50s and early '60s.

"Most of the fishermen around here had spent all their lives fishing for smallmouth bass," McKinnis said. "After the dams were built, they stayed mad for the next five years because their smallmouth were gone. All the time these trout were growing like a son-of-a-gun. The trout might average six or seven pounds. The fish wouldn't fit in our live boxes, so we'd always carry an ice box, and we'd fill it up after the livewell got full.

"I don't think anybody will ever see that kind of trout fishing in a three- or four-year period again. There are too many people fishing the river now, and they are too sharp now days."

Both McKinnis and Wood have ideas about how to bring White River trout fishing back to a semblance of those glory days. McKinnis favors a reduced creel limit plus a slot limit, like the regulations on the Green River in Utah. The daily limit is two trout - you may take only one over 22 inches long, and all trout between 14 and 22 inches must be released.

"I never saw so many three- to four-pound trout in all my life," said McKinnis, who taped a session for "The Fishin' Hole" there. "They don't have any more fish than the White River, but they are bigger."

Wood favors an increase in the minimum flow of water from Bull Shoals Dam. Under current management, power generation may be discontinued for several days in a row and stream flow slows to a trickle.

"Food production in the White River would increase about 400 percent if they improved the minimum flow," said Wood, a long-time cattle rancher. "Any farmer in the country knows that. Cattle are the same way. You dry up their pasture, and they won't produce."

Two men as successful as McKinnis and Wood are, naturally, going to look for ways to make anything the best it can be. Don't read any bitterness into their comments about what the river once was and is now. It's still one of the top trout streams in the world.

And McKinnis and Wood are here for the long run. They are protective of what is possibly the most important factor in their lives - the White River. McKinnis shudders at the thought of not seeing the magazine article that led to his first White River float trip.

"Would I have seen another magazine article on the White River?" McKinnis said. "Just what would have happened? It's really kind of scary because I would sure hate to have missed out on this life."

Pat Perdue Prefers A Natural Approach

Worms gathered from river bank prove to be favorite trout food

There were already two boxes of worms in the cooler. Pat Perdue had just launched his boat at White Hole Access. It seemed he hardly needed more worms.

But Perdue eased his johnboat to the bank and began running his fingers through clumps of moss that had been caught on limbs and rocks during higher water levels. Like magic, he started pulling earthworms from the moss. The worms were darker-colored, shorter and skinnier than what you'd find in your backyard garden and what you'd buy in the local bait shop.

"I've always said that in trout fishing, the more natural you can keep the bait the better off you are," Perdue said. "If it doesn't look natural, instead of being in the pole position, you are four or five rows back."

When you're fishing with Perdue, you're always in the pole position. Perdue has been guiding on the White River for 24 years, just over half his life. He prides himself on observing trout behavior.

"I'm a studier," he says. "I keep notes and file them away." His studies have paid off in the form of big trout he's caught. That list includes a 15-pound, 6-ounce rainbow, a 13-pound rainbow (both were 4-pound-test line class records), a 25-pound brown and a 7-pound cutthroat trout.

Perdue averages about 250 guide trips a year out of Bull Shoals Boat Dock. By far, the majority of those will be for just "fishing trips," not trophy fishing trips. Because of his knowledge of trout behavior, Perdue may be as good as anyone when it comes to catching numbers of trout, especially rainbows.

The "river worm," as Perdue calls the ones he finds along the river banks, is just one example of that knowledge.

"They make a big difference," Perdue said. "Other worms, as soon as they hit that cold water, they are dead. These stay fresh a whole lot longer.

Pat Perdue displays a rainbow trout that hit a "river worm" gathered from a bank along the White River near White Hole.

When the water goes up and down and the bank stays wet, it creates a perfect environment for them to live and reproduce."

Perdue says he "stumbled on to river worms." He was cleaning trout one day when he noticed small, dark worms in the fish stomachs. He had never noticed worms like that before. He started digging through moss and gravel at the river's edge and found them. It's something he has done many times since then.

"River worms were a secret for a while," Perdue said. "You don't want the word to get out when fishing is competitive as it is here. Once the word gets out and everybody's using it, a bait doesn't work near as well as before."

Although the word is out on these worms, they're still effective. Another key to making them more effective is how you place them on a hook. Perdue caught his 25-pound brown trout from the White Hole in 1975 on a mass of wiggling worms.

It's always a good idea to try something different, but on most occasions Perdue defers to the most natural presentation possible.

With river worms, that means threading one worm on a No. 4 hook. Start the hook point at one end of the worm; slide the worm all the way over the hook shank and eye and up the line. You are running the hook right through the middle of the worm, covering the hook completely. Stop just before the hook point comes out the other end of the worm, leaving a quarter-inch or less of the worm's body dangling. Again, no part of the hook should be visible.

It's easier to explain this than do it. Perdue can thread a worm on a hook as quickly as most people can pop on a few kernels of corn. It's difficult to keep the hook point running through the middle of these skinny river worms. It takes practice.

If Perdue can't find any river worms, he'll use a plastic worm made by Creme that matches the size of the natural bait and thread it on a hook the same way. One guide has nicknamed this lure "the magic worm."

Drag Chains: For Experienced Boaters Only

Pat Perdue wasn't the first White River angler to drag something along the river bed as a way to slow down his boat. But he doesn't mind being credited as the first to use a drag chain, at least the way it is used here now. And there are some anglers who think Perdue deserves blame, not credit, for the drag chain.

It's dangerous to drop an anchor in the White River when the power generators are running at Bull Shoals Dam. The anchor is likely to get hung on the bottom. The force of the current prevents you from loosening the anchor. This results in a capsized boat, which can be deadly in 50-degree water and strong current, or a lost anchor, provided you can cut the anchor rope and get yourself out of this predicament.

However, anglers need something to slow down their drift speed during heavy generation. Some of the old-timers would fill a plastic jug with gravel, attach it to a rope at the boat's bow and drag that downstream. It wasn't as heavy as an anchor and was less likely to get hung on the bottom.

The idea is to slow down the boat enough to fish more effectively. The current at the surface is faster than that along the bottom, where it gets slowed by the streambed. Trout will hold and feed in the slower moving water near the bottom. To present a lure or bait most effectively, it should be drifting at the same speed as the water. Unless the boat is slowed somehow, it will move at the same rate as the surface current and, therefore, pull a bottom-fished lure or bait unnaturally fast.

Perdue may or may not have been the first to attach an 18-inch section of half-inch chain to a rope and drag it down the White River. But he, at least, helped popularize it.

"Everybody used to turn the boat sideways and cast upstream," Perdue said. "But that can spook the fish when you drift over them like that. A drag chain slows the boat down and positions it so you don't drift over the fish. When I first started using it, people would yell at me to get my anchor in or I was going to sink."

Some anglers yell at Perdue for other reasons. They believe the use of drag chains destroys aquatic vegetation on the streambed. In 1981 the Arkansas Game and Fish Commission backed up that theory by banning the use of drag chains in the North Fork River.

"I can't see where chains are hurting the river at all," Perdue said.

The drag chain issue basically boils down to a power struggle between fly fishers and anglers like Perdue. "Fly fishermen and bait fishermen have been in a silent war," Perdue said. The drag chain issue broke the silence. Perdue counters that a wading fly fisher does more damage to aquatic vegetation than an 18-inch section of half-inch chain.

Drag chains aren't a perfect answer for drift fishing success. "Even with the drag chain out, you sometimes can't get the boat to drift just right," Perdue said. "So I just keep the motor running to either slow down or speed up."

And there are many bait fishermen who won't use a drag chain in the White River, where it is allowed. Despite their light weight and slim profile, it's common for a drag chain to hang up on the bottom. If you happen to be standing in the boat, or simply leaning to one side, the jolt when a drag chain hangs is likely to send you swimming.

A fishing guide is often out of his seat, as helps a client or maneuvers the boat. Perdue admits he has taken a swim before, due to a drag chain. He doesn't know many guides who haven't. That must be a horrifying sight for two first-time White River trout fishers, to see their guide go in the river as they sit in a boat they know nothing about operating.

The message on drag chains is clear. If you're in the North Fork River, you can't use them. If you're anywhere else, use them with extreme caution.

Canceled Trip Meant Big Fish For Perdue Family

For Pat Perdue, it was love at first sight of the Bull Shoals area. Born in Missouri, Perdue decided to "come down here and hack out a living," after a tour in the Air Force. Fishing guide has been his profession ever since. "I'll guide until I can't pickup that (outboard) motor anymore, I reckon," Pat says. "It's just an enjoyable profession."

Perdue enjoys being on the river, period. He was booked for a guide trip on August 8, 1976, but his client canceled. So Perdue scheduled a family fishing trip. Pat and Carole Perdue's sons Jeff and John were 8- and 6-years-old at the time. They caught so many trout that day they couldn't hold a fishing pole any longer.

"I cast out and tried to hand the rod to Jeff," Pat said. "He said, 'No, dad. I don't want to fish no more.' It could have just as easily been him as me holding that rod."

But Pat Perdue was holding it when a big trout hit. At that time, Perdue held the International Spin Fishing Association's 4-pound-test line class record for rainbow trout of 13 pounds. A month earlier, he caught the big rainbow on, he thought, 2-pound-test line. But the line sample he submitted tested just over 2 pounds, so Perdue's catch was put in the 4-pound class.

The Perdue family was fishing at the lower end of Wildcat Shoals when this big one hit. One hour, 10 minutes later and 2 miles farther downstream, Purdue had smashed his own record. The rainbow trout weighed 15 pounds,6 ounces. It was caught on 4-pound-test line, and the line tested at 4 pounds when submitted to the International Spin Fishing Association.

"I've always said it pays to take your wife and kids fishing," said Perdue.

When water is low, Perdue searches through moss and grass along the banks to find earthworms.

Perdue fishes worms on a standard White River drift rig - drop sinker and 12- to 18-inch leader. He'll anchor and cast it downstream into dropoffs and gravel bar edges during low water.

But Perdue would much rather trout fish when the power generators are running. Both his line-class-record rainbow trout were caught in high water.

"The fish are a lot less wary and they are in more of a feeding mode," Perdue said. "Think you are a lot more likely to catch a big one on high water than low."

Trout tend to move up on the gravel bars to feed during high water. The key is to keep the bait moving at the same speed as the current near the bottom, which will be slower than the flow at the surface. You don't want to be dragging your bait down the river; you want it to drift naturally, at the same speed everything else is moving.

This is where an experienced boat operator makes a big difference. It's easy to spot the amateurs. They'll be floating with the boat pointed at the bank, drifting lines upstream. They aren't only drifting too fast, but also their boat is passing directly over the fish before their bait arrives. In this clear water, trout are easily spooked by a boat passing over them.

The better method, as practiced by Perdue, is to point your boat upstream, keep the motor running in order to slow down the drift, and cast your line to one side, away from the boat. Perdue also uses a drag chain to slow the drift of his boat. (See related story.)

In addition to worms, either natural or artificial, Perdue likes to fish with salmon eggs, either natural or artificial. His 13-pound rainbow hit a worm; the 15-6 was caught on a salmon egg. Perdue has been swayed by the effectiveness of Berkley Power Eggs as a salmon egg imitation.

"I don't believe in endorsing anybody's product," Perdue said, "but it works. In my line of business, where I'm usually with somebody who fishes one or two times a year and wants to catch fish, I've got to use what works."

Again, Perdue keeps the presentation as natural as possible. During trout spawning periods, any kind of egg imitation drifting down the White River will draw some interest from trout. An egg pattern is one of the top producers for fly fishers. You are "matching the hatch," because real eggs are a common food source for trout.

"It's not natural to put two or three eggs on a hook," Perdue said. "I try to duplicate the natural food by putting just one egg on a number six hook."

Perdue fishes salmon eggs or Power Eggs just like he does worms, on a drop sinker and leader.

Another key to natural presentation, according to Perdue, is line. Perdue prefers 4-pound-test. He'll increase to 6- or 8-pound-test if a client wants to go strictly for big fish. Perdue favors Maxima's green line, but any neutral colored line will work.

"Just so it's not fluorescent," Perdue said. "I just shudder when I see fluorescent line on a reel because I know they would be doing so much better if they had a neutral colored line."

It's important to load that line on a spinning or spincasting reel that has a good drag system. If the drag system freezes up or isn't set properly in the first place, you have no chance to land a big trout on 4-pound-test line. Perdue recommends a medium action rod 6 feet or longer.

"Something between ultralight and heavy duty," he says.

Perdue has fished with just about every kind of trout bait. Many years ago, Velveeta cheese molded on a small treble hook was popular. In fact, cheese produced an Arkansas state record rainbow in 1968 (15 lbs., 8 oz., from the Little Red River).

But you won't see many people using cheese anymore. Perdue believes it is important to experiment.

"If you start out using corn and catch one, two or three fish, a lot of times they'll quit hitting it," Perdue said. "If you put on a worm, you might catch two or three more, then you might get a couple more on Power Bait.

"You need to keep alternating baits. It's like that in crappie fishing, too. If they quit hitting one color jig, you can change colors and they'll start hitting again."

The following are some tips from Perdue on other baits:

Corn: "I'm not a big corn fan," Perdue said. "Trout tend to pick it up and spit it out. They don't hold on to it. A worm or something soft they tend to hold on to longer."

Crawfish: The meat from a crawfish tail has caught some of the biggest rainbow trout in the Ozarks. Perdue likes to combine a crawfish tail and a worm. He threads the worm over the hook and brings the barb out one end, then he covers the hook point and bark with the crawfish tail meat.

"I don't know what that's supposed to imitate," Perdue said. "All I know is they like it."

Crickets: This is a natural food source for trout and one often overlooked by anglers. Perdue starts a No. 6 hook at the cricket's tail and brings it out, but just barely, right behind the head.

Jackie Due's Trout Knowledge Ranked Among Best On The River

A driving rainstorm finally forced Jackie Due to pull his johnboat into a nearby commercial dock, where he could wait this one out. A few minutes later, as Due bailed the rain water from his boat, a White River guide with 15 years experience watched and said, "I'd like to pick through that guy's brain. He's seen more on this river than most of us ever will."

As Jackie Due approached his 40th birthday, he had 27 years experience as a fishing guide. Yes, your math is correct; Due started guiding when he was 13. "I'd like to give it another 30 years," he said with a smile.

Jackie's father, Walter, was a fishing guide on the White River before Bull Shoals Dam was built. When the dam came, Walter changed from guiding for smallmouth bass to guiding for trout. There were 10 kids in the family, 4 boys. Walter owned a farm along the Blue Hole section of the White River, but guiding was his life. All of his sons became fishing guides, too.

"I grew up with it," Jackie said. "I used to clean boats in the summertime when I was out of school. One day a guide called in sick. My dad said to go ahead and take (the clients) out. On the first cast, this guy caught a 9 1/2-pound rainbow. We came in with the biggest string of fish that day."

That day marked the end of Jackie Due's formal schooling and the beginning of his reputation for being able to put a client on big fish.

"Once you start getting it in your blood, that's all you want to do," he said. "After I first started guiding, I started playing hooky from school so much they kicked my butt out."

Due does schoolwork with his kids now. "I've seen the mistake I made," he says. "A man must have an education in his day and time."

But all those days he spent on the river instead of the classroom gave Due an edge in his chosen profession. A lot of people know that. Due has had an

unlisted phone number for the last 10 years. He lets the folks at Bull Shoals Boat Dock, where he's booked out of, take all the calls. "It keeps people from driving me nuts at night," Due said.

Due has been around long enough to watch White River trout fishing techniques improve from primitive to innovative. "We used to drift sideways with a No. 5 sinker that was as big as the end of your fishing rod and 10- or 12-pound-test line," Due said. "But we started wising up."

The guides slowly adapted from bass to trout fishing techniques. Meanwhile, rainbow trout were growing incredibly fast, and there was little fishing pressure on them. As the anglers discovered baits like crawfish and salmon eggs, their fishing success improved.

"My biggest rainbow trout ever weighed 15 pounds, 11 ounces," Due said. "I caught it on a crawfish tail in the Armstrong Hole (near Cotter) in the early '60s."

Artificial lures, like Countdown Rapalas, also became popular. "When they first came out, a good Countdown cost 10 dollars," Due said. "You had to rent them around here, they were so scarce."

That was the golden era for the White River's rainbow trout. By the mid '70s, the overall size of rainbows had noticeably decreased. "Back then, there was no such thing as catch and release," Due said.

Now, if you want to catch a trophy-size trout in the White River, you've got to go for browns.

"The brown trout fishing is the best it has been in 20 years," Due said. "It's getting better every year, due to catch-and-release. I've released browns up to 18 pounds. Browns are considered a trophy species now on the river. This will continue to improve. People have learned to protect the environment."

And people, like Due, have learned how to catch brown trout. On New Year's Day, 1984, Due landed a

Jackie Due considers sculpins the No. 1 bait for catching trophy-size brown trout. He caught a 28-pound, 9-ounce brown trout on a sculpin in 1984.

pounder.

"I'm going to try to get it back," Due said.

He'll probably try to do that with a sculpin. These big-headed, prehistoric-looking baitfish are plentiful in the White River. As guides have learned, sculpins are an important part of a brown trout's diet.

"Troy Lackey was one of the first ones to use them," Due said. "He was the first one to learn how to hook them up. He kept it a secret for about a month, then all the guides knew."

Lackey, a long-time guide who once held the Arkansas brown trout record of 31 pounds, 8 ounces (caught on a crawfish in 1972), started threading a sculpin on a No. 2 hook and bringing the hook out one side, behind a pectoral fin. Lackey then made a half-hitch with the line and stuck the sculpin's tail through it. The result was a harness of sorts. A sculpin fished this way causes less line twist and gets better hook sets than any other typical method for hooking live bait, according to Due.

That brings up another aspect of using sculpins. Most anglers kill sculpins before using them as bait. Because it lives among rocks, fishing a live sculpin usually means staying hung up in the rocks.

If you are drifting a sculpin in strong current, a trout won't have time to tell if the bait is dead or alive. And brown trout will pick up dead sculpins even in low water and little current.

But Due likes to add some life to his bait when the power generators aren't running. In a variation of a common nightcrawler technique, Due takes a syringe and adds just a touch or two of air just under the skin of the sculpin's tail section.

"A sculpin is more of a natural bait for big brown trout than anything else in the river," Due said.

On low water, you've got to sight fish. After you spot a school of brown trout, anchor to the side, as far away as you can cast. Once the bait is in place among the fish, it's a waiting game.

"You may fish all day long for one bite," Due said.

But it's the best way Due knows to

28-pound, 9-ounce brown trout. The big brown went for a sculpin.

Today, Due considers sculpins the No. 1 bait for catching trophy-size brown trout, with softshell crawfish running a close second. Nightcrawlers have their place here too, but Due thinks nightcrawlers are better for catching browns up to about 8 pounds.

And, of course, you can mix and

match these baits to give the fish something they don't see often. In 1990, one of Due's regular clients, Dr. Jim Smith of Horseshoe Bend, Arkansas, caught a 16-pound, 4-ounce brown trout, which established a new IGFA record for 2-pound-test line. The big brown hit a combination of a nightcrawler and crawfish tail. Shortly afterward, White River guide Carl Jones broke the record with a 20-

catch a lunker.

"If I'm going to fish for big fish, I want low water," he said. "I will set up on them and sight fish."

Due believes light line is a key for getting these fish to take the bait. Then, after you've hooked a big brown trout on 2-pound-test, you've got to have a soft touch.

Both for casting distance and fighting big fish, many anglers, including Due, are starting to use long rods, as long as 9 feet.

If he can't get a big brown to hit a sculpin in low water, Due will put a nightcrawler on a No. 8 hook. The key is to hook the nightcrawler once, in the very tip of the head end, so it can drift naturally in the water.

"I catch a lot of 4- to 7-pound browns that way," Due said. "They go absolutely wild over it."

When he uses artificial lures, Due prefers old standbys like Countdown Rapalas (sizes 7 and 9) and Helfin's Flatfish (sizes 5 and 7). His favorite color pattern is black and silver. His favorite time to throw them is when the current is running at the equivalent of one generator.

Once you know what baits and lures to use and how to present them, you have to know where to fish them. Since brown trout are primarily nocturnal feeders, you'll seldom find them cruising near riffles and shallow gravel bars during daylight hours. They prefer deeper holes. Brown trout relate to structure like bass do.

During high water levels, Due drifts sculpins and nightcrawlers near the bottom over gravel bar dropoffs and rock ledges. Or he may anchor on the downstream side of an island and cast to the edge of an eddy.

Most of Due's fishing time is spent between the Bull Shoals Dam and Cotter. He knows every sunken log, cut bank, gravel bar dropoff, rock ledge and boulder in those 18 miles of the White River, as he should.

Due guides about 250 days a year, and he's spent over half his life as a guide. It's no wonder then that even long-time guides respect Due's knowledge of the White River.

Herding Trout: New Technique Goes Bad, Finally Banned

Pat Perdue and Jackie Due, long-time friends and fishing guides, were floating down the White River one day in separate boats. They stopped fishing for a moment and motored closer together to talk. Their 20-foot johnboats were end-to-end and perpendicular to the banks as they conversed their way through the White Hole. They happened to look down into the clear water at the same time, and neither man could believe his eyes.

"Every brown (trout) in the White Hole was below us," Due said. "There must have been 150 fish down there."

If two men who knew less about trout fishing and the White River had seen this, it might have passed as simply an unusual sight. But Perdue and Due have been making their livings too long with both eyes wide open on the river to let something like this be so easily dismissed. They quickly translated it into a way to catch brown trout.

Perdue and Due experimented with the technique and discovered you could herd brown trout into a small area and keep them there. By using an underwater ledge or gravel bar on one side and johnboats on the other, the fish could be bunched tighter and tighter, unless you moved the boats too close and forced them to scatter. It wasn't like shooting fish in a barrel, but it did increase your odds of catching a big brown trout.

It's hard to keep a secret on the White River. News about a new lure or a new way of fishing an old lure moves quickly through the circle of fulltime guides. Keeping something as visible as trout herding a secret was impossible. And when the word got out, the technique was refined into a brown trout massacre. As many as 15 boats would encircle a group of herded trout. Then every angler in each boat would toss a baited line into the middle of the bunched up browns.

Thousands of brown trout were caught this way; most were snagged.

"That's part of the past I'd like to forget," Perdue said. "I'm not proud of it. I'm not proud of it a bit."

The standard White River drift rig includes a small bell sinker attached on a dropper line. The hook is attached to another 24 inches or so of line. By pumping air into a nightcrawler, threading a marshmallow over the hook or adding a plastic glow worm, you can float the bait off the bottom. Some guides noticed that after the trout were herded up, you could toss handfuls of gravel into the circle and excite the fish. They would start working their jaws, biting at nothing but the irritation from above.

The fish that didn't get snagged in the tail or the belly, swam with open mouths into one of these floating lines, then hooked themselves. You could easily tell a fish that had been caught this way. The hook was stuck in the outside corner of the jaw. Once the line got in the fish's mouth, the moving fish would set the hook, like a dog running to the end of its leash.

"It's our fault it got started," Due said. "But we did not throw rocks, and we did not snag fish. The fish we caught were caught legitimately."

"All kinds of crazy stuff was going on," Perdue said. "Lots of big fish were taken out of here."

In the May 1981 meeting of the Arkansas Game and Fish Commission brown trout were declared "in eminent peril" because of herding. An emergency regulation was passed and went into immediate effect. The regulation is written as follows: (#31.12) Herding Trout Prohibited. It shall be unlawful on any trout stream in Arkansas to drive, pursue, harass or rally trout with the use of boats, wading, throwing objects, disturbing with noises, or by an other means for the intended purpose of concentrating or congregating trout.

Carrying On A Family Fishing Tradition

Carl, Paul Jones following in the footsteps of an Ozark fishing pioneer

When Bull Shoals Dam turned the White River from a small-mouth bass stream into a trout stream, it threw anglers for a loop. Trout aren't native to the Ozarks, and few people knew how to fish for them.

The late Preston Jones was one of the original White River trout guides. He'd worked as a guide before Bull Shoals Dam was built. In the early 1960s, Jones guided a fisherman from Kansas City who brought a jar of salmon eggs with him. Nobody had seen that bait here.

"They started drifting with salmon eggs and catching big fish," said Jerry McKinnis, host of ESPN's Fishin' Hole and a former White River guide. "Preston wouldn't say how they caught them. Preston is catching the hell out of these big trout, and nobody knows how he's catching them.

"We finally got on to it. We ordered salmon eggs and off went the big fish explosion."

That big fish explosion and learning its secrets are a big part of the Jones family history. Preston and Della Jones raised three sons and a daughter. Two of those sons, Carl and Paul, started guiding as teenagers with their father - Carl at age 14 and Paul at 16. Preston Jones guided for 28 years. He died of emphysema in 1981 at the age of 62. By then he had inflicted a powerful fishing fever on Carl and Paul.

"He had some fun with those salmon eggs for awhile," Paul recalled. "He wouldn't tell anybody."

That's part of a good fishing guide's makeup - the desire for a competitive edge. In their younger days, after Carl and Paul finished their guide trips, they'd often get together and fish half the night, even though another guide trip was scheduled early the next morning. More time on the river meant, one, more time doing what they loved best and, two, a competitive edge.

Carl and Paul now have over 50 years of guiding experience between

Carl Jones set the International Game Fish Association 2-pound-test-line class record in 1987 when he caught a brown trout weighing 20 pounds, 12 ounces.

them. They've worked for various trout docks along the White River from Bull Shoals Dam to Calico Rock.

Carl claims he and his fishing clients have caught 26 brown trout weighing over 20 pounds. Carl set the International Game Fish Association 2-pound-test line brown trout record of 20 pounds, 12 ounces in 1987. He was featured in a book series entitled "Secrets of the Fishing Pros," pub-

lished by The Hunting and Fishing Library.

Paul has a 20-pound brown trout and 14-pound, 8-ounce rainbow trout to his credit. They can't begin to guess how many trout over 10 pounds have been caught from a boat with Carl or Paul Jones at the helm.

From spring through fall, a well-known trout guide often works seven days a week here. Sometimes the days would mount up to 100 in a row on the river.

"It's rough on a marriage," said Carl. "You leave before daylight a lot of times, and you don't get home until late."

If a marriage survives trout fishing season, it is usually tested again with deer hunting season.

"Your wife says, 'You've got to do what?' But most guides like to hunt," Paul said. "That's our vacation time, deer season."

It's no coincidence, this love for both fishing and hunting that many of the best guides have in common. Especially in clear Ozark waters, where fish are easily spooked, you can understand the similarities in stalking a trophy deer and catching a trophy trout.

"Paul is one of the best deer hunters I've ever been around," Carl said. "If there's a buck in the woods, he'll find it. As big as he is, you wouldn't think he'd be able to slip up on anything."

What we're really talking about here is not just an enjoyment of the fishing and hunting but a love of the outdoors. A love greater than anything else. Carl and Paul Jones are "country boys." They grew up on a farm near Clabber Creek. The closest town, Yellville (population 1,181), was 18 miles away.

Although Carl and Paul may not always be trout fishing guides, they will always be part of the tradition of Ozark outdoorsmen. It's a tradition on the decline.

"I wish we had more young guys interested in learning how to guide on the river," Carl said. "I hate to say it, but we've got some guys that can run a boat and drink a beer and that's about it."

Carl has a son who tried the guiding business for a short time. Carl understands that his wish for more young guides and the reality of the business aren't compatible.

"I wouldn't recommend a young guy going into it," Carl said. "But if I had it to do over again, I'd do the same. I enjoy being outside."

Keeping Up With The Joneses

The following is advice from brothers Carl and Paul Jones on how to catch trout on the White River below Bull Shoals Dam.

Prime water conditions: In the first years that trout fishing was a possibility here, no one knew how to catch fish when the power generators were running. Everyone thought you had to have low water to catch trout. That thinking has changed completely.

"I like it when the water is high, four generators and up," said Paul. "My favorite is five or six generators. One reason I like fishing high water is the fish aren't as spooky. Fish are going to feed at all levels of water flow. But they'll be feeding in different areas at two generators, four generators and six generators."

Paul would much rather catch the river on the rise than on the fall. "When the water starts falling, those fish have noticed it before you have," Paul said. "Only two or three times in 24 years have I seen fishing good on falling water."

It is the fluctuations in water levels, so characteristic of this section of the White River, that irritate Carl.

"Where you caught fish one day, it

Paul Jones prepares to release a brown trout caught on a nightcrawler during low water conditions. Jones says fishing is best when the water is on the rise.

Both Jones brothers agree that a sculpin, like the one above, is the best bait for big brown trout, but they differ in their methods of putting one on a hook.

will be dry land the next," he said. "The main thing is consistent water - either real high or real low is fine, if it will be the same for two or three days. Brown trout don't feed well on low water until about the third day. They'll feed even better on the fourth and fifth days.

"It's the same way on high water. If it stays that way for a week, they'll feed better."

Sculpins for big browns: The two brothers differ in their techniques for hooking sculpins, the baitfish that are a favorite brown trout food.

Paul prefers the most common White River technique. A No. 6 long shank hook is stuck through a sculpin on one side of the tail and the barb is brought out the same side, just behind the pectoral fin. The line is looped around the sculpin's tail and held in place by a half-hitch.

"It's a matter of opinion, but I think that half-hitch weakens your line," Carl said.

So he threads the sculpin on a hook. He prefers a No. 4 long shank hook, which he weaves through a sculpin's tail three times, before bringing the barb out behind a pectoral fin.

"I started doing this 15 years ago," Carl said. "I fish a sculpin a lot. It's a good big-fish bait all the way around. But I think it works best early in the year. By around July, the fish have seen so many of them."

A sculpin hooked in both methods described here is, obviously, dead. Because of a sculpin's preference for laying in tight places between rocks, it's difficult to use one as live bait. Trout may become more wary of a dead sculpin during the months of heavy fishing pressure.

Although he'll sometimes use a big sculpin when going after a big brown trout, Paul prefers a medium-size bait.

"You don't have to let them take it as long," he said.

When fishing sculpins in low water conditions, Paul will cast and let the bait settle to the bottom. He takes the slack out of the line, then opens the bail on his spinning reel and holds the line with his index finger. If he feels a bite, he releases the line, so the fish can't detect any tension.

With a thick bait like a sculpin and the hook hidden behind a pectoral fin, sometimes it's difficult to get a good hook set.

"The main thing is to set the hook when the fish is moving away from you," Paul said.

Paul favors 6-pound-test line for fishing sculpins in low water. Carl sometimes moves up to 8- and 10-pound-test when he has a chance at a bigger than usual brown.

"Once a brown trout gets over 20 pounds, it's got some mean teeth," Carl said. "A lot of times with a sculpin, the fish will have it deep in its mouth, and those teeth will saw the line."

There's one other trick for fishing a sculpin: Skin it. Take hemostats or needlenose pliers and strip the sculpin's dark skin - from the pectoral fins back to the tail - exposing the light-colored meat.

"Some days that works, some days it doesn't," Paul said. "I don't know why, but some days it makes a difference."

Throwing hardware: That's what Carl calls fishing with artificial lures - throwing hardware. When the power generators are running, Carl enjoys casting artificial lures, mostly on spinning tackle, but sometimes on baitcasting gear. His favorite hardware includes: Shad Raps, Countdown Rapalas and Luhr Jensen Krocodile Spoons.

"We throw a lot of hardware in the winter," Carl said.

Winter is the time when threadfin shad in Bull Shoals Lake die because of cold weather. Any kind of shad imitating lure works well then. Paul prefers a 1/8th-ounce marabou jig. Carl uses a pearl-colored Krocodile Spoon - 1/4th-ounce on five to six generators and 3/8th-ounce on seven to eight generators. He slow-rolls the spoon off gravel bars.

Most of the year, Carl favors Countdown Rapalas in sizes 7 (2 3/4 inches long) and 9 (3 1/2 inches) in shad color patterns. He casts them on spinning gear and 6-pound-test line. But in the winter, he steps up to a CD11, which is 4 3/8 inches long, and he casts it with baitcasting gear and 8- or 10-pound test line.

"It's an awful big bait," Carl said. "But it will occasionally produce a great big fish. I jig it. Let it sink, then crank it about six feet, flash it."

He casts a Countdown Rapala at an upstream angle to give the lure a chance to sink. But he casts a Shad Rap at a downstream angle to let the current work on the longer-billed lure, giving it both action and depth. This can be exciting fishing because you can see fish chasing the lures, all the way to the boat at times.

However, if you want to catch a lunker, the lure has got to make a close pass.

"Big fish won't run a bait," Carl said. "The big fish here won't chase a bait two feet. Fish up to 10 pounds

> "The big fish here won't chase a bait two feet. Fish up to 10 pounds will chase it all the way to the boat, but all the great big fish I've caught on a lure hit while I was working it real slow."

will chase it all the way to the boat, but all the great big fish I've caught on a lure hit while I was working it real slow."

Just fishing: If you are out just to catch trout - numbers of trout, not trophy trout - there is no doubt about the best bait.

"In our business, there are so many women and kids out here who just want to fish, they'd have a tough time if it was all artificial," Paul said. "If I could only use one bait, it would be little red worms. They'll work on high water and low water."

Carl agreed, saying, "Red wigglers are as good a bait as you can use."

As for other baits, Paul says he usually carries a little bit of everything, including corn and Berkley Power Bait. Waxworms are a good choice. He puts two of them on a No. 8 short shank hook. He floats them off the bottom with either a small piece of Styrofoam on the line, near the hook, or with a little air (from a syringe) in the second waxworm. Crickets are also a good natural bait choice.

"Any kind of bug you can put on a hook will work," Paul said. "I've caught trout on butterflies and June bugs."

Trophy fishing: "There's nobody on this river who can catch big fish every day," Paul said. "I don't care who he is, and I've fished with just about all of them."

Patience is definitely the key. If you don't have it, don't waste your time with this aspect of Ozark trout fishing. If you hire a guide to go "trophy fishing," you need to know this can mean waiting on one big fish all day, and it can mean catching nothing.

"I used to ask people: do you want to fish for big fish or just fish," Paul said. "It helps to let the guide know the score."

There are more big brown trout in these waters than ever, but the number of trophy-size rainbows has dropped significantly. That has also changed the rules of the trophy fishing game.

"I used to say that anytime the river was low and I could find a big rainbow, I could set up on it and catch it," Carl said. "Brown trout aren't nearly as cooperative.

The first step is finding the fish. Both Carl and Paul have developed the ability to see fish that most people would never notice.

"I look for fins," Carl said. "They'll stand out in the water. Even if a fish is laying still, its fins will keep moving. You can see the outside edge of them. You can pick a big rainbow out of a bunch of browns because the tail fin is squared off and the rainbow will have a darker back."

Landing Record Brown Became Work After An Hour

Carl Jones didn't need a record to establish his reputation as a guide who knew how to catch big trout. But he had set a goal for himself, and he was determined to achieve it.

"I wanted to catch a fish over 20 pounds on 2-pound-test line," Carl said. "I really didn't care whether it was a record, I just wanted to make the 20-pound mark."

In fact, Jones may have set a record before reaching his goal. He caught a 16-pound, 2-ounce brown trout on 2-pound-test. Since it didn't top the 20-pound mark, he never submitted the catch to any of the record-keeping organizations.

Seven proved to be a lucky number for Jones. Seven years into pursuit of the goal, Jones had hooked "four or five" big brown trout, including two he was certain weighed over 20 pounds. But the 16-2 was the biggest he had landed.

Jones was one of the guides booked for a seven-boat group of anglers. The power generators were off, and Jones had spotted a school of big browns below Tucker Shoal. He watched as a big fish swam down the river to join the school.

"I was joking about it," Jones recalled. "I said, 'There's you a record fish.' One of the guys I was guiding said, 'If you think it's that big, bait up.' He wanted to watch the show."

A few minutes later, Jones had coaxed the fish into hitting a nightcrawler. "I enjoyed the fight for about an hour, then it turned into work," said Jones of the one-hour and 45-minute struggle.

Jones had to follow the fish up and down the river until it tired. The brown trout officially weighed 20 pounds, 12 ounces, and became an International Game Fish Association 2-pound-test line class record.

No More California Dreaming For Wilson

West Coast native finds fly fishing finally catching hold in the Ozarks

Hank Wilson will never forget the first day he took his fly rod to the White River. Wilson moved from Sacramento, California, to Bull Shoals, Arkansas, in 1978.

"Guides actually used to tell people to leave their fly rods in the cabin because trout don't hit flies over here," Wilson said.

The first day out with fly rod in hand, Wilson went to Cotter and walked upstream to avoid hearing the derisive comments of other anglers. In 45 minutes, he caught a limit of good-size trout.

"They asked me what I caught them on," Wilson said. "I showed them the little fly, and they wouldn't believe me."

Times have changed on the White River. Wilson, as much or more than anyone, has observed the influx of fly fishing here. He began working as a fishing guide in 1980. Although Wilson grew up in San Diego,

California, with a fly rod in his hand, he learned the methods of other White River guides - how to use bait and lures on spinning tackle.

"I didn't have anything to prove," Wilson said. "I listened to what a guy had to say, and I learned. I did a lot of overnight camping trips when I was first guiding. I always brought a lot of change to the nightly poker game, and I never minded giving it away."

There weren't many calls for fly fishing guides then. When a client did want to fish with a fly rod, many of the other guides would defer to Wilson.

"I probably did five or six fly fishing trips that first year," Wilson said. "The next year it was about 25, then it was probably 60 the next."

In 1993, Wilson guided 260 days out of Gaston's White River Resort, and 150 of those were fly fishing trips. Within that obvious statement about the increasing popularity of fly fishing is a message about Wilson, too. His

love of fly fishing, no matter how popular it gets, won't cause him to turn up his nose at other methods of fishing.

"You've got to have fun," said Wilson, as he cut a glance up to the sky. "I'm afraid that's going to be one of the questions they ask up there. Did you have fun?"

It was the pursuit of happiness that brought Wilson and his wife, Sarah, to the Ozarks in the first place. California's aerospace industry attracted many people from Arkansas, Missouri and Oklahoma in the 1960s and '70s. Wilson was employed as an aircraft tool designer, and he heard stories from the Ozark transplants about the White River.

"The industry kind of folded up," Wilson said. "From the stories I'd heard, this area reminded me of California back in the '50s, so I came out and took a look at it. The stories were surpassed by reality - all these great, friendly people, no crowds, no

Hank Wilson remembers the days when many anglers thought White River trout couldn't be caught on a fly rod.

crime, clean water. I remember back when California had that."

Wilson tried the cleaning business first. All the work was at night, and he could fish all day. Guiding soon became his fulltime job.

Wilson is the resident fly fishing expert at Gaston's White River Resort. He is the instructor at Gaston's two-day fly fishing schools, and Wilson ties all the flies available in Gaston's tackle shop.

Obviously, Wilson is benefiting from fly fishing's popularity. However, some aspects of this phenomenon trouble him, like clothing, for example. Heliotrope hats and chartreuse shirts aren't going to help anyone approach a trout in clear water.

"They might as well have a neon sign flashing, 'Predator, predator,'" Wilson said. "I kind of like to get everything down to earth."

Sometimes that means teaching anglers to keep both feet on dry land.

"I think 90 percent of us could use wading lessons," Wilson said. "Just because it says chest waders on the box doesn't mean it's a mandatory thing.

"I can walk the bank on a good day and in three hours catch 30-plus trout, without ever getting my boots wet. I can catch brown trout from two to four pounds just up from Gaston's without ever getting my boots wet."

Wilson says he has trouble convincing people how close the trout are. Loud clothes and wading will send the fish scurrying. But with a quiet approach, a beginning caster can catch fish.

"I try to get people to slow down and fish within 40 feet of the rod tip," Wilson said.

Wilson relies on his eyes. He looks for trout in "skinny water" - especially gravel bars, where an abundance of scuds attracts hungry trout. And Wilson would much rather cast to an actively feeding trout than one resting near the bottom of a deep pool.

Even big brown trout will make regular feeding runs through shallow water, Wilson says. A pair of polarized sunglasses is crucial for figuring out the feeding patterns.

"Feeding brown trout will pick up food in two or three spots and no other place," Wilson said. "They ignore everything else in between. The trick is to get the fly into the spot where they are feeding."

If you think this is strictly an early-morning routine, Wilson has some advice: Stay in bed, the trout will wait on you. Most guided fishing trips on the White River begin about 7:00 or 7:30 a.m. Prime feeding time for trout is often an hour or two away, according to Wilson.

"A lot of fly fishermen are used to fishing western streams," Wilson said. "They'll pound the river here until eight or nine o'clock, then leave convinced there are no trout. But this is not a real early morning proposition. You can do a lot of fly fishing in the fog with very few results. Eight-thirty seems to be turn-on time, especially in the summer. You can almost set your watch by it."

On this particular early fall day, the trout didn't make a liar out of Wilson. At 8:30 a.m., Wilson beached his 20-foot fiberglass johnboat just below Wildcat Shoals and began fishing to a pod of rising trout. A size 16 peacock herl creation that Wilson calls his "What-A-Fly" produced several rainbow trout up to 14 inches.

It was that way the rest of the day - simple patterns, short casts, feeding fish. With two power generators running at Bull Shoals Dam, the water level was higher than most fly fishers prefer on the White River.

But, as you might expect from a California native living in Arkansas, Wilson has learned to adapt. He kept his casts close to the bank, where the fish tend to congregate as the current increases.

Six weeks earlier, Wilson made a point of counting the anglers from Gaston's down to Wildcat Shoals. Of the 48 fishing from the bank or wading, 35 were fly fishing.

"I was astounded," Wilson said. "I'd never seen that many people fly fishing on this river."

Wilson smiled. It now seems like a century ago when they said you couldn't catch White River trout on a fly.

Hank's Tips For Fly Fishing The Bull Shoals Tailwater

There are four distinct seasons in the Ozarks, and trout fishing can be good in all four. Hank Wilson offers some basic guidelines for fly fishing the Bull Shoals Tailwater, plus some seasonal advice.

Concerning the basics, Wilson recommends a 6-weight, 8- or 9-foot fly rod, if you are limited to one. From April through October, a second rod should be in the 2- to 4-weight range for fishing smaller stuff, like scuds, sowbugs, emergers and dry flies. From October through March, a second rod choice might be a 7- or 8-weight, for casting bigger sculpin and shad patterns and slinky rigs during the brown trout spawn.

Sowbugs and Scuds All Year: The White River carries huge populations of sowbugs and scuds year-round. If you carry nothing else in your fly box, include sowbugs and scuds in sizes 14 through 18.

Sowbugs are most plentiful from the dam to Wildcat Shoals, but the pattern will work all the way down the river. Wilson thinks a light gray color is important, something that won't get dark when wet, so he prefers a light gray, fine chenille for body dubbing material.

He usually ties sowbugs in sizes 14 and 16, and he weights some of them with fine lead wire. The shellback can be made of clear Mylar or a plastic bag strip; Wilson prefers Mylar for its durability. For durability and definition, Wilson uses 2-pound-test monofilament for ribbing.

"The most important thing with a sowbug is to keep it light," Wilson said. "I like to fish them with a good cross-stream cast, put a big mend in the line, then let the line flow down past me. I don't like to use them on a strike indicator. A strike indicator casts a big shadow on a clear, sunny day, plus, it will also make the leader butt sit up high and cast a big shadow."

Scuds are best fished on the light-colored gravel bars that are so common in the White River. Wilson says many anglers mistakenly pound the dark, shady side of the river during low water conditions, when actually the trout will be feeding in shallow water on the gravel bars.

Just as with the sowbug, color is important when tying a scud. A peachy-tan color is best, tan with a hint of orange. Wilson achieves this color by blending squirrel belly fur and camel dubbing, but you can also buy a dubbing material in this color.

Most of the time Wilson ties scuds on a size 14 hook. He'll vary it by using both scud hooks and regular hooks. He also ties two versions of the scud - one with a solid wire rib and Mylar shellback, and another with an oval gold wire rib.

"I'll fish them in knee-deep water on gravel bars and catch fish all afternoon," Wilson said. "I use a 12-foot leader and 5X or 6X tippet. It's a good thing to do on a dog-day afternoon."

Spring: Late March and early April is good bug-hatching time on the White River, especially for caddisflies. A Red-Butted soft hackle, sometimes called a Red Ass or Red Ass Kelso, is Wilson's favorite pattern this time of year. He uses dubbed rabbit fur and partridge hackle tied on the upper third of short size 12 and size 14 dry fly hooks - 12s early in the spring and 14s later. He adds just enough red thread to show above and below the body.

"Look for rising fish," Wilson said. "Fish it wet. Make a downstream and across cast, give it a little jerk to get it under the surface, then use a basic wet fly swing.If nothing hits it on the swing, give it a short twitch or two."

As the hatch gets busier, Wilson will go to a caddis dry fly with tan or light gray wings. Wilson varies from the standard Elk-Hair Caddis pattern. Sparseness is important because the caddis will be fished in slow water primarily, and Wilson wants the fly to sit lower in the water.

The body is made from Kauffmann's scud blend in a green color that is tied with white 6/0 thread.

Wilson doesn't add any hackle, and the wings are on the small side. For the wings he uses coastal deer hair, which is denser and finer and doesn't flair as much as elk hair.

Also at this time of year, olive Woolly Buggers and Red Fox Squirrel nymphs are good patterns.

May - June: The mayflies start hatching. Wilson carries only one dry fly to match the mayfly hatch, and it's his favorite dry fly pattern on the White River - a size 16 yellow Comparadun. Materials include: Mustad dry fly hook, coastal deer hair wings, microfibets tail and yellow superfine dubbing. An emerger imitation with tan soft hackle and a creamy-tan rabbit fur body in size 14 also works well during the mayfly hatch. You can get away with a size 14 Red Fox Squirrel nymph if you don't have the soft hackle emerger.

Another of Wilson's favorite patterns comes into its own in May and continues to work well through October. It's a peacock herl pattern; Hank calls his version of it the What-A-Fly.

"I had a client who was catching lots of fish on it," Wilson explained. "He kept saying, 'What a fly! What a fly!' every time he caught another trout. I thought I'd invented the pattern, but later I read John Gierach describing the same thing."

Wilson ties four or five strands of peacock herl at the base of the hook, usually size 14, with black thread. He then twists fine copper wire and the peacock herl together, which both binds the herl and gives the fly some weight. To this body he adds a sparse, brown hen hackle, about a turn and a half.

"Probably half the big brown trout I catch in the summer will be on that fly," Wilson said. "In hot months, it will keep on working. I've tied it without the hackle and it seems to work just as well, but it doesn't sell as well. If you added a white hackle to it, you'd have a Renegade."

Two flies are better than one, especially from May on, according to Wilson. He likes to combine a size 12

weighted Red Fox Squirrel nymph with a size 14 unweighted scud. He casts it across and downstream, then retrieves with a slow twitch-and-pause retrieve.

Summer: Crawfish and sculpin patterns are important now, in addition to Woolly Buggers, sowbugs and scuds.

Wilson ties crawfish patterns in rust, dark olive and gray for the White River. He generally uses a size 6 streamer hook, 4X-long, and bends down slightly the first quarter of the hook shank. He adds a couple turns of .03 lead wire at that new bend in the hook. The claws are little sections of Zonker strips that are lashed to the hook where the lead wire has been added. The body is made of shaggy yarn and the carapace of foam.

"I'll either weight the leader with split shot or use a sink tip line," Wilson said. "I'll cast it into fast water that enters a slow pool, let it sink, and the fly ends up in the seam. Get it on the bottom, then twitch it back. A crawfish pattern works best from Wildcat Shoals down. There seems to be more crawfish down there. This pattern will work all summer."

Wilson isn't as concerned about the looks of the sculpin pattern he uses as he is about how its fished. Rather than slowly working a sculpin through a deep hole, which Wilson considers boring, he works them in shallow water next to the bank.

It's a sight-fishing technique that Wilson uses in the first two hours after the fog lifts in the morning. He watches for brown trout feeding patterns. Then, from either a boat or the bank, he casts the sculpin into a brown trout's feeding lane. If he's casting from the bank, Wilson stays several feet away from the shoreline, so he won't spook the fish.

Fall: This is a big time for Woolly Buggers. A No. 8 olive Woolly Bugger heavily weighted is a White River standard year-round, but it's best in the fall, and Wilson has a big fish story to back that up.

"We usually have lot of low water in the fall, so I do a lot of sight fishing with Woolly Buggers," Wilson said. "I caught my best rainbow, 8 pounds, on No. 8 Woolly Bugger in October 1988.

"I spotted two fish, one was about 8 pounds and the other one was bigger, maybe 10 pounds. I was in the boat, so I set the anchor down immediately, and cast to where I'd last seen them."

Wilson got a strike immediately. He was fishing with a 5-weight rod and a small Hardy reel with no backing.

"It would run until I had about three wraps of line left on the reel, jump, then come back the other way," Wilson said.

He finally landed the fish, weighed it at Gaston's dock and released it.

"I didn't make another cast that day," Wilson said. "I told myself, 'It won't get any better than this.' Ever since, the olive Woolly Bugger has been one of my favorite fall patterns."

Wilson ties some with Flashabou and some without. He prefers black patterns on dark days and olive the rest of the time. They work best when drifted into the seams or current lines, then retrieved with a varying strip and pause.

"Fall can be a weird time," Wilson said. "You're not doing much nymphing. It's mainly Woolly Buggers and the occasional Blue-Winged Olive or caddis hatch every now and then. The Red-Butted soft hackle is also good during caddis hatch in the fall. But drop down to size 16."

Winter: More big fish are caught during the winter than any other time of year in the Bull Shoals Tailwater. That's because of the brown trout spawning run, which starts in late October and continues through early February, and the threadfin shad kill in Bull Shoals Lake. Therefore, egg imitations and shad patterns are the most popular winter patterns.

Glo-Bugs, size 10, in bright colors like chartreuse, yellow, red or orange are hard to beat this time of year. You can fish them with a strike indicator or without. Wilson prefers 6-pound-test tippet.

Wilson makes two variations of the standard Glo-Bug. One involves no fly-tying at all. Buy a bag of pom-pons

Red Butt

Hook: Mustad 94838 or any dry fly hook, sizes 12-16
Thread: Red
Body: Dark olive rabbit dubbing
Hackle: Soft partridge or mottled hen

The Red Ass or Red Ass Kelso has become a popular pattern in the White River System, as have soft hackles in general. Hank Wilson ties a variation of the Red Ass and calls it a Red Butt. He uses a dry fly hook instead of a scud hook, and he uses rabbit dubbing instead of peacock herl for the body. Plus, Wilson adds some red thread in front of the hackle.

"I've grown to like this fly a whole lot," Wilson said. "The river has such heavy caddis hatches, and this can imitate everything from a nymph to an emerger to an adult. It's a good pattern all year, but it's best from mid-March into July.

"I step it down to a size 16 in the colder months, and it can pass pretty well for any of the small emerging mayflies out there."

When tying this pattern, Wilson leans toward the sparse side. Also, he doesn't wind the thread down into the bend of the hook, like on most Red Ass patterns. He tends to clamp hemostats in the hook bend when releasing a fish, so the fly doesn't tear up so quickly if it doesn't have thread there.

Wilson fishes the Red Butt on a quartering downstream cast. He twitches it to pull it under the surface. If he sees any rising fish, he'll let the fly tight-line drift to them.

"If I don't get a strike, I'll make a few short strips, then pick it up and cast again," Wilson said. "You can also grease the leader and fish it in the film, or dress it with a paste-type dry fly floatant and fish it upstream."

from a craft store, put a small amount of Super Glue on a size 10 egg hook, then slide one of the pom-pons on the hook. To make the other Glo-Bug, simply wrap fluorescent tensile-core chenille around a size 10 hook. Make two wraps close together, then criss-cross with a couple more wraps.

Wilson's favorite shad pattern is Zonker variation tied on a No. 6 hook. It features a tensile chenille body instead of a Mylar tubing body. "You get a lot more sparkle off the tensile chenille body," Wilson said. Rabbit strip is tied Zonker style at the front and the rear of the hook.

Both the egg and shad patterns can be highly effective during power generation, but Wilson stresses that the flies must be fished near the bottom.

Wilson often uses a slinky rig during high water conditions. It's simply a piece of 3/16ths-inch parachute cord with split shot inside, sealed at both ends and attached to a snap swivel. The length of the parachute cord varies with the number of split shot inside.

Wilson uses it like the fly fisher's version of the White River drift rig. He attaches 10 feet of 10-pound-test tippet to the eye of the snap swivel, then ties a 24-inch dropper of 6-pound-test tippet to the same snap swivel eye. Add an egg or shad fly to the other end of the dropper. From a drifting johnboat, cast this rig at a 45-degree angle upstream, then let it bounce along the bottom.

If the water is low, and there is a hatch, mayflies than can be successfully imitated with a size 18 or 20 emerger, like Chuck's Emerger, created by the late North Fork River fishing legend Chuck Davidson, or one of Wilson's creations called a Blue Meany. The main difference in the two is that Chuck's Emerger has a yellow body and Wilson's Blue Meany has a blue body.

Wilson thinks Chuck's Emerger works best in imitating light colored mayflies, usually late April through May and June. The Blue Meany is a Blue-Winged Olive imitation and is most effective October through March. Wilson looks for rising fish, then casts these tiny emergers on 6X tippet.

Watchdog For The White River; Gaston Has Eye On Big Picture

Jim Gaston can't recall the last time he went trout fishing. Yet he's done as much as any man to protect and enhance trout fishing on the White River.

As the owner of Gaston's Resort it is in his best interests, of course, to be concerned about the health of the White River. But since he came here in 1958 to help his father, Al, manage a six-cabin resort, Jim Gaston has proven his interest in the river is far greater than just business.

When President Reagan's Secretary of Interior James Watt put the Norfork National Fish Hatchery on a list of federal projects to be shut down, Gaston's office became a local crisis management center. When low dissolved oxygen problems caused fish kills in White River below Bull Shoals Dam, Gaston became the point man for bringing federal, state and local interests together.

The results: the Norfork Hatchery remains open, and new devices have been added to the turbines at both Bull Shoals and Norfork dams to help alleviate annual fall low dissolved oxygen problems.

Gaston doesn't take credit for those results, as he shouldn't. But he was at least the catalyst for bringing them about. Gaston has a rapport with Arkansas politicians and a reputation for getting things done. When he calls, they listen.

"Jim thinks of the river first, himself second," said Don McFadyen, who owned Rainbow Drive Resort and served as the vice president of the White River commercial outfitters association before returning to his home state of Florida in 1992.

"He has never deviated from that. Never. That's why he is so well-respected."

Gaston's eye on the bigger picture rather than simply his own resort is reflected in his service on the Arkansas State Parks, Recreation and Travel Commission. Gaston was appointed by then-Governor Dale Bumpers in 1973. He has been reappointed as a commissioner at the conclusion of each term since.

"I'd be lying through my teeth if I said I didn't want to be on the commission," Gaston said. "I enjoy it. One of the main reasons I enjoy it is because once a month you're with 15 or 20 different people from all over the state with different perspectives. It's intellectually challenging. If it wasn't for that, I'd be exposed only to my little world right here."

> "Jim thinks of the river first, himself second. He has never deviated from that. Never. That's why he is so well-respected."

Gaston's world does get awfully small at times. On a typical day he will arrive at the resort between 10 and 11 a.m. and go home between 10 and 11 p.m. Most of those hours will be spent in his wood-paneled, antique-filled office, where he can usually be found working on his computer or talking on the telephone.

But a good resort owner ought to know something about having fun. Gaston has grabbed his share. As a former stunt pilot, Gaston still enjoys flying over the Ozarks in his two-seat, single-engine Bellanca Citabria airplane.

Gaston is also a motorcycle fan. He makes an annual cross-country tour, and he owns a Harley-Davidson Electra Glide Classic.

Jim Gaston came to the White River in 1958 to help manage his father's six-cabin resort. He says he never wants to leave.

Gaston's hobbies have carried him to many other parts of the world. He prefers the Ozarks.

"There is no better place to ride a motorcycle in the fall and the spring than the Ozarks," Gaston said. "I can honestly say that every time I take a trip, when I end up back here the Ozarks has more value to me. It amazes me when I notice that much more beauty after I've lived here this long."

Gaston was born in Herrin, Illinois, in 1941. He was raised on a farm near Flint Hills, Kansas. Al Gaston was employed in the oil field construction business when he bought 25 acres on the White River in 1958. Jim thought he would end up in the construction business, too, but his father asked him to go look after the resort for awhile.

"That's what I did, and I never left," Gaston said.

Gaston's Resort is now a small city that includes: 300 acres, 73 cottages, convention center, 3,200-foot grass airplane runway, restaurant overlooking the river, nature trail, over 100 employees, and, of course, a boat dock and trout fishing guide service.

Located about four miles below Bull Shoals Dam, the boat dock, restaurant and long row of trademark pink-painted cottages make up one of the most well-known landmarks on the river. Gaston's Resort has been mentioned in every major U.S. travel magazine.

"Jim Gaston is like a treasure for the state of Arkansas," said ESPN outdoors show host Jerry McKinnis. "He does so much to promote our state, and he has got the finest resort in mid-America."

McKinnis was a guide on the White River when Gaston's was a six-cottage resort. McKinnis owns some White River property. But he can't imagine how much Gaston's Resort would be worth in today's market.

"I've had the opportunity several times to sell out," Gaston said. "What people don't understand is that this is more than a resort to me. I don't ever want to leave."

Although Gaston doesn't fish or hunt much anymore, he is an avid nature watcher. Looking at bald eagles, ospreys, wildflowers and native grasses gives him more pleasure than catching a trout. The White River provides him the perfect setting for that hobby.

"I can honestly say I really enjoy what I'm doing," Gaston said. "The White River supplies a lot of different uses for a lot of different people. Perhaps it supplies a little different use to me than most people."

Fly Fishing Perfect Pursuit For Whitlock

Creative interests in drawing, writing, photography combined in sport

"Like the sculptor or painter, the fly tier has a variety of tools at his disposal; the bottom line is always how well he uses them to create."

"The chief difference between the angler who fly-fishes for trout and the angler who uses bait or who spin-fishes is that the fly fisher enjoys a much greater latitude for self-expression."

Dave Whitlock
"Guide to Aquatic Trout Foods"

It was the urge for creativity and self-expression that brought Dave Whitlock out of Oklahoma and into the Ozarks. In 1970, Whitlock leaped from the field of petroleum engineering into the stream of fly fishing.

He and his first wife, Joan, came to the White River for the first time on their honeymoon in 1956. By the time they moved from Muskogee, Oklahoma, to Norfork, Arkansas, 14 years later, Whitlock had established himself as one of the best fly fishermen in the world. And, more importantly, he could afford to walk away from the petroleum industry.

Fly fishing seems to bring together all Whitlock's interests - especially the creative ones, like drawing, writing and photography. He had felt those interests pulling him from an early age, but was discouraged from following them.

"My folks were very poor," said Whitlock, who was born in Muskogee in 1934. "I was going to be the first person in my family to get to go to college. I thought I would like to be a writer and a professional fisherman. But my parents said, 'Whatever you do, don't major in art and journalism. You'll starve to death.'"

Whitlock followed that advice and earned degrees in chemistry, physics and biology from Northeastern State University in Tahlequah, Oklahoma. Thus, he was prepared for Oklahoma's petroleum industry.

"I kept in the back of my mind that

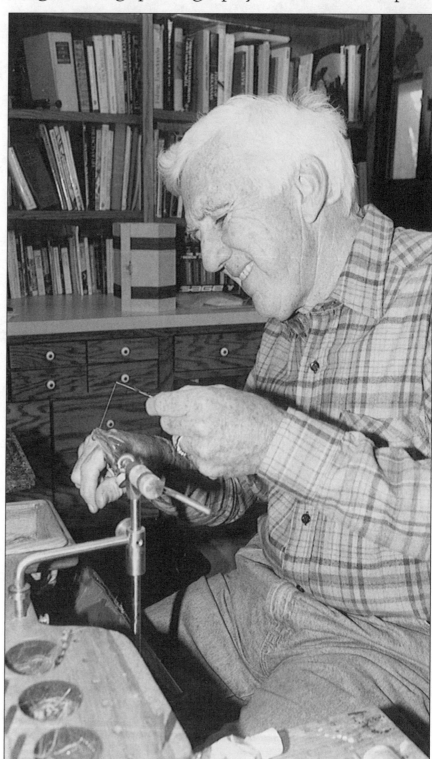

Dave Whitlock's fly tying creations number "somewhere between 60 and 100," he says, and they include many standard Ozark trout fishing patterns

I wanted to be a writer and an artist," Whitlock said. "As I began to understand fly fishing, I knew that was the area I wanted to be in."

It's easy to look back now and recognize Whitlock's fly fishing talent. He has written three books, chapters in several other books and hundreds of magazine articles about fly fishing. He and Lefty Kreh are the "editors-at-large" of Fly Fisherman magazine. Whitlock has illustrated 22 books, including former President Carter's "Outdoor Journal," and been employed for his fly fishing expertise by L.L. Bean, Bass Pro Shops and Gander Mountain.

Whitlock's fly tying creations number "somewhere between 60 and 100," he says, and they include such standard Ozark trout fishing patterns as Dave's Red Fox Squirrel Nymph, Dave's Hopper and the Whitlock Sculpin.

For those who are new to the sport, Whitlock's attitude is refreshing. He hasn't forgotten how difficult it was to cut through the, in his words, "mystique, tradition and downright bullshit" of fly fishing. Consider this passage from "Guide to Aquatic Trout Foods:" "...all aspects of fly fishing have traditionally suffered from far too much complication spawned by 'experts' using their hard-earned knowledge to bewilder and discourage (if not consciously) the newcomer.'"

Whitlock says he has always been interested in bugs and things that crawled under rocks. Water has forever attracted him, too.

"As I began to learn how to fish, it interested me that fish fed on all those smaller things, yet most of the stuff we were using then was big, wooden lures," Whitlock said. "When I was eight or nine years old, I learned about fly fishing from reading. It seemed to be the answer to catching fish on those little things."

That approach makes all of Whitlock's work so accessible - for the beginner and the advanced fly fisher. Whitlock can write about and illustrate fly fishing from the standpoint of a boyhood curiosity, not an attitude steeped in the sport's mystique. That's

Dave's Red Fox Squirrel Nymph

Hook: Sizes 2-18, 2X or 3X long
Thread: Black or orange, 8/0 or 6/0
Tail: Red fox squirrel back hair fibers
Abdomen: 50-50 blend red fox squirrel belly, similar color Antron
Rib: Gold oval tinsel or gold pearlescent Flashabou
Thorax: 50-50 blend red fox squirrel back hair, similar color Antron
Hackle: One turn of brown speckled hen or partridge

This Dave Whitlock original, created in the mid 1960s, is an Ozark tailwater standard pattern that every fly fisher should carry.

"I've fished it all over the world," Whitlock said. "It works everywhere. It's a lot of people's favorite."

What does it imitate? Well, a little bit of everything.

"It's like a Hare's Ear nymph and a Woolly Bugger in that it's so suggestive," Whitlock said. "It imitates so many different foods - scuds, sowbugs.

"The smaller sizes imitate mayfly nymphs, caddis pupae and larvae. The larger ones imitate softshell crawfish, stonefly nymphs and burrowing mayfly nymphs."

Whitlock usually weights this pattern with 10 to 12 turns of lead wire the same diameter as the hook wire.

As for other tying tips, Whitlock says, "This is dubbed fairly loose. It's not a real tightly dubbed nymph."

Whitlock usually fishes it on a dead drift, casting upstream and letting it drift down.

"If the trout are hitting emergers, you can sink it and then bring it to the surface," Whitlock said. "That can be a very effective technique."

Whitlock believes nymph fishing is by far the most productive method for the White River System. He'll often fish two at a time - combining a Red Fox Squirrel nymph with a sowbug or scud.

Whitlock's Sculpin

Hook: Sizes 8 to 5/0, 4X long, heavy wire
Thread: Yellow single strand tying floss
Belly: Cream colored rabbit, Antron mix
Body: Cree neck hackles, gold or olive
Pectoral fins: Back feather of cock pheasant
Gills: Red Antron
Head, collar: Cream, olive, gold, black deer hair

Because sculpins are such an important food source in the White River, Dave Whitlock was compelled to create a sculpin fly pattern in the late 1950s.

"The Muddler Minnow was popular then, but it wasn't really a sculpin imitation," Whitlock said.

"McClane's New Standard Fishing Encyclopedia and International Angling Guide," published in 1965, noted, "The Whitlock sculpin is perhaps the best exact imitation of the sculpin minnow."

Sculpins tend to have a chameleon characteristic, in that their colors vary to match that of the stream bottom. Whitlock combines various shades of deer hair to match the sculpin colors he observes wherever he's fishing. The head should be trimmed and shaped in the wide, flat diving plane that is typical of sculpins. This not only makes the pattern look like a sculpin, but swim like one, as well. Sculpins hug the river bottom. Whitlock also adds 20 to 25 wraps of lead, the same diameter as the hook wire.

Typically, he'll cast sculpins on a sink tip or full sinking line with a 2- to 6-foot leader. There are several ways to fish this pattern. Whitlock usually casts straight toward a cut or structure-holding bank and strips the sculpin back, or casts into the tail end of riffles and lets the sculpin drift into the pools below.

why Whitlock's "Guide to Aquatic Trout Foods" is important. It debunks much of that mystique with practical observations. For example, there is the following passage from a chapter about mayflies:

"It has finally been established and accepted by most fly fishers that fishing the nymph in several fly designs and methods is the best method for hooking the greatest number of the largest and most selective of the hatch-feeding trout. Traditional fly-fishing snobbery put subsurface flies on the same plane as bait. Such is not the case. Fishing the nymph is as much if not more sophisticated and complex a technique as the floating-fly techniques once touted by the dry-fly purists.

"The deep-fished nymph, the rising or swimming nymph, and finally the surface-film, floating, nymph-emerger present the most challenging and deadliest methods of fishing the hatch. On most hatches I've fished, ten to fifteen nymphs are usually consumed to every winged dun. Trout stomach samples verified this."

Practical advice gleaned from careful observation - that's the essence of Whitlock on fly fishing. So if you want to know about food sources for trout in the White and North Fork rivers, there is no better source than Whitlock, who lived near the confluence of the streams for over 20 years.

"There are three primary food sources in any really successful trout river - aquatic insects, minnows or small fishes, and crustaceans," Whitlock said. "A fourth source would be terrestrials, like ants or beetles or worms."

When the dams changed the White and North Fork from warmwater to coldwater streams, aquatic insect life changed just as dramatically. In fact, the aquatic insect populations may just now be starting to show signs of adapting to the change.

"I have seen a really healthy increase in the mayfly and caddis populations in the last four or five years," Whitlock said. "There are good caddis and mayfly hatches in the spring and summer now that didn't used to be here at all."

There are four or five species of mayflies that Whitlock sees regularly, including pale morning duns and pale evening duns.

"I don't think that's particularly significant other than the fact that they usually run from size 12 to 18, and all are primarily cream-colored or white in the water," Whitlock said.

April through July are primary mayfly hatch months, but Whitlock discourages fly fishers from coming to the White and North Fork expecting to fish hatches. Crustaceans and minnows, in that order, are much more significant food sources for these trout, therefore nymphs and streamers are the most productive fly patterns.

"The primary food, day-in and day-out, is the crustacea," Whitlock said. "That includes the scuds, the sowbugs and the crawfish."

Scuds and sowbugs are available year-round. Crawfish hibernate during the winter, but provide a valuable food source eight months a year. Big fish, especially, seem to key in on crawfish during the spring, summer and fall. Crawfish are so plentiful in certain sections of the White River that bucketfuls can be gathered at night with the aid of a flashlight.

Among the minnows and small fish, a significant food source for big fish comes in the form of sculpins. The prehistoric-looking, bottom-dwelling fish are as abundant as crawfish in the White River.

"As soon as trout carry over for about six months and get about 15 or 16 inches long, they really begin to feed heavily on the sculpins," Whitlock said.

Other significant fish food sources for trout include minnows like dace, darters, shiners and chubs. As a bonus, cold weather usually causes a threadfin shad kill in the lakes each winter and trout fatten up on the millions of shad that come through the generators.

"I've seen the river sometimes in February when it would just be silver with those fish," Whitlock said.

Once brown trout reach 3 to 4 pounds start feeding on the 10-inch rainbow trout that are stocked in the river from the hatchery.

Because of the high water fluctuations in these tailwaters, especially below Bull Shoals Dam with its eight power generators, terrestrials become an important food source, more so than they would be without all the fluctuation. During non-generation periods, earthworms, ants and beetles move out on the exposed mud banks and gravel bars, then are swept into the river during the rapid rise of power generation.

"I liken it to an ocean. The dynamics of the food sources and the richness of the food sources are constantly stimulating the fish to eat, and what they eat is the richest they can get. It's a great big wonderful soup of nutrient."

With all the these food sources available, fly fishers may offer trout a smorgasbord of patterns. Again, Whitlock recommends concentrating on nymphs and streamers.

A wide range of sizes is important, too. Size should correspond to power generation - during high flow, use large flies and drop down in size accordingly as water releases decrease.

"For instance, when water is at minimum flow I'll catch fish on a size 8 or size 10 Woolly Bugger," Whitlock said. "To catch those same fish on high water, I'm going to have to use a No. 2 Woolly Bugger.

"It's still imitating the same food, but, because the water is so high, it's much harder for the fish to see it. A big fly becomes more effective."

The abundance of all these trout foods makes the White and North Fork rivers special.

"I liken it to an ocean," Whitlock said. "The dynamics of the food sources and the richness of the food sources are constantly stimulating the fish to eat, and what they eat is the richest they can get. It's a great big wonderful soup of nutrient."

That's also the source of Whitlock's frustration. He remembers a time when a 10-pound trout wouldn't get a second look around here. Whitlock remembers an Arkansas Game and Fish Commission survey at Cotter Trout Dock documented approximately 1,600 fish weighing from four to 17 pounds - all caught during a six- or seven-month period.

"That is probably more trophy rainbows and browns than are caught in any 25 other rivers in this country," Whitlock said. "And that was just out of one dock on the White River."

A sharp increase in fishing pressure and emphasis on keeping a six-trout limit, no matter how big or small the fish are - has made stocker-size rainbow trout, rather than trophies, the more common catch now.

Because of their nocturnal feeding patterns and protection in the form of minimum length limits, brown trout have escaped some of the pressure. Therefore, many more big brown trout than big rainbows are caught here now.

Whitlock understands that every fishery has a maximum carrying capacity. However, he doesn't think the maximums in the White and North Fork are being even remotely approached.

"It's like having the world's best garden," Whitlock said. "You put the seeds in it, but as soon as they pop up out of the ground you harvest them instead of letting them mature into a crop."

Whitlock thinks it is important that newcomers to the White and North Fork rivers have this perspective. As he puts it, "These rivers don't need any more fishermen, they need more friends."

Troy Lackey (left) and David Capps gather worms from the river bank before power generation begins.

Rising Water Can Make Fishing Easier

But you have to study current to take advantage, like Capps, Lackey

Finally, the horn sounded at Bull Shoals Dam signalling that power generation would begin. It was 1:45 on a September afternoon. David Capps and Troy Lackey had spent most of the morning waiting on the water to come.

"I just don't like fishing this low water," Lackey said earlier. "It's boring."

Capps and Lackey pulled up their anchors and eased the johnboat next to a gravel bar. You could hear the water coming. Within minutes, the White River was trickling over the gravel bar that had been dry. Soon the gravel bar was submerged under several feet of water. And the fishing action picked up just as quickly.

"Now this is our type of fishing," Lackey said as he set the hook on a 2-pound brown trout.

In the next hour and 15 minutes, Lackey and Capps would land and release 10 trout - six browns up to 4 pounds and four rainbows up to 2 pounds.

"You can pattern these fish just like you can pattern a bass," Capps said. "There's a pattern out here every day."

These are two guys who ought to know. Lackey was born in 1949 and started guiding on the White River when he was 15 years old. Capps was born in 1963 and started guiding at age 15, also. Between them they've got over 45 years of experience on the White River.

Lackey is by far the veteran of the two. After almost three decades on the river and two back surgeries, Lackey says his guiding days are over. However, his days of fishing the river and sharing his knowledge of it aren't about to stop. Lackey and Capps formed a partnership in 1994 called Top Guide Productions. They began making videotapes on how to trout fish in the White River.

"When you get old, you'll catch them anyway you can," said Capps, as Lackey landed a brown trout that was foul-hooked in a pectoral fin.

"We've had more fun fishing together this year than I've ever had," Lackey said. "We've had a lot of laughs."

And they've caught a lot of big fish, fish that have been captured on videotape. The first hour-long video featured jig fishing for brown trout from winter through early spring. The second videotape focused on using red worms to catch browns and rainbows from late spring through summer.

There is a common theme in the videos - how to use the power generation at Bull Shoals Dam to your advantage.

"The key is understanding the water levels," Capps said. "At some point, the rising water is going to trigger a feeding response.

"If you pay close attention when you catch a fish, you can follow that water level right down the river."

This might be the most important lesson for someone learning to fish any of the White River System Tailwaters. No matter what your method of choice - from bait fishing to fly fishing - understanding what the trout do at various water levels is the key to success.

This has developed into a science at the Bull Shoals Tailwater. There are eight power generators in Bull Shoals Dam - twice that of any other White River System dam. The fishing guides here have had to adapt to the various levels of rising and falling water.

It's also important to note that it wasn't always this way. When Lackey first started guiding, most people thought you couldn't catch trout when the water came up. They fished only on low water. Now Lackey would just as soon stay off the river when it's dead low.

Lackey and Capps have found a more effective way to spend their time when the power generators aren't running. While waiting on the water to rise, they dig through dirt and moss along the banks, gathering earthworms.

The moisture left there from a previous high-water period creates the perfect environment for earthworms. That's the key to the worm fishing method Capps and Lackey utilized this day. The banks of the White River below Bull Shoals Dam are like one big tidal worm farm. The water comes up,

moistens the ground, recedes and attracts the worms; then, when it rises again, many of these worms are washed into the river.

The trout are in tune to the process, and so are Capps and Lackey. As the water first starts rising, they will drift red worms through the deeper holes and dropoffs where the fish were holding in dead low water. As the river rises, it pushes the fish toward the banks, where they can get more protection from the current. That also happens to be where more worms will be washing into river.

"Look for the grass lines along the banks," Capps said. "The higher the water gets, the closer you should get to the bank. It's really just common sense. You see the browns out there in low water, and you know they're going

to move in to the grass lines when the water comes up."

The tackle they use is standard for White River drift-fishing: spinning reel with a good drag system; 4-pound-test clear, green or brown monofilament line; and a 5- to 6-foot rod with a limber tip.

Capps and Lackey prefer the standard White River drift rig, also. On a 36-inch length of monofilament, they attach a small bell sinker to one end and a hook to the other. The main line is attached to the leader about 8 inches above the drop sinker.

There are two points of emphasis here: 1) the bell sinker should be as small as possible, a No. 10 when up to six power generators are running, then a No. 9 on seven and eight generators; 2) the leader should be long, so the

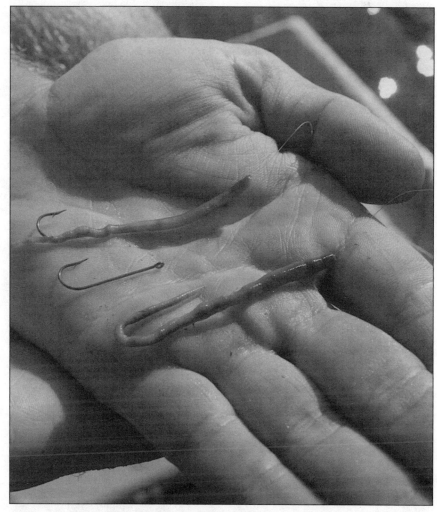

Most often, Lackey and Capps completely cover the hook with a worm, like the nearest example. But to counter "short bites," they expose the hook point.

worm drifts well behind the bell sinker.

The bait is also important. You don't have to gather worms from the river banks. The red worms sold in most bait shops will work most of the time.

Capps and Lackey have noticed days when a river worm seems to catch more fish than a bait shop worm and vice versa, so it's a good idea to have both.

Length is more significant than where the worm came from. Three to 4 inches is the optimum size. You don't want nightcrawlers.

"You can catch them sometimes on nightcrawlers, but it takes the fish longer to suck it in," Capps said. "They can inhale these little red worms, plus they are used to seeing them washed out of the bank every day.

"Another thing I like about fishing a red worm is that you've got a chance to catch good browns and some good rainbows."

Added Lackey, "I think a red worm is really just the best all-around bait for trout."

Placing the worm on the hook is another point of emphasis. Capps and Lackey prefer a No. 4 hook, which is threaded through the center of the worm so that none of the hook is exposed.

This requires manual dexterity and practice. You start the hook point at the very tip of the big end, or head, of the worm, and gradually work the worm up the hook shank, over the hook eye and up the line. Leave about a half-inch of worm dangling.

If the trout seem to be biting short, Capps and Lackey vary this procedure slightly, bringing the hook out of the worm about three-quarters of the way down. Instead of a J-shaped worm with no hook exposed, the worm is straight and the hook bend and point are exposed.

"Keep a pretty good worm on your hook," Lackey said. "If it's wadded up, take it off. If the tail is torn off, take the whole thing off. A big fish won't hit that."

Capps and Lackey use a drag chain to slow down the boat's drift, and, if

Lackey Got Lucky After Seven Years Of Stalking Brown Trout

Two or three times a week for seven years, Troy Lackey would attempt to catch the big brown trout that he'd watched as often as his television set. The fish's hangout was the Partee Hole on the White River. Several other trout fishing guides knew about it.

"I probably fished for it a 1,000 times," Lackey said. "My dad got it to bite one time, but it broke his line."

Lackey had watched the fish grow into what he thought was a new state record. The mark at that time was 28 pounds, 3 ounces.

"I thought the fish weighed over 30 pounds," Lackey said. "Me and Preston Jones got into an argument one day. He said it wouldn't go an ounce over 25."

But on this day, May 24, 1972, Lackey didn't figure he'd have a chance to fish for the big brown. He was working a guide trip. In his boat were two women. Their husbands were in another boat upstream.

"They wanted to wait on their husbands," Lackey said. "We were at the Partee Hole, but I didn't even look for that fish. I was just stalling for time when I cast over there."

Lackey had also noticed another guide, Ray "Paddlefoot" Warren, in that spot earlier. He figured the fish had seen too many fishing lines for one day. But he didn't have anything better to do, so he made a cast to the same place he had cast so many times before.

"I just lifted the shell off a crawdad and threw it over there," Lackey said. "It didn't stay there very long."

Lackey battled the fish for right at an hour. His reel was spooled with line labeled 8-pound-test, but it later tested at 12 pounds. After he landed the fish, he took it to Sportsman's Dock and made a phone call.

Lackey was working out of Rivercliff Trout Dock on the first day of an overnight camping trip. He didn't

have any more time to waste on the big brown trout. After he called Rivercliff to inform his bosses of the catch, he left the fish at Sportsman's and continued the guide trip - just another day at the office.

That evening, Lackey and the rest of the guided party were camped at Hardy Bar near Cotter when Phil Cullen and Roy Tillary, the owners of Rivercliff Dock, came driving up. They took Lackey back into town for a steak dinner. The brown trout had been certified at 31 pounds, 8 ounces.

> "I didn't even look for that fish. I was just stalling for time when I cast over there."

It was the first to break the 30-pound mark in Arkansas. Lackey's state record stood for almost five years, until Leon Waggoner of Flippin topped it with a 33-8 in March 1977.

In looking back, Lackey thinks Warren, the guide who fished the Partee Hole before him, had something to do with making the fish bite that day in May.

"Ray Warren had been there for two or three hours," Lackey said. "I didn't know it at the time, but he chummed that hole with a bunch of bait. When someone sits on a fish like that, sometimes it moves down to the next hole.

"I think that's what happened. I think when Paddlefoot left, that big fish moved back into its hole."

And that's when Lackey made his cast.

"It was a once in a lifetime thing," Lackey said.

needed, supplement that with power from the outboard motor, kicking it in and out of gear.

"Cast straight to the bank or slightly upstream," Capps said. "Use the motor to keep the line straight out from the boat."

If the line drifts too far upstream or downstream, or if you feel moss or leaves building up on the line, reel in and cast again.

Debris can be a problem on rising water. At some point, especially when the water starts rising after several hours of no generation, the water becomes clouded with moss, leaves and other debris. Capps and Lackey call this "trashy" water.

Trashy water usually follows the initial surge. When the water starts rising, Capps and Lackey will follow that initial water surge down the river, all the way from the dam to Cotter if the fish are biting.

Then they'll motor back upstream and start over, after the trashy water has cleared out.

"There are basically two patterns we try to fish - the front end and the top end (of power generation)," Lackey said. "You'll catch the biggest fish when the water peaks."

This sounds easier than it is. Power generation varies widely at Bull Shoals Dam. It may start with two generators and gradually increase to all eight, or it may start with two and stay that way all day. There are numerous possibilities, and there is no way to predict what will happen from one day to the next.

Your best bet is to do like Capps and Lackey, take whatever comes and work with it. Develop your powers of observation to the point you can be as in touch with the water fluctuations as the trout are.

If you're catching fish, then suddenly the action stops, move downstream and catch up with the same water conditions that turned on the fish before.

"It seems like there's a lot of guesswork," Capps said. "The key is not to panic. The fish will tell you when they want to feed."

A white jig is one of the most effective lures you can use when threadfin shad are flowing through Bull Shoals Dam and trout are gobbling them up.

White Marabou Jig Becomes Top Trout Lure When Shad Are Dying

If you want to catch Bull Shoals Tailwater trout in the winter, you must take advantage of the threadfin shad "hatch." As water temperatures drop in Bull Shoals Lake, hundreds of thousands of threadfin shad die, flow through the power generators and spill into the river, where they provide a gravy train for trout.

Becoming aware of this annual phenomenon will not only help your fishing, but also help you understand another aspect of why White River System trout grow so quickly.

Threadfin shad are a subtropical and southern temperate fish. They are native to the Arkansas River, but threadfin shad were introduced in these U.S. Army Corps of Engineers lakes, like Bull Shoals, to provide forage for gamefish.

Most of the year, the lake provides the warmwater environment threadfin shad require. But during the winter, when water temperatures drop below 40 degrees, the shad begin to die. During power generation, huge numbers of dead and dying shad are sucked through the turbines and dumped into the tailwater. Trout quickly tune-in to this seasonal food source.

Threadfin shad are thin, silvery white and usually 2 to 4 inches long. When they start showing up in the tailwater, some anglers scoop the dead shad from the river and use them for bait, fishing them on a drift rig just like they would a worm.

However, any white or silver artificial lure shaped like a shad will work, too. Small crankbaits, like Rapalas, are popular imitations.

When David Capps and Troy Lackey want a threadfin shad imitation, they choose a white marabou jig. The "chrome dome" jig, with a silver head and white marabou is the top choice on the Bull Shoals Tailwater.

On most water levels, they'll use a 1/16th-ounce jig. But when eight generators are running at Bull Shoals Dam, they'll go up in weight to a 1/8th-ounce jig.

Capps and Lackey employ many of the same tactics and tackle they use for drift-fishing worms - johnboat, drag chain, spinning gear and 4- or 6-

pound-test line. As they drift downstream, they cast the jigs close to the bank, then retrieve them with an up-and-down motion.

"It's a slow pumping action," Lackey said. "The more current there is, the slower you pump the rod tip. Ninety percent of the strikes will come as the jig is falling."

"You'll feel a light peck," Capps said. "It's not a hard yank at all. It feels almost like your jig hitting the bottom. So if you feel anything at all, set the hook."

When Capps and Lackey decided to team up and make videotapes about White River trout fishing, the threadfin shad-white jig story was the first one they told. Although you'll catch every species of White River trout on a white jig during the shad kill, it's primarily a brown trout lure.

"Around the first of February they really turn on to the shad," Capps said. "They'll stay on them until it starts to warm up in the spring."

Trout caught during this time are so gorged with shad they'll often leave a trail of the regurgitated baitfish as they are reeled to the boat. It's also common to hear anglers complain that the trout are so full of shad they aren't biting anything else.

Capps and Lackey don't buy that theory. Just like with their red worm method, the key to fishing jigs during the shad kill is understanding water fluctuation.

"As the water rises, the fish move into the banks to feed," Capps said. "They're going to get behind any kind of obstruction - logs or rocks or islands - where they can get out of the current."

"In our experience, we think the water is usually into the seventh generator when the bigger fish move into the bank. The best action usually comes at the peak of the rise and in the first foot of fall after the peak."

Those general guidelines don't always hold, though. And, just as in drifting red worms, the power of observation is crucial. If you can pinpoint the water level that's turning on the trout, you can follow it down the White River.

Lackey Stumbled Into Method For Using Sculpins As Trout Bait

Troy Lackey started working as a fishing guide in 1964, when he was 15 years old. In those days, everyone noticed the little, prehistoric looking fish darting among the rocks in the Bull Shoals Tailwater, but nobody used a sculpin for trout bait.

"Sometimes you just stumble into stuff," Lackey said.

Lackey had been guiding for about 15 years when he discovered how useful a sculpin could be.

"Me and two other guys were fishing a big school of browns above Gaston's," Lackey said. "I didn't know how to catch a sculpin then, but I'd found a dead one and had it in the boat with me. I put it on a hook and threw it out there. Those big brown trout started fighting over it.

"I caught three browns on one sculpin, and that told me something."

Lackey started looking for dead sculpins on gravel bars. Almost every time he used one for bait, he caught a big brown trout.

"Jackie Due was the first one I told about them," Lackey said. "I pitched two or three in his boat. I didn't keep anything a secret. We were all trying to make a living out there. The more big fish we'd catch, the more money we'd make."

The word about sculpins spread among the fishing guides and soon the bait wasn't quite as effective as it was when only Lackey was using them.

"I let a lot of my secrets out that I should have kept to myself," Lackey says with a laugh.

Sculpins remain one of the most commonly used baits for brown trout on the White River. Most people know how to catch them now, too, without looking for dead ones.

By putting a small piece of worm on a hook, just enough to cover the hook point and barb, then dangling it among rocks on the stream bed, you can catch sculpins just like you would any other fish.

A small piece of worm, dangled from a hook along rocky areas of river bottom, can be used to catch sculpins.

However, most anglers kill sculpins before using them as bait. If you are fishing along a chunk-rock bottom, a live sculpin will keep you hung up in the rocks most of the time. It's just doing what comes natural - looking for a rock to hide under.

"If I'm fishing a gravel bar, I'll use a live sculpin," Lackey said. "You can tease a fish into hitting them there, and the sculpin can't get you hung up."

Lackey has two other secrets for fishing sculpins. If the water is cloudy, he'll skin a sculpin before putting it on a hook. He thinks the white body of a skinned sculpin is easier for the fish to see.

If he needs to make a long cast, Lackey will stick a small bell sinker in the sculpin's mouth and sew it shut with a few stitches of monofilament. The extra weight gives him more casting distance without the loss of sensitivity that occurs when weight is attached to the line.

Lackey thinks sculpins will always be one of the top baits for catching big trout in the White River.

"I think a worm is as good as anything you can use for catching a brown trout up to 10 pounds," Lackey said. "But if I want to catch one over 10 pounds, I'll go to a sculpin or softshell crawfish."

Cobb Conducts Trout With Jig Movement

Rather than subtle approach, he makes jig dance to a rapid beat

It's easy to spot Pete Cobb on the White River. He's the one waving his fishing rod like a symphony orchestra conductor.

"I made this up myself," Cobb said, as he repeatedly jerked his rod tip straight up, then slowly lowered it. "A lot of people tell me I'm jigging too hard."

It is a violent movement. Picture a clock face. The rod tip jerks from four o'clock to one o'clock, then drops back to four o'clock. If you count it out, there's one beat for the upswing and two for the downswing. ONE, two, three. ONE, two, three. ONE, two, three.

On the other end of the 4-pound-test monofilament line strung through Cobb's fishing rod is a marabou jig, usually 1/16th of an ounce.

"I like to flash it," Cobb said. "The jig really doesn't move as much in the water as you'd think it would. I want to make it flash."

Cobb would change if his method didn't work. His arm gets tired jigging that jig all day. But there is both rhythm and method to this madness. Cobb has been guiding on the White River for over 15 years. For the last seven, he's been throwing a jig whenever he can. Like many other veterans of this river, the more time Cobb has spent here, the fewer lures he's needed to catch trout.

"My two favorite baits are a jig and a Red Fin," Cobb said.

The jig rates No. 1, especially when there are three power generators or less running at Bull Shoals Dam. If more water is running, Cobb will continue to throw a jig, but he will step up in size to 1/8th ounce. Bigger lures, like the Red Fin and similar stickbaits, become more effective in high water, too.

Many White River guides use jigs in January and February when cold weather causes threadfin shad kills in the lake. Trout feed on the shad after they come through the dam into the river. Cobb grew up in a family of guides. His dad and both his grandfathers guided anglers on the White River. Cobb saw how effective a jig was in January and February. By experimenting with color and action, he has made it a 12-month technique.

Brown is one of Cobb's favorite jig colors most of the year. Rather than imitating a shad, a brown jig looks more like an aquatic insect, a crawfish or a sculpin. Gray is also an effective color. A gray jig may look more like a minnow or an aquatic insect.

> ## "That's why I like fast-moving water. They know they've got to hit it quick."

When Cobb adds that violent jerk, a trout has to make a quick decision.

"That's why I like fast-moving water," Cobb said. "They know they've got to hit it quick. There is less chance to examine it."

Cobb prefers a 5-foot rod with some backbone for jig fishing.

"You don't want a real limber rod because you can't set the hook," he said.

The key is to keep the rod tip moving in an up-and-down motion, not side-to-side. The quick upward movement of the jig seems to attract the fish and cause them to give chase. Most strikes will come when the jig starts falling. Any side-to-side jerking of the rod tip detracts from this action and drags the jig away from the strike zone.

In fact, it's important to keep this whole presentation in a vertical plane. Cobb slows his boat with a drag chain or keeps the outboard motor in gear so his boat drifts as slowly as possible. The idea is to give the jig a lot of movement up and down, but keep the movement in one spot. Cobb will reel only slightly between each up-and-down movement of the rod.

Trout tend to congregate in certain places as the current increases. Boulders, wood structure and the banks provide protection from the current and ambush points for feeding.

"That's the thing about a jig," Cobb said. "You can get it into a lot of places you can't get a bigger lure."

At times, it's important to cast the jig right next to the bank. Six inches can mean the difference in getting a strike or not.

Cobb prefers 4-pound-test line, both for the action it gives the jig and it's lack of visibility. He uses either clear or green line and avoids fluorescent. Using 4-pound-test line in heavy current requires a reel with a good drag system. Cobb has landed brown trout up to 12 pounds with this method.

In the clear water of the White River, it's easy to follow a light-colored jig as it hops along, and it's not unusual to see several trout racing up to the lure.

"The more you can get coming after it, the quicker one is going to take it," Cobb said.

Cobb relies heavily on sight. Although this technique requires feel for the bite a trout makes on a falling jig, often you can see the strike before you feel anything.

That can cause problems for the beginner. It's difficult to maintain the ONE-two-three motion of the rod tip when a 3-pound brown trout is approaching the jig.

But the jig won't mean a thing, if it ain't got that swing. Pete Cobb has proven, if you've got the rhythm, you'll catch the trout.

"I've found that a lot of people like to fish this way, because you're doing something all the time," Cobb said. "They think it's more fun than drift fishing, where you're just sitting there waiting on a fish to bite."

Fulton Lured By Chance To Contribute

Ozark fly fishing is in its infancy compared to knowledge of the West

In 1987, Dale Fulton realized he had a decision to make. Fulton had worked as a fly fishing guide and guide service owner in Montana and Colorado for over 20 years. Seventeen of those years had been spent primarily in the West Yellowstone, Montana, area, which has as rich a fly fishing tradition as anywhere in the world.

And that was part of the problem. Fulton, the son of a college professor, grew up and went to college in Fayetteville, Arkansas, home of the University of Arkansas. He came back to the state every winter. Finally, Fulton and his wife, Ronna, decided to come back for good.

"It's a neat area, and I wouldn't put it down at all," Fulton said of West Yellowstone. "But a lot of talented people have been fishing there for a long time. I wasn't contributing anything. I was starting to do it by rote. If you go to the Madison (River), and it's cloudy, you do X and Y and Z. There is no place in Montana where you can't get a total description of what to expect."

Fulton and partner Craig Mathews of West Yellowstone opened Blue Ribbon Flies in Mountain Home, Arkansas, in 1987. Fulton bought Mathews' interest in the Mountain Home store in 1992. Even though he is committed 12 months a year to the Ozarks now, Fulton still maintains a Montana outfitter's license.

Fulton's father was a fly fisherman, so Dale grew up with the sport. But the Fultons did their fly fishing for trout at Roaring River State Park in Missouri.

During those years, the prevalent myth was that trout in the White and North Fork rivers wouldn't hit a fly. The myth died slowly, and it pointed to the fact that these rivers had such a short fly fishing history. The chance to make a contribution is what lured Fulton back fulltime.

"The difference in time between the two places is incredible," Fulton said. "Here, there has hardly been anything done on fly fishing. It's always bothered me that the fly fishermen here are so focused on low water. They weren't interested in the system as a whole. Out West, if you didn't look at the

Dale Fulton spent 20 fishing seasons in Colorado and Montana before returning to the Ozarks on a year-round basis.

whole system, you couldn't make a living."

That's where Fulton is making his contribution. If you grew up in the Ozark fly fishing school of thought that taught you to cuss the U.S. Army Corps of Engineers when river levels are high, Fulton can change your attitude.

"The real problem with fishing only in the daytime on low water is that you don't catch a lot of big fish," Fulton said. "What we're doing here is a different discipline of fly fishing."

Rather than try to fit the White and North Fork rivers into some other niche in the fly fishing world, Fulton believes the fly fisher needs to adapt to some unique conditions. He doesn't try to candy-coat it for anglers inquiring about the area.

"People call me all the time," Fulton said. "They ask, 'How much dry fly fishing do you have?' I say, 'Practically none.' They ask, 'Are there a lot of bait fishermen?' I say, 'Thousands.' They ask, 'Are they killing a lot of fish?' I say, 'Millions.' I make no effort to convince people to come here to fish. The point of our business is we want to help the people learn that do show up."

Fulton is continuously amazed by the White and North Fork rivers.

"It's one of the richest river systems in the world, and it has been one of the most abused," Fulton said. "No other river - and I've fished a lot of them - could have tolerated what is fairly commonplace here. It's a testament to the fertility of this river system."

Fulton views the White and North Fork rivers as having the rare combination of an abundance of hatchery-raised trout, plus the fertility to go beyond a typical put-and-take hatchery system. Large rainbow trout used to be an indicator of that. Now, because the rainbows are harvested so quickly after they are stocked, brown trout have become the evidence of a great fishery.

"The browns are turning into the sport fish of the river," Fulton said. "With the way it's headed, you've got a fair chance to catch a 3- to 5-pound brown here. The number of people who would come here to do that is just

Beadhead Hare's Ear Nymph

Hook: Dai Riki 135-C, sizes 12-16
Head: 5/32nd-inch brass bead
Thread: Gray or cream
Body: Hare's mask tied in dubbing loop
Rib: Gold wire

In 1994, this was the third-most popular pattern sold at Blue Ribbon Flies, next to a sowbug and an olive Woolly Bugger. It doesn't resemble the standard Hare's Ear nymph other than the fact that it is tied with hare's mask.

"It's just a real good all-purpose fly that doesn't look like anything," Dale Fulton said.

Beadhead patterns have grown increasingly popular. Beadhead Caddis and Beadhead Woolly Buggers are also commonly used patterns among White River System fly fishers.

"Most of the beadhead patterns originated in Europe," Fulton said. "Now Americans are sticking beads on everything. It's a pretty effective way of adding a lot of weight.

"Out of all the ones I've tried, I think the Beadhead Hare's Ear works best here. The fur is a little fuzzier. Most of the other stuff is tied a little soft."

A Beadhead Hare's Ear nymph can be fished effectively on the swing during the late spring and early summer when caddis emerge. However, most of the time Fulton fishes it on a dead drift under a strike indicator.

"It's such a heavy fly, there's no question about it getting down," Fulton said. "You don't have to add weight, which can make a fly less effective."

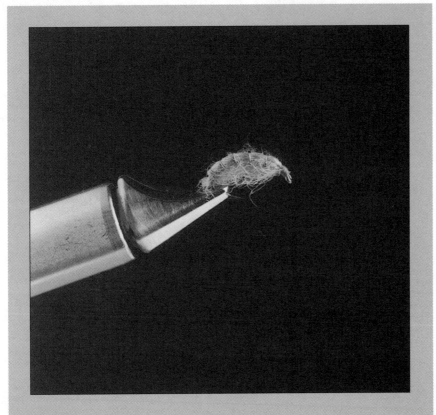

BRF Shrimp

Hook: Dai Riki 135-C, sizes 12-16
Thread: 6/0 olive
Weight: .015 lead wire wrapped under body
Body: Equal parts of beaver and green damsel Antron blend for dubbing
Shellback: Light olive zelon
Rib: Silver wire

The White River System features an abundance of crustaceans, in the forms of crawfish, sowbugs and scuds. Most fly fishers focus on sowbugs first.

Dale Fulton thinks many anglers underestimate the importance of scuds, also called freshwater shrimp. The BRF (Blue Ribbon Flies) Shrimp addresses that.

Although sowbugs are more numerous than scuds, on a one-to-one basis, scuds are a richer food source. And there is another important difference.

"Sowbugs can't swim," Fulton said. "Shrimp can beat it through the water. They are really strong swimmers."

Therefore, a scud pattern can be stripped slowly through pools of still water and present a natural attraction for trout.

This is a good general purpose pattern for both the White and North Fork rivers. It can also be fished dead drift with a strike indicator.

"It really works well with an indicator when there is a light chop on the water," Fulton said. "That gives it a natural swimming action."

Although scud colors and sizes vary in the White and North Fork rivers, Fulton says a light olive color in size 16 is the best all-around choice. He adds 8 or 9 wraps of lead. The zelon is important because of its light-reflecting qualities.

incredible."

That worries Fulton. As a businessman, you'd think he would want all the customers he could get.

"I don't like crowded fishing," Fulton said. "That destroys the point of it for me."

His dislike for crowds is one reason that Fulton doesn't put down bait fishers, like so many fly fishers are wont to do.

> "The total fishery is the key. We don't need to exclude other people. Everyone needs to become more aware of their impact and fit their impact into what's best for the fishery."

"Fly fishermen don't have a feel for the idea that if fishing is better for them, it's going to be better for everybody," Fulton said.

"The total fishery is the key. We don't need to exclude other people from the resource. Everyone needs to become more aware of their impact and fit their impact into what's best for the fishery."

To minimize the impact of his operation, Fulton's guided trips are run strictly on a catch-and-release basis.

"Besides, I don't think there is any advantage in trying to replace spin fishermen," Fulton said. "In Montana, there are thousands of fly fishermen. They get in your way. There is nothing more uncomfortable than trying to fish around a place with 10,000 fly fishermen. They are going to be doing the same thing you are."

No, that's the last thing Dale Fulton wants to be doing - the same thing 10,000 other folks are. That's why he's here.

Fulton Focuses On Hatchery Factor, Water Fluctuation

If you are schooled in the traditional methods of fly fishing and you're preparing for your first trip to the White River System, Dale Fulton has one piece of advice for you.

"Take 90 percent of the books - about matching the hatch and knowing insects - and throw them out," Fulton said. "Most of the time these fish are motivated to feed by no natural occurrences."

Your time will be more productively spent trying to understand the behavior quirks of hatchery-raised fish and the overriding influence of the constant water fluctuations in these tailwaters.

"Those are the two things addressed least by fly fishermen, and they are, I think, the two most interesting things about this area," Fulton said.

Fulton notes that hatchery-stocked tailwater trout fisheries in the U.S. are like accelerated experimental testing grounds, cycling huge numbers of fish through them.

"In the wilderness, it would take 10 years to do what is done in one year here," Fulton said.

That's how the White River System has been able to produce two world record brown trout during its relatively brief existence as a trout fishery.

Although these rivers now have a significant population of naturally reproducing brown trout, it's still primarily a hatchery-driven fishery, as almost three million trout are stocked each year in the five tailwaters.

In this age when most wild trout populations are maintained by strict catch-and-release regulations, Fulton thinks the term "wild fish" has lost its significance.

"There's hardly a place left on Earth where anyone is catching fish that haven't been impacted by man," Fulton said. "If a fish is raised in a hatchery and caught once, is it less wild than one born in the river but caught-and-released 50 times? I'm

Arkansas Beadhead

Hook: Dai Riki 730-C, size 8
Thread: 6/0 white
Head: 3/16ths-inch nickel bead
Wing: White marabou with gray Krystal Flash overwing
Eyes: : Stick-on plastic

This simple pattern is a good threadfin shad imitation. But its use isn't limited to the late winter months when the shad are dying.

"Most of the stuff I use is multi-purpose," Dale Fulton said. "I'm not into changing flies a lot.

"There's not doubt that brown trout like white. This is a good pattern for browns on any of the higher water levels, but I haven't done real well with it on low water."

It can be fished dead drift under a strike indicator or stripped as a streamer.

When it's stripped, the brightness of this pattern aids the angler. Fulton fishes it around logs and other thick cover. It's easy to follow the fly and set the hook as soon as a trout strikes it.

"I like something I can see underwater," Fulton said. "If I can't see it, I can't really tell if I'm getting any reactions to it. Plus, it's fun when you see fish follow the fly."

The Krystal Flash serves two functions. In addition to adding some silvery sparkle that is typical of threadfin shad and other baitfish, it helps keep the marabou straightened and flared properly.

The plastic eyes might seem insignificant. At one time, that's what Fulton thought, too.

"The first ones I tied didn't have eyes," Fulton said. "They worked OK. Then I started putting eyes on them. When I had some of each, there was no doubt the fish were taking the ones with eyes more often."

BRF Gold Matuka

Hook: Dai Riki 730-C, size 4
Thread: 6/0 black, plus 6/0 red band on head
Weight: .025 lead wire
Body: Cream rug yarn
Wing: Grizzly body feathers dyed gold
Hackle: Grizzly body feathers dyed gold
Rib: Small oval gold tinsel

Dale Fulton's gold version of the standard Matuka pattern features grizzly body feathers that are tied so they cup out at the tail instead of laying flat.

"The old flat Matukas aren't real effective," Fulton said.

For the best action, Fulton suggests using matching pairs of body feathers on the wing.

This is another good brown trout pattern. It is most effective on high water, during low light conditions or at night. It should be tied heavy.

Fulton often uses this pattern at night. He works it more slowly than he does during daylight hours. He casts it on a 9-foot, 3X leader, and sometimes steps up to 2X.

More so than the action of the fly, its color is the secret to success.

"Gold is the single best color there is for brown trout," Fulton said. "When you are stripping streamers, gold is a big help."

more concerned with what the fish ate than where it was born."

So Fulton's philosophy is not to get hung up in the hatchery vs. wild fish debate, but to take what's here - a bunch of hatchery-born trout that are primarily influenced by manmade water fluctuations - and figure out how best to catch them on a fly rod.

For instance, Fulton says, "The tendency to follow things on the swing is more a characteristic of hatchery fish."

Swinging a fly is one of the most common fly fishing techniques on the White River. It accommodates wading anglers and those fishing from a boat.

"It's the easiest way to get most people started," Fulton said.

Position yourself at the bottom of a riffle or at the top, above the "lip" of the riffle. Make an across-and-downstream cast, mend the line upstream, then follow the fly with your rod tip. As the fly swings down below you, continue to mend, or strip the fly slowly. Give it a couple of short strips after the swing is completed. Most strikes will come near the end of the swing. Woolly Buggers and soft hackle flies are the most effective patterns to fish on the swing.

The single best method for coaxing a strike from a White River trout is a dead-drift. With the abundance of forage and current fluctuations, trout are accustomed to picking off food as it floats by. Fulton enhances a dead-drift technique by adding a strike indicator and a second fly, tied on a dropper. A typical two-fly combination would include a Glo-Bug and a sowbug, with the sowbug as the bottom fly.

"Most of the hits will be on the sowbug," Fulton said. "We used to do this on the Madison River all the time. It's real well-known."

The strike indicator increases the effectiveness of the dead-drift. Fulton doesn't go along with those who dismiss strike indicators as a tool for beginners.

"It's not fishing with a bobber," Fulton said. "It's a discipline of fishing. I'm not making excuses for it. It's the only way to get a long drift on flat water, so it's important. Using it to indicate a strike is secondary.

Suspending the fly is the key to it."

This technique, when used while fishing from a boat, applies for all water levels on the White River. As water rises, add weight, in the form of split shot or heavier flies, and increase the size and brightness of the flies.

"You can do this in any water," Fulton said. "On any given day, I'll fish half the time like this."

But you need to know where to fish at different water levels. The water fluctuations caused by eight power generators at Bull Shoals Dam, in essence, create several different rivers. A gravel bar might be submerged when six generators are running, but half-exposed at four generators and completely dry at two. The trout will move accordingly.

"It's pretty much different every day," Fulton said. "The fish don't know this is an artificial deal. They are completely tuned into it. There's a lot to be said for match-the-hatch fly fishing, but this is so much more complex and interesting."

If you want to experience all these fly fishing possibilities on the Bull Shoals Tailwater, the key piece of equipment is a boat. Maneuverability is important when the White River is both high and low. In low water, a boat is the answer to avoiding crowds. During power generation, an outboard-powered boat allows you to fish various water conditions up and down the river.

At one time Fulton owned a McKenzie drift boat, which is commonly used on Western streams. But he sold it in favor of a 20-foot fiberglass johnboat powered by a 15-horsepower outboard motor. It's the standard rig for all types of fishing on the Bull Shoals and Norfork tailwaters. Its shallow draft and slim design allow you to maneuver through shoals that other boats can't.

Most bait fishermen would rather concentrate their efforts on rising water. But Fulton doesn't mind fly fishing on falling water (often referred to as "tailwater").

"The problem with fly fishing the rise is the cloudiness of the water," Fulton said. "I don't think the fish see

Randy's Leadeye Sculpin

Hook: Dai Riki 700-C, size 4
Thread: Size A tan
Weight: .025 lead wire under body, 1/36-ounce nickel-plated lead eyes
Body: Cream rug yarn
Tail, wing, walking fins: Gold rabbit strips
Head: Gold and white deer hair, spun and trimmed around lead eyes

Unlike most other patterns Dale Fulton ties, this has one purpose and one purpose only.

"It's for stripping off the bank in high water," Fulton said. "As far as I know, that's all it's good for."

He fishes it on a sinking line or sink-tip line and a 4-foot, 3X leader.

"You need a little stronger tippet than usual because (brown trout) hit it so hard," Fulton said.

Getting some depth on the fly during high water levels is important, and two features of this pattern add to that.

The lead eyes cause it to nose down. When you strip the fly, it goes down, not up, like most sculpin patterns.

The deer hair is trimmed so there is a diving skirt around the top of the back of the head. This also forces the fly down when it's stripped.

But depth is a relative term. Fulton doesn't bump the river bottom with this fly. He just wants something that will get down around logs and other fish-holding cover.

"The white color in the head throws a lot of people off," Fulton said. "It's there entirely for visibility."

As Fulton emphasizes in using patterns like the Arkansas Beadhead, visibility can add to the fun of fly fishing, as well as the effectiveness.

"There's something exciting about catching a fish you can see," Fulton said.

Fulton's Favorite White River Fly Patterns

SPRING	SUMMER	FALL	WINTER	HIGH WATER ALL SEASONS
Wet patterns	**Wet patterns**	**Wet patterns**	**Wet patterns**	Glo-Bugs, 12
Beadhead Hare's Ear, 12-16	Beadhead Hare's Ear, 12-16	Beadhead Hare's Ear, 12-16	BRF Gold Matuka, 4	*(peach, fire orange,*
Various sowbugs, 12-16	Prince Nymph, 14-16	Various sowbugs, 14-18	Various sculpins, 4	*chartreuse)*
Squirrel Nymph, 14-16	Red Ass Kelso, 12-14	Woolly Bugger, 8-12	Various shad streamers, 6	San Juan Worm, 10
Hare's Ear Nymph, 12-16	Various sowbugs, 14-16	*(olive, black)*	Arkansas Beadhead, 8	*(fire orange)*
Arkansas Beadhead, 8	Woolly Bugger, 8-12	Red Ass Kelso, 12-14	Olive Woolly Bugger, 8-10	Beadhead Hare's Ear, 12
Caddis Pupa, 14-16	*(olive, black)*	BRF Shrimp, 12-14	Squirrel Nymph, 10-12	Arkansas Beadhead, 8
(tan, green)	Brassie, 14-16	Soft Hackles, 12-14	Glo-Bug, 12	Various shad streamers, 6
Sulphur Nymph, 14-16	Soft Hackles, 12-14	*(yellow, orange)*	*(chartreuse, peach)*	Various sculpins, 4
RS2 Emerger, 16	*(yellow, orange)*	Glo-Bug (peach), 12	**Dry patterns**	
Brassie, 14-16	BRF Shrimp, 12-14	**Dry patterns**	Blue Wing Olive, 18-20	
Soft Hackles, 12-14	**Dry patterns**	Hopper, 10-12	Midge, 20-24	
(yellow, orange)	Sulphur Dun, 16	Midge, 20-24		
Dry patterns	Hopper, 10			
Light Cahill, 14	Midge, 20-24			
Sulphur Dun, 16				
Elk Hair Caddis, 14-18				

your stuff. Falling water is gentle and easy to fish. There aren't as many boats. It's not fast action, but there are a lot of browns still around.

"I can get more action on water like that than I can on 100 percent generation.

"As the water recedes, the fish get less active in proportion. The worst fishing is that last foot of drop. It's pitiful. But until you get to that point, there's usually something going on."

It's not enough to have a boat. You have to know how to operate it.

"That's the secret of a McKenzie boat," Fulton said. "The guide is actually doing the fishing. You keep it in a position so (the customer) is always casting the same length of line. All we're doing is adapting the McKenzie boat techniques to a more practical craft for this area."

As water levels increase, anchoring at the head or tail of a riffle is no longer an option. Anchors and rising water are a dangerous combination.

Your fly fishing options from a boat are basically: 1) dead-drifting, using a strike indicator, as described previously, and 2) casting the banks with streamers.

By keeping the nose of the boat pointed upstream and the motor in gear at low throttle or in neutral, you can keep the johnboat within casting distance of the bank and control the rate of downstream drift.

For safety reasons, this is pretty much a two-person operation - one operating the motor while the other fishes. But it's worth the sacrifice of taking turns with a fly rod. (A fishing guide is the obvious answer for those who want to fish all day.) As water levels rise, so do the chances of catching bigger fish.

Trout, particularly brown trout, will relate to structure along the banks more and more as the water rises. The closer you can cast to half-submerged logs, fallen trees, overhanging branches, boulders and cut banks, the more strikes you'll get.

Fulton's favorite pattern for this type of fishing is Randy's Leadeye Sculpin, which he and friend, Randy Sublett, designed. Another top choice is Fulton's Arkansas Beadhead.

The visibility of whatever pattern you choose is important. Fulton's sculpin has a touch of white on it. The Arkansas Beadhead is solid white with a silver bead.

"I like to use white because you can follow it in the water," Fulton said. "If I can't see the fly, I can't tell if I'm getting any reaction to it. And brown trout just like white."

That brings us to one of the most exciting aspects of this method - following the fly and watching trout rush out for a closer look.

The retrieve is made in short strips. Some will hit it, some won't. But the

passes are almost as thrilling as the strikes.

Fulton noted that a trout will seldom strike after it makes one pass. You can spend your time more wisely by moving on to the next piece of structure, rather than trying to coax another pass from a trout that has already taken a look.

This isn't just a brown trout method, especially when you're using something like the Arkansas Beadhead.

"If you slow it down and let it go deeper, you can pick up rainbows," Fulton said.

A 9-foot, 6-weight rod is a good all-purpose choice for both drift fishing and casting streamers on the White River. Fulton sometimes steps up to a 7-weight when he's throwing big flies, like sculpins.

You can get by with a floating line for both methods, but a sink tip or full sinking is better when casting streamers. Dead-drifting requires 12-foot, 5X or 6X tippets. Fulton uses short (3 to 5 feet) 3X tippets when casting sculpin patterns.

The single most important piece of equipment is an open mind.

"Fly fishing has evolved around wild fish in natural rivers," Fulton said. "All the books are focused on that. This is a totally different thing. You can take that knowledge and open other possibilities here. That's what fascinates me."

Chatelain Enjoys 'Running The River'

One trip began at Bull Shoals Dam and ended at Mississippi River

There is one thing Ralph Chatelain enjoys more than catching trout on the White River. That is the White River itself. All of it. From the Boston Mountains to the Mississippi River. Just looking at White River, experiencing it from a boat, meeting people along the way, is Chatelain's favorite way to spend a day. It's why the profession of White River fishing guide has suited him perfectly since he was 15 years old.

Dean Brandenburg, an insurance company owner from Murphreesboro, Illinois, has been coming to the White River to fish with Chatelain for over a dozen years. They had often discussed the idea of floating the White River to its mouth at the Mississippi River.

"Everyone we talked to about it would say they'd always wanted to do that but hadn't gotten around to it," Chatelain said. "We decided we were going to get around to it."

On Jan. 28, 1992, Chatelain and Brandenburg left Rivercliff Boat Dock below Bull Shoals Dam in a heavily-loaded 20-foot johnboat powered by a 25-horsepower outboard motor. They covered 418 miles of the White River in the next 4 1/2 days.

Chatelain's wife, Becky, met them at the Sylamore bridge, almost 80 river miles from Bull Shoals Dam. They trailered the boat to Batesville and launched again, thus avoiding the three lock-and-dams in between.

On Feb. 1, Chatelain and Brandenburg crossed the Mississippi River, set foot in the state of Mississippi, then came back to the Arkansas side of the river, where Becky was waiting for them again.

During the trip down the White River, they caught trout, bass and catfish, watched bald eagles, blue herons, snow geese and mallard ducks, camped next to roaring driftwood fires that kept the winter chill away and met many friendly people. Trips to the shore in search of gas stations were common, as few docks were open at that time of year.

It was on this once in a lifetime adventure when Chatelain realized the value of a river trip - not a fishing trip, but simply experiencing the White River by boat. It's a service he is happy to provide now. Chatelain started his own business, Bull Shoals Famous

Ralph Chatelain, shown here at the Cotter Bridge, has been showing folks the White River since he was 15 years old.

Floats, in 1994. He offers a variety of both fishing and sightseeing trips. For instance, he will take you on a one-day float from the dam to Calico Rock, 62 miles, show you the sights and tell you some stories along the way.

Chatelain knows the Bull Shoals Tailwater as well as anyone. When the national news media started showing up on the White River shortly after President Bill Clinton was elected in 1992, Chatelain was the perfect tour guide for them.

The reporters wanted to see Whitewater Estates, the 230-acre tract along the White River at the mouth of Crooked Creek. They were investigating the story about the financial dealings of Bill and Hillary Clinton and the failed Whitewater land development venture.

Chatelain is quick to point out that he knows nothing of the deal involving the Clintons, but he does know all about the land itself. He grew up on it.

It's difficult to think of Ralph Chatelain as a native Texan. He was born in Houston in 1952. His family moved to the Ozarks when he was 14, after Ralph's father, Ray, bought 2,000 acres along White River and Crooked Creek.

That acreage included what would later be called Whitewater Estates. Chatelain planned on developing his 2,000 acres as White River Valley Ranchettes. An Arkansas Game and Fish Commission public access point along here still carries that name, Ranchette.

"That was dad's dream, to develop that land," Chatelain said. "He donated the land where the public access is now and built the road in there."

Ralph got into the fishing guide business as a way of showing potential buyers White River Valley Ranchettes.

"My dad made me start guiding," Chatelain said. "I was taking customers out to show them what the river was like."

No one got sold on it more than Ralph Chatelain.

"All this land was open range," Chatelain said. "We had to put up fences to keep the cattle out. I had a big area to hunt and fish when I was a

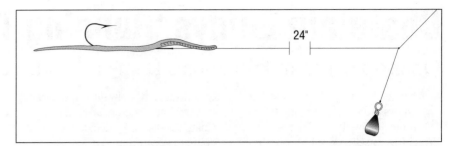

A typical White River drift rig includes a small bell sinker, as shown above, but Chatelain sometimes uses split shot on the dropper line at low water levels.

kid. I had it made."

But Ralph's father was diagnosed with cancer during his second year here. One year later, Ray moved back to Houston to be near the M.D. Anderson Clinic.

Three years of fishing and hunting in the Ozarks were more than enough to convince Ralph that Houston wasn't for him. Even if it meant living for a year in a one-room building with no heat or running water, which it did, Ralph was staying. He finished high school at Flippin and worked nights at Ranger Boats.

"Forrest and Nina Wood took pretty good care of me when I was growing up," said Chatelain of the founders of Ranger Boats.

In the years since, as he has married and raised three children, Chatelain has labored on offshore oil rigs, delivered milk and worked as a fry cook, but only for short stints. Chatelain's occupation is White River fishing guide, and he is proud of it.

"A lot of people ask me why I don't leave the river and get a real job," Chatelain said. "I've never gone hungry. The river always gives something back to me."

Like most fulltime guides, he has developed a variety of techniques for accommodating the various water levels of the river and fishing abilities of his customers.

"The No. 1 artificial lure on this river is a Countdown Rapala," Chatelain said. "A lot of people are going to Rogues now, too.

"But I get more action with a small willowleaf spinner in front of a Woolly Worm. You get more strikes, and you still have chance of catching a good size fish.

"A Flatfish also works real good. Black with orange spots is No. 1. I think the trout think they are a sculpin. Silver is a close second. In the winter and early spring, when a lot of shad are coming through the dam, a silver Flatfish looks like a crippled shad. They are good big-fish lures when the water is moving."

Chatelain uses a 25-horsepower outboard motor on his johnboat. Fifteen-horsepower motors are more common on White River guide boats, but Chatelain wants the extra horsepower for running the river.

Power generation usually starts early in the morning. He wants to follow the rise in the river and fish it as long as possible.

An average power generation rate, when four or five units are operating, takes five to six hours before it raises the river level at Cotter, located 18 miles downstream from Bull Shoals Dam.

If Chatelain gets on the river after the generators have been turned on, he'll run down until he catches the rising water, then start fishing.

"In the spring, they start running water earlier, so you have to go down the river farther to get in front of it," he said.

High water requires larger lures, like Rapalas, Rogues and Flatfish. Chatelain likes a Colorado spoon, too, because of its ability to catch numbers of average-size fish, plus an occasional lunker.

Low water demands smaller lures. Although Chatelain doesn't fly fish, he'll use a variety of size 10 and 12 nymphs, cast on spinning tackle with a plastic bubble for weight, when the river is at its lowest.

"Anything in a cinnamon color works real good," he said. "If people can't cast a fly on a bubble, I'll put on a small jig for them."

Most days, however, Chatelain's clients will be fishing with bait - usually red worms or crawfish tails. The bait is attached to a No. 4 or No. 6 hook and 4-pound-test line. It's weighted with a bell sinker, usually No. 10, attached on a dropper - the typical White River drift rig.

If water conditions are low, and a lighter drift rig is required, Chatelain clamps various sizes of split shot on the dropper line in place of a bell sinker.

Chatelain prefers the worms that can be gathered from the moss along the river banks during low water, but any worm will do.

If he has some crawfish and fishing is slow, Chatelain will take the white meat from a crawfish tail and stick it on a hook, behind the worm.

"It just adds a little sweetness to it," said Chatelain.

Chatelain is aware of the pros and cons of using bait. Tops on the pro side is catching fish.

"If you want to catch fish, use bait," Chatelain said. "No artificial lure catches as many fish as live bait."

On the con side is fish mortality, the rate of which corresponds to the river level.

"If you anchor up in low water and fish with bait, you're going to kill fish," he said. "They'll swallow the hook."

When water is high, you are better able to feel the fish's tug and set the hook before it swallows the bait.

Chatelain has a 13 1/2-pound rainbow trout mounted on his wall at home. He says he has caught and released a 20-pound brown trout. He has witnessed a decline in the number of big rainbow trout in the White River.

"So many people know how to catch them now," he said. "It's not like it used to be. There is more pressure."

But one thing hasn't changed in the last quarter-century. Chatelain is still running the White River.

"The river has been good to me," Chatelain said.

Cotter, Arkansas, Claims Title Of 'Trout Capital Of The World'

With its location on the White River, 18 miles downstream from Bull Shoals Dam, and with the river's history as a world class trout stream, Cotter Mayor Rex Bayless Jr., didn't see anything inappropriate about referring to this town as "Trout Capital of the World."

"I started using it as a slogan in 1967," said Bayless, who served the town as mayor from 1967-86 and took office again in 1991. "Trout Capital of the World" was printed on city hall stationery and painted on the town's water tower.

Cotter's slogan was reduced in scope but made official in 1993. Arkansas General Assembly Act 740 stated that Cotter "shall hereafter be known and may be referred to as the Trout Capital of the USA."

Indications of trout fishing's importance are everywhere. Cotter is centered around a riverside park. An Arkansas Game and Fish Commission-built launching ramp there is one of the most popular put-in and take-out places for White River boaters.

Two commercial trout docks - Cotter and Miller's - are located nearby. The park, which also includes a large spring and a hiking trail along the river, lies just below Cotter's most famous landmark - a multi-arched, 1,850-foot White River bridge that was built in 1930.

The 1990 census listed Cotter's population as 687. Its history includes a "boom" period when the population was as high as 1,500, according to Bayless.

The town was incorporated on July 7, 1904. The boom came with the extension of the St. Louis, Iron Mountain and Southern Railroad from Batesville in 1905.

The railroad ended the White River's steamboat era, which had begun in the 1830s. Railroad construction laborers came to Cotter, and many stayed when a roundhouse and repair station for the railroad company were built.

"There was a boom atmosphere," Bayless said. "We had about five hotels, four or five stores, three doctors, a pool hall, and we had the only movie house in Baxter County."

Bayless represents the fifth generation of his family to grow up along the White River. The family name is on a White River landmark. The island just upstream from the Cotter bridge is called Bayless Island.

"I became the owner of it in the 1940s," Bayless said.

Cotter's population stayed near 1,000 until 1940. That's when Mountain Home surpassed it as the biggest town in Baxter County.

Before then, Cotter's reputation was that of a town where you could get anything you wanted. The whiskey from local moonshiners flowed into Cotter and "made it a rough outfit," Bayless said. Card games were common along the river banks.

"A lot of those railroad boys had money," Bayless said. "Cotter had more cash than about any town around here, so there was a lot of gambling."

All that led to some wild Saturday nights on the town. That reputation seems centuries old now as Cotter caters to trout fishing, tourism and retired folks.

"We are a bedroom community of Mountain Home," Bayless said.

He predicts another boom for Cotter, spurred by the railroad again. March 16, 1960, marked the last time a passenger train came through Cotter. In November 1993, a trial run was made on a scenic railroad excursion train from Branson, Missouri, to Newport, Arkansas, with a stop in Cotter.

"If that becomes a reality, it will make the White River country expand like never before," Bayless said.

Before Elvin Weaver goes after a big brown trout, he feels his way through moss beds, gathering softshell crawfish.

Strictly A Trophy Fishing Proposition

Elvin Weaver: 'If I couldn't fish for big fish, I probably wouldn't fish.'

Elvin Weaver looked like a man who'd dropped his eyeglasses in the White River. As he leaned over the back of a johnboat with a boat cushion under his stomach, Weaver used his bare hands to feel through a moss bed along the river bottom.

Weaver smiled as he found what he wanted. It wasn't glasses; it was alive.

"That's a dandy," he said, as he put a softshell crawfish in a Styrofoam bucket. "That one there is soft as butter. That's one big brown (trout) for sure."

Weaver only needs a dozen softshell crawfish for a day of fishing. He's not into numbers of fish. He's after a few big bites.

"If I couldn't fish for big fish, I probably wouldn't fish," Weaver says.

It's called "trophy fishing." Some people don't have the patience for it. It appeals more to those with a big-

game-hunting mentality, those who know both the thrill of the chase and the odds of coming home empty-handed.

When you start asking around for the best big-fish guide on the White River, you're sure to hear Elvin Weaver's name among the first mentioned.

His big trout from the White River include a 25-pound brown, two 16-pound, 6-ounce rainbows and a 9-pound cutthroat, which might have been a new state record. The Arkansas record cutthroat at that time was 9 pounds, 4 ounces. (A new mark of 9 pounds, 9 ounces was set by Scott Rudolph of Ozark in 1985).

"I had that 9-pounder in the boat all day before I weighed it," Weaver said. "The reason I didn't weigh him sooner is I thought the record was 10 pounds. I knew this fish wasn't 10. I've

caught so many big fish over the years that I can usually guess the weight within a quarter of a pound."

Weaver is an easy man to find. Everyone around Cotter and Gassville knows him. He has served as the Gassville city marshal since 1981. (Towns of less than 5,000 people have a city marshal instead of a police chief. Gassville's population is 1,167.)

Weaver was born in Gassville in 1943. He started guiding on the White River when he was 16 years old. He left for Indianapolis, Indiana, in 1968, and that's where he got into law enforcement work. Weaver was back on the White River in 1971, working as Cotter's city marshall at night and as a trout fishing guide during the day.

If you can't find Weaver at city hall or patrolling the streets, you'll find him at Miller's Fishing Service or on the river, where he guides on his two-days-off a week, on holidays and during his vacation time.

Weaver claims he enjoys every part of law enforcement work. Three murder cases during his 20-plus years of duty have involved the most intense labor.

But Weaver is most famous for patrolling the banks of the White River. If you see a skinny man with both arms buried to the biceps in a moss bed, it's most likely Elvin Weaver. His favorite bait for big White River trout is a softshell crawfish.

"If I'm after big fish, I use softshell crawfish unless I don't have anything else to use," Weaver said.

Usually this is an April to October fishing technique. The crawfish are most active during those warmer months, and that's also when they grow fastest.

Periodically, a crawfish sheds its hard shell, so it has room for more growth. As the new shell forms, it is soft and doesn't have the camouflage of a hard shell. Thus, the crawfish becomes both easier for a trout to see and easier for a trout to eat.

"I've seen trout go right up to a softshell and instantly take it," Weaver said. "A hardshell crawfish can be right next to it, and they'll never even pick it up. I've always thought it was because they look different, but a softshell may give off a different smell, too."

A softshell crawfish in the Cotter area of the White River, where Weaver usually fishes, will have a light gray color.

"Especially on the mossy river bottom, like we've got around here now, that bait looks as white as cotton," he said.

Just before a crawfish sheds its hard shell, a separation forms between the head and tail sections of the carapace. Weaver calls these crawfish "peelers." If he finds one, it goes in the bait bucket, too, since it will soon be a softshell. Otherwise, Weaver takes only enough crawfish to use that day.

"I don't keep what I can't use," he said. "I could use the tail on the hard ones, but I keep throwing them back so I'll have a good supply of softshells.

"The only time I use a crawfish tail

is when I want to catch a nice string of rainbows, or I don't have any softshells."

Weaver knows how valuable the moss beds are as both trout and crawfish habitat, so he searches them with his bare hands, rather than a net.

"If you scoop with a net, you tear up the moss," he said. "I don't tear up the moss when I just feel in there with my hands."

You don't have to look in moss beds to find softshell crawfish. They'll be among the rocks, too.

> ## "What you catch with a softshell crawdad is worth a little pain. I get pinched once in a while..."

"But I've found out there are usually more softshells in the moss than the rocks," Weaver said. "Plus, in the rocks you'll usually run into more snakes than you do in the moss.

"I think that's why most people don't want to catch crawfish this way. They are afraid of what they can't see in the moss."

A crawfish may be more vulnerable during its soft-shelled state, but its pinchers still work. Weaver sometimes pays the price for his barehanded method.

"What you catch with a softshell crawdad is worth a little pain," Weaver said. "I get pinched once in a while, but the moss kind of cushions the pinchers.

"Don't try to pull it off, if a crawfish grabs hold. The pinchers will cut like a knife. Just sit there and grin and bear it until he lets go."

Weaver follows the old fishing maxim of using big bait to catch big fish.

"The bigger they are, the better I like them," he said. "I'll find some crawfish that are five inches long."

Weaver uses a No. 1 or 1/0 hook. He starts it at the tip of the crawfish's tail, on the underside, and brings it out near the chest. Weaver thinks the bend in a Tru-Turn hook is important.

"Browns have a habit of grabbing the bait, and, when you hit them hard, they'll try to spit it out," he said. "A Tru-Turn hook seems to help you hang on better."

Weaver fishes a crawfish on a typical White River drift rig, weighted with a bell sinker off a dropper, and 6-pound-test line.

The real key is knowing where to cast the crawfish. Like all good guides, Weaver sees fish that the average person doesn't. Three decades of guiding on the river have helped him develop this awareness. It's not simply sharp eyesight. It's the ability to notice a shadow or a movement in the water and relate that instantly to fish behavior.

Weaver's crawfishing technique requires low water conditions - particularly for gathering the bait, but also for catching fish. It's easier to spot the fish and keep the bait in position during low water flow.

If Weaver sees a school of brown trout, he will anchor his boat either to one side or upstream, being careful to keep his distance and not spook the fish.

If he is upstream, Weaver will cast downstream, but not directly on top of the fish. He makes a short cast and lets the current carry the bait to the fish. If he is to one side, he will cast upstream and, again, let the current carry the bait to its proper location.

If the fish are on a gravel bar, Weaver will anchor upstream, make a quartering cast downstream and let the current swing the bait over to the fish. Then, the waiting game begins.

"I usually leave it there a good while," Weaver said. "I move it occasionally. If the fish act like they aren't feeding, I'll move and try it from a different position. You can usually tell if they are in a feeding mood. But they might go 30 minutes without feeding, then start eating like crazy. You can't predict it."

That's why this type of fishing isn't

for everyone. It's angling's version of sitting in a tree stand, waiting on that big buck to come by. And, because of Weaver's track record of success, it can be just as addicting as deer hunting.

"I normally guide the same customers every year," Weaver said. "When I lose a customer, because someone passes away or something like that, there's always another one waiting on me."

Weaver and his customers have taken a ton of big trout from the White River. But he has seen a gradual change in that practice of keeping everything you catch.

"There used to be no such thing as catch-and-release," Weaver said. "Nobody ever thought about it. We would keep a limit of rainbows that weighed between 5 and 14 pounds. If we'd known about catch-and-release, and it would have been pushed, chances are there would be more big rainbows right now.

"That's the biggest change I've seen in this river. There used to be a lot of big rainbows, especially from Wildcat Shoals to Cotter. Now there are hardly any big rainbows, but the river is full of big browns."

Weaver is optimistic about the future of the river. People aren't keeping the big brown trout like they did the big rainbows in years past.

"I release every one I can," Weaver said. "Most customers I guide have caught a big brown. They have one mounted on the wall. Most of them don't want to keep any more fish."

Weaver has guided on five-day float trips, so he has fished the Bull Shoals Tailwater from the dam to Guion.

And he's comfortable with a variety of trout fishing methods - from other baits, like sculpins and shiner minnows, to artificial lures, like Countdown Rapalas.

But Weaver doesn't work the five-day floats anymore. He concentrates his fishing between Wildcat Shoals and Ranchette.

For one thing, crawfish are more abundant from Wildcat down. And Elvin Weaver has made a name for himself fishing with crawfish.

Attention To Detail Aided Morris In Catching Record Book Brown

When Mike Morris went fishing at Rim Shoals on April 15, 1992, he made certain his first cast was perfect. And it was.

Two months earlier, on his first-ever trout fishing trip to the White River, Morris and his buddy, Hal Fraim, had caught and released over 150 trout up to 4 pounds.

During that trip, Morris had noticed a large tree in the river, just up from the first shoal. It still had the root wad attached.

Rim Shoals attracts as many fly fishers as any place on the White River. Two long, narrow islands feature shoals on both sides and classic fly fishing water.

"In February, I had noticed some big fish feeding in what I call the flat-water area (above the shoals)," Morris said.

"After we got our wading gear on, I told Hal I was going to fish that area once, before fishing the shoals."

Living in Rubicon, Arkansas, near Benton, Morris doesn't get many chances to fish for trout. Most of his fishing time is spent pursuing smallmouth bass in the Saline River. Being a bass fisherman, he knew a good piece of fish-holding structure when he saw one. He tied on a brown No. 8 Muddler Minnow.

"I cast across the river, so the current would take it down to the tree," Morris said. "When it got where I wanted it, I started stripping line to make it look like a frightened baitfish. That's when I saw the torpedo come out after it."

Morris set the hook as hard as he could, and his 7-foot, 9-inch Orvis Green Mountain 5-weight rod bent double.

"There was no movement," Morris said. "It felt like I had hooked the stump."

But just for a moment.

"Then it jumped about four feet in the air," Morris said.

His reel, which was loaded with 80

feet of fly line and 180 feet of backing, was nearly empty after the big brown trout made its first run

"I could see most of my spool," he said. "I thought, 'This is starting to get serious.' And I started wading downstream."

That was the beginning of what would be a 30-minute struggle, during which the fish jumped eight times.

"It was a seesaw battle," Morris said. "He'd go out; I'd get him in. I finally got him into shallow water. I latched on to him, and he latched on to me."

The trout's sharp teeth left Morris with two lacerated fingers.

Morris didn't think anything about the record book. He just knew he'd caught the biggest trout of his life. His previous best was an 11-pound brown trout from the Little Red River. There were no scales to weigh his latest catch, but Morris knew it was bigger than that 11-pounder.

The fish had been out of the water about 20 minutes when Jerry Nixon, who has a home at Rim Shoals, saw it and suggested that Morris might have a line class record fish. Morris was using an Orvis 4X tapered leader.

It was 30 minutes later before Morris' brown trout was put on an official scale. The fish weighed 15.64 pounds. It measured 33 inches in length and 18 3/4 inches in girth.

The 4X tippet passed the National Fresh Water Fishing Hall of Fame test, and Morris' fish became a record in the 4-pound-test fly fishing category.

Morris has one more memory of that record-setting catch. When he made the cast and saw the "torpedo" going for his Muddler Minnow, he actually saw two torpedoes. One was half again as big as the other. He hooked the smaller of the two.

"I could see them both plain as day," Morris said. "They were swimming side by side."

With another perfect cast, one day that fish may enter the record book, too.

Calcasieu Pig Boat, .56er, Help Nixon Keep Shirt Unstuffed

Tom Nixon tends to philosophize when he ties flies. And Nixon ties lots of flies.

"When tying flies, you've got to watch yourself or you'll become a stuffed shirt," Nixon said.

There's no chance of that happening with the man who named one of his fly patterns the "Calcasieu Pig Boat." (Ed Zern, the outdoor humor writer for Field & Stream magazine, liked the name so much that he worked it into several columns.)

Nixon is best known for tying black bass and bluegill patterns. He wrote a book on the subject, and he has written articles about fly tying for most of the major fly fishing magazines.

"Don't forget the most important thing about fly fishing is supposed to be fun," Nixon said, philosophizing again. "All this technical stuff is just to augment the fun."

As Nixon talked, he was tying another of his creations, the .56er. (He calls it a "Point Fifty-Sixer" or just

Tom Nixon emphasizes the fun part of fly fishing, as you might expect from the Calciseau Pig Boat creator.

.56er

Hook: Mustad 3665A 6X long or 79580 4X long (sizes 4-18)
Thread: Black
Tail: Wood duck flank feather
Body: Gray wool
Belly stripe: Yellow, orange or green wool
Hackle: Grizzly saddle hackle

The Woolly Bugger is by far the most popular streamer pattern in the White River System. If the trout tire of Woolly Buggers, the .56er is a good streamer alternative.

It seems to be an especially good pattern in the Rim Shoals area of the White River. That might be due to the fact that Tom Nixon's brother, Jerry, has a vacation home at Rim Shoals and uses the .56er often there.

But Jerry has another idea. He thinks it imitates the many crawfish found in the Rim Shoals area.

"The main test is when the crawfish are hibernating, the effectiveness of that fly drops off about 70 percent," Jerry said. "If you're fishing that fly in January, you're wasting your time."

The smaller patterns are effective in winter months, when they probably imitate a scud more than a crawfish.

Tom varies the belly stripe color of the .56er from green to yellow to orange. He varies the hook size from No. 4 down to No. 18. He weights it with 8 to 10 wraps of lead, the same diameter as the hook.

Fish a .56er just like you would a Woolly Bugger - with a cross-stream cast, letting it swing. Give it a couple of short strips back before repeating the cast.

"Fifty-Sixer.")

"I was asked to write an article for the Fly Tyers Roundtable in Boston about this bluegill fly I used in Louisiana," Nixon said. "The old saying was that New England dry fly fishermen were 99.44-percent pure."

Thus, Nixon's pattern, a streamer, represents that .56 percent of impurity found in even the purest of the pure.

Tom often ties .56ers in the vacation home of his brother, Jerry. The house is located just above Rim Shoals on the White River. Jerry and Tom Nixon have been fishing the White River since 1958, when their father would bring them here on camping trips. Tom says his brother hasn't always been a fly fisherman.

"He was a worm fisherman," Tom said. "I used to get a separate tent, so I wouldn't have to sleep in the same tent with a worm fisherman."

Jerry laughed in acceptance of the label "former worm fisherman."

The .56er may have started as a bluegill fly, but in Tom's visits to the White River he has found it's an excellent pattern for trout, too.

Now, about that Calcasieu Pig Boat. "In the first World War, German subs were known as pig boats," Nixon said. "I developed the fly on the Calcasieu River in Alabama."

It's more or less a fly fisher's version of a bass jig. Its main feature is medium or fine black rubber hackle.

"I won a bass club tournament with it on Toledo Bend in 1965," Nixon said. "You'd be surprised what some people called a fly rod then, and where they said you could put it."

Nixon said he got some funny looks when he first started fly fishing on the White River.

"People would float by and say, 'What's the matter, mister, did you lose your boat?' They'd never seen anyone wading," he said.

Tom Nixon now finds plenty of fly fishing company when he visits his brother on the White River.

"In my opinion, the White River is the best big-trout stream in the U.S.," Tom said. "There isn't any place that gets the play this place does and survives."

Wapsi Fly, Inc., Is World's Top Wholesaler Of Tying Materials

If you were new to fly fishing, the Wapsi Fly, Inc., warehouse might send a shiver down your spine. It could pass for a witchcraft mail order house.

Here you'll find cock necks, Indian hen saddle patches, goose shoulders, turkey flats, squirrel tails, deer belly hair and hare masks (with ears). All that's missing, it seems, is eye of newt and hair of toad.

But if you know fly fishing, you probably know Wapsi. And the only shivers you'll have are those of delight. Prime dry fly Indian rooster necks, Woolly Bugger marabou, Hungarian partridge feathers, ringneck pheasant skins, whatever, if it's commonly used in fly tying, it can be found in this Mountain Home warehouse. Wapsi is the largest wholesaler of fly tying materials in the world.

"I had great visions of being a Madison Avenue executive's wife instead of being belly button deep in feathers and hair," said Ann Schmuecker, who helps her husband, Tom, run the business.

"This is actually an outgrowth of my husband's hobby. He started tying flies when he was a little boy. It has gotten out of hand."

What's "gotten out of hand" is the need for fly tying materials. Growth in the sport of fly fishing created a niche for Wapsi, which started out as a fly tying business in Independence, Iowa, in 1944.

Lacey E. Gee created Wapsi, which was named after the nearby Wapsipinicon River. The company employed about 25 women who tied flies that were then sold to retail shops.

Tom and Ann Schmuecker are both University of Iowa graduates. Tom's degree is in business and advertising; Ann majored in education and taught school for awhile.

After college, Tom raised Angus cattle for 10 years. As part hobby and part work, Tom and Ann also spent time developing a good strain of

Barred Rock Grizzly, which they sold to Lacey Gee and Wapsi Fly.

"That was kind of our going out to dinner money," Ann said.

Tom was a member of the Iowa Hawkeye Fly Fishing Club. In 1973, his hobby got the best of him, and he bought Wapsi Fly from Gee. Within five years, the Schmuecker family began taking a new approach to their business.

Commercial fly tying shifted toward cheap labor in other countries or one-man, specialty shops in the U.S. Tom had become familiar with acquiring and dyeing the various feathers and furs needed as materials for his own fly tyers at Wapsi, so he shifted the emphasis of his company.

"If dyeing were a science, you could write a book on it, and everyone could do it. But you can't. It's like cooking; it's an art."

Because of high energy costs in Iowa, the Schmuecker's also started looking for a new place to locate their business.

"We looked for two years," Ann said. "There was no single reason why we came to Mountain Home. The general environment was just very appealing."

Tom says, "I came here because of the White River."

In 1988, the Wapsi Fly warehouse was gutted by fire. Friends, neighbors and people the Schmuecker's didn't even know volunteered to help cleanup and rebuild.

"We were able to keep everyone employed and were showing a profit

Tom Schmuecker (right) turned his hobby of fly tying into a business that now employs sons Karl (left) and Joe.

within a month," Ann said. "We took orders on a phone outside."

The Schmuecker's oldest of four sons, Karl, was between jobs, so he came home to help reorganize the business. Karl and another son, Joe, have become important parts of this family-run business, which has about 30 employees.

In addition to supplying the major retailers and mail order catalogs in the fly fishing business, Wapsi Fly helps fill the needs of fly shops all over the world.

For example, Wapsi has customers in Norway, Japan, New Zealand, Argentina and Iceland. And the international element of this business goes both ways. Wapsi's sources of fly tying materials include China, India and Africa.

Foreign animal products have to ride a sea of customs regulations before entering the U.S.

"There are lots of rules and regulations about what can be used and what can't," Ann said. "We are careful about what we use."

Many of these fly tying materials are leftovers from another industry. Marabou is a body feather from a white domestic turkey. Wapsi Fly sells literally tons of marabou each year, after the feathers have been dyed and packaged for their many uses in fly tying.

Tom's ability to dye fly tying materials is another factor in Wapsi's success. Consistency is crucial. Tom is passing on this art to son Joe.

"It takes a different recipe to dye bucktails pink than it does to dye chicken feathers pink," Joe said. "There are a whole lot of recipes for the same colors. If dyeing were a science, you could write a book on it, and everyone could do it. But you can't. It's like cooking; it's an art."

If you are into fly tying, and you had never heard of Wapsi Fly before, you've probably come in contact with Wapsi products without realizing it. Again, Wapsi Fly is a wholesale house. And in an effort to be a complete fly shop supplier, Wapsi also handles various tools, threads, tinsels, wires, waxes and hooks used in fly tying.

The warehouse even handles a wide selection of books, including founder Lacy Gee's classic, "How to Fish with Jigs."

The Schmueckers didn't know an invoice from a packing list when they moved Wapsi Fly to Mountain Home, according to Ann. But, like every other business, what is now the largest supplier of fly tying materials in the world had to start somewhere.

"We've been in the right place at the right time," Ann said. "But it wouldn't have worked if we hadn't worked hard."

Fox Statler Applies Math To Fly Fishing

Counting bugs part of formula for figuring best patterns for trout

At the age of 44, Fox Statler was forced to retire as a Mountain Home Junior High School math teacher. His hearing had deteriorated to the point where he couldn't do his job.

But Statler doesn't have to hear well to catch fish, and he applies his math principles as much on the river as he did in the classroom.

"By the end of the day, I'll prove to you that fishing is simply numbers," Statler said, one August day as he pulled on his waders and walked toward the White River below Cotter bridge.

Statler has been a fly fishing guide since 1981. He also has become the chief number cruncher on the White River. Fox isn't a bean counter; he's a bug counter.

"I've counted bugs all the way down to Black River," Statler said. "After reading Charlie Brooks' book 'Nymphing for Larger Trout' I was convinced I needed to go out and dig up some gravel."

Statler once dug up a square yard of gravel below Bull Shoals Dam and sorted through it. He counted about 7,000 sowbugs and 500 scuds.

"Sowbugs go as deep as there is gravel," Statler said. "Scuds go only about three inches deep in the gravel."

With that sowbug-to-scud ratio of 14-to-1 in mind, Statler started counting the bugs in the stomachs of trout. This time the ratio was only four sowbugs to one scud.

"Why?" Statler said. "Why not 14-to-1? Then I found out that a scud has about five times more protein than a sowbug. The scud is the preferred bug."

It didn't seem right to hear those words coming from Fox Statler's mouth. This is a fly fisherman who has billed himself, "Mr. Sowbug."

He has sold thousands of the simple sowbug pattern he ties, and thousands of trout have been caught on his sowbugs.

But on this particular day of fly fishing on the White River, Statler never tied on a sowbug. And his knowledge of White River trout food defied such a one-dimensional label as "Mr. Sowbug."

"If you just go out and look and dig, you'll see all the food that trout can utilize in this river," Statler said. "In terms of numbers, No. 1 is sow-bugs, No. 2 is scuds, and you'll see more minnows than mayflies."

In certain sections of the White River, other food sources figure in the equation. From Cotter down, crawfish are common. Statler explained the crawfish pattern he ties - in sizes 8 to 12.

"For every adult crawfish, there are 12 to 350 smaller ones in the same

Fox Statler gave himself the title "Mr. Sowbug," but he has also counted every other bug and trout food he could find along the White and North Fork rivers.

area, depending on the species," Statler said. "Sometimes people can't see the forest for the trees. The trees are the big crawfish; the forest is all the little ones.

"It's the same way with sculpins. I tie what I call a 'micro sculpin' on a No. 12 hook."

Statler's number-crunching and bug-counting add up to five-step philosophy on fly fishing:

1) Ninety percent of the fish in a river will be in a place where there is no current, like the stream bed.

2) Ninety percent of the bug life in a river is on the bottom also.

3) Fish feed on what is most available to them at the time.

4) Success to a fisherman should be assessed in number of bites, not number of fish caught.

5) A fisherman will be more successful if he is using a pattern that imitates what the fish are biting most.

"You can take those five concepts and go to any river in the world and catch fish," Statler said.

The Statler five-step philosophy came about through reading and personal experience. Brooks' book informed him of the fact that a trout can spend only 45 minutes per day in current of three miles per hour. Statler's own digging in the gravel showed him where the food was.

"Even most caddis live three years in the gravel," Statler said. "A fish's brain is not even big enough to feel pain, yet we give them all these mystical powers.

"If a fish spends 90 percent of its life near the bottom, and 90 percent of the food is on the bottom, why couldn't 90 percent of its feeding activity take place on the bottom?"

Although Statler is an advocate of catch-and-release, he's spent much of his research time looking through the stomach contents of trout. He doesn't apologize for that.

"I've killed lots of fish," he said. "I was poor and I ate every damn one of them."

One day Statler was cleaning fish and examining the stomach contents when another angler stopped and said, "I know what you caught that fish on -

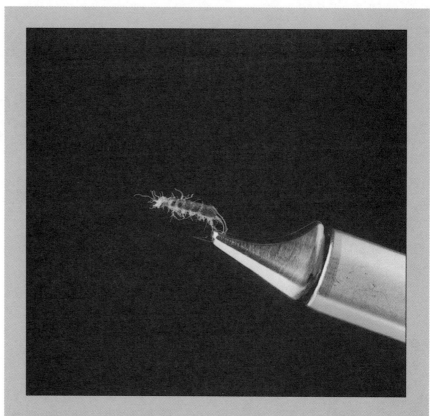

Statler's Sowbug

Hook: Dai-Riki 305 or 310 dry fly hook, sizes 14-20
Thread: 8/0 tan
Weight: 10 turns of lead wire the same diameter as the hook shank
Body: Equal parts white zelon, gray zelon, sand Antron, calibaetis Antron
Shellback: Swiss straw, dyed olive

Simplicity is emphasized in all Fox Statler's fly patterns. He wants something that you can tie in less than two minutes.

"I don't want it to be special in any way," Statler said. "I want it to be just another bug. You can't use a fly you're going to feel bad about losing."

Statler prefers dry fly hooks because they penetrate easier when using light line, and they'll dissolve quicker than heavy wire hooks if they are broken off in a fish. He matches lead with the hook shank - .025 for a No. 12 hook, .020 for No. 14, .015 for No. 16 and .010 for Nos. 18 and 20 - and adds about 10 turns on each, except for the No. 20 hook,

which will take only about eight wraps of .010 lead.

The Swiss straw can be found in craft stores and fly shops. He dyes it for a natural color, then opens it up, flattens it out and cuts strips the width of the sowbug he's tying. He ties in the Swiss straw and covers the lead with it.

"Undercolors are as important as any," Statler said. "That's why I don't leave any bare lead."

Statler adds the dubbing, then squeezes the fly flat with pliers before bringing the straw forward for the shellback. If you flatten it after the straw is brought forward, the straw will crack and tear.

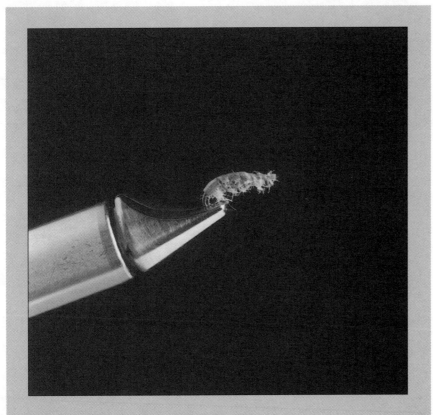

Statler's Arkansas Scud

Hook: Dai-Riki 305 or 310 dry fly hook, sizes 12-20
Thread: 8/0 tan
Body: Same Antron, zelon blend as sowbug, except copper or brown zelon is substituted for white zelon
Shellback: Swiss straw
Lead: 8 turns of .020 on a size 14 hook

This is another of Fox Statler's two-minute patterns. As with his sowbug, color and silhouette are the points of emphasis.

"Scuds come in three colors in the White River," Statler said. "In the pre-molt stage they are dark chocolate. When they are molting they are copper-orange. Most of the time they are red-brown. If you are fishing a deteriorating gravel bar, the molting scud is the best. In big open pools, chocolate is best. Overall, the red-brown shade is the one I like."

Statler matches lead size to hook size with the same formula he uses in his sowbug. But instead of 10 wraps, he uses 8 on the scud. Just like in the sowbug, the Swiss straw completely covers the lead. But the lead is wrapped near the hook bend to give the scud a curved silhouette. After the body is dubbed, Statler squeezes it with pliers to flatten it vertically, not horizontally like a sowbug. The straw shellback is cut off just past the thread in order to give it a tail.

"A scud is the best wind bug there is," Statler said. "If there's a light chop on the water, a strike indicator makes the scud bump along the bottom. A sowbug doesn't swim like this, but a scud does."

When Statler fishes a size 16 or smaller scud, he'll offset the hook slightly or turn the fly on the hook, because a scud's vertical body shape tends to crowd into the hook gap.

a minnow."

Statler had separated five minnows - two sculpins and three shiners - from the stomach of one big trout.

"Is that all you see?" Statler asked. "What about this pile of green stuff?"

The "green stuff" that made up the bulk of the fish's stomach contents was sowbugs.

"There must have been 500 of them," Statler said. "In other words, I had five chances to catch that fish on a minnow and 500 chances to catch it on a little bug. My decision on what fly to use is going to be based totally on the highest number. It's simple math."

And the longer you're around Statler, the more math lessons you get.

"Nymph and streamer fishermen shouldn't false cast because it dries the fly out," said Statler, later that day, as he made a cast, then landed his sixth trout in 30 minutes from a riffle near Smith Island. "The longer your fly stays at the bottom, the more strikes you'll get,"

Statler has been fly fishing since age seven, when his father introduced him to the sport. His parents were from Walnut Ridge, Arkansas, but had moved to Fort Wayne, Indiana, where he was born William Fox Statler. (Fox is a family name dating back to some Native American ancestry.)

Statler grew up fishing for bass and bream until he moved to Imboden, Arkansas, after a four-year hitch in the Navy. Statler was working as a carpenter when he discovered the Spring River and trout fishing.

Statler's carpentry career ended with a head-on car wreck that broke both his legs. He enrolled at Arkansas State University as a 28-year-old freshman. After graduation, he was hired as a teacher in Mountain Home.

For 9 1/2 years, that was a perfect setting for Statler's pursuits - fulltime teacher and parttime fishing guide. In 1992, Statler gave in to his hearing problems and retired from teaching.

But he's still teaching math, trout fishing math, and it's hard to argue with Statler's numbers.

"I've got tennis elbow," Statler said with a smile. "My doctor says it's from catching too many fish."

Statler Specializes In Fly Fishing The Ultralight Way

Fox Statler had tried just about everything in his search for the perfect strike indicator. None of the indicators he found on the market fit his need for sensitivity.

"Round indicators aren't worth a damn," Statler said. "They only tell you half of what you need to know."

He'd even experimented with Super Gluing small pieces of Styrofoam pie plates to his leader. That didn't work either.

One day his wife asked him to buy some double-sided picture mounting tape for a project she was working on.

"I brought the tape home and looked at it," Statler recalled. "I said, 'This stuff will float.' I cut a piece and threw it in her coffee."

Eureka! The perfect strike indicator had been discovered. Statler's fishing, not to mention his marriage, would never be the same.

"When I found that tape, it changed my fishing totally," Statler said. "I could fish the depth I wanted and bring the sensitivity up by cutting the tape to the size I needed. After that, if a fish so much as farted on the fly, I could catch it."

Statler's fly fishing tools of choice lean heavily toward the sensitive side. He prefers 2- and 3-weight, 9-foot rods that have a flexible tip and stiff butt. They allow him to fish with a line that features a 20-foot leader and 6X to 8X tippet.

"Ultralight fly fishing is exactly what we should call it," Statler said.

But if you think Statler is fishing strictly for high numbers of small fish, you're wrong. The ultralight equipment allows him to make the best presentation possible.

It follows that if you catch more fish than the average angler, you'll catch more big ones, too. Statler has landed White River brown trout over 20 pounds on 6X tippet.

"I fish the first six feet of my drift as good as any man alive," Statler said.

Statler's Crawfish

Hook: Dai-Riki 730C, sizes 8-12
Thread: 8/0 tan
Weight: 8 to 10 wraps of .025 lead wire
Body dubbing: Same Antron-zelon 4-part blend as sowbug and scud, but matched to color of crawfish in the stream
Body feather: Body shaft or blood feather, also called gimp feather
Shellback: Swiss straw

Most White River anglers have noticed the abundance of crawfish in the river, particularly from Cotter down. But few anglers have noticed them to the extent that Fox Statler has.

"For every adult crawfish, there are 12 to 350 smaller ones in the same area, depending on the species," Statler said. "Sometimes people can't see the forest for the trees. The trees are the big crawfish; the forest is all the little ones."

Applying his math principles again, Statler concentrates on imitating all the little crawfish with another of his two-minute patterns.

Color, as always, is important.

Statler tries to match it with the various colors of crawfish he finds.

"Look at the crawfish in the river and look for the highlight colors," Statler said. "In the North Fork River, the crawfish are blue-gray. In the Spring River, they are brown-red. In the White, I like to use a fleshy brown-gray."

After the body is dubbed, Statler places the feather on top of the hook, near the bend and ties it in with two wraps of thread before bringing the Swiss straw back toward the hook eye.

"Most guys throw away the gimp feathers on a saddle," Statler said. "But they work perfectly for this."

Statler's Sculpin

Hook: Dai-Riki 700, sizes 4-12
Thread: Red 6/0
Body: Olive chenille
Pectoral fins: Olive or brown hackle
Tail: Light olive marabou feather

Just as in his observations of crawfish, Statler noticed that for every large sculpin you see in the White River, there will be dozens of smaller ones that are seldom noticed. It's why he ties this pattern in a "micro sculpin" size 12.

"I caught a 27-pound brown trout on a No. 10 sculpin," Statler said. "It looks almost like a little jig."

Statler kept sculpins in an aquarium for several years and observed how they propelled themselves in the water.

"They use those big pectoral fins for the first stroke, and that's it," Statler said. "A sculpin swims by tail vibrations. When you see them swimming, the tail is just a blur."

Statler imitates the pectoral fins with 2 or 3 turns of olive or brown hackle, just behind the chenille head. The key feature in this pattern is the movement of the marabou tail.

"Pluck off enough marabou to make a good, full-bodied silhouette, about 1 1/2 hook shanks long," Statler said.

"This works as well as a Woolly Bugger, if not better, and it takes half as long to tie," Statler said. "I use it unweighted on a sinking tip line. I like unweighted streamers.

"If you see any minnow in the current, he's at the mercy of the current. Sinking tips and unweighted streamers give you more action than anything else you can do."

While that point might be debated, there is no doubt that Statler has spent hundreds of hours working on his nymphing techniques. The search for the perfect strike indicator was only part of it.

""When I watch most people fishing a nymph, I want to go up and thump them in the ear," Statler said. "They're not imitating anything that's in the river. Nymphs don't swim against the current."

Statler places a strike indicator at the same depth of the water he's fishing. He adds as little lead as possible to his flies and seldom uses any split shot between the fly and the indicator.

"You must mend so the fly drifts downstream first," Statler said. "With the right mending technique, you don't need a lot of lead. Too much lead and you have no sensitivity. Any time you put weight between the indicator and the fly, you numb it. It's best to tie the weight in the fly and eliminate the split shot."

Statler believes that weight, or lack of it, is also an important consideration in using 8X tippet. "The fish don't feel it, so they hold it longer," he said.

The long leader length figures in this equation, too.

"If you are fishing with an indicator, grease the line right to the indicator," Statler said. "The long leader allows you to keep more light line on the surface, not down in the water. That helps you set the hook. It's simple geometry - the shortest distance between two points is a straight line."

Statler is constantly looking for simple answers in fly fishing. The picture mounting tape strike indicator is evidence of that. (By the way, he prefers Nanco, Bulldog Jordan and America 3 brands.) That is also evident in the fly patterns he ties.

"I don't want it to be special in any way," Statler said of his sowbug pattern. "I want it to be just another bug. You can't use a fly you're going to feel bad about losing. As a guide, you look for simple flies that perform."

Statler didn't care to spend half the night tying flies in preparation for a guide trip the next day. Just as in forming his nymphing techniques,

Statler has studied the real thing and then looked for the easiest way to imitate it. The result is a selection of "two-minute patterns." With minimal fly tying skills, you can tie them in two minutes. Statler ties his sowbug in 1 minute, 40 seconds.

"The sowbug took me eight years to develop," Statler said. "There wasn't any zelon or Antron when I started. I used mink and muskrat."

Statler combines several colors of Antron and zelon to get the overall dubbing shades to match the sowbugs wherever he's fishing. He dyes the Swiss straw. Then he tests these materials in water.

"I'm interested in the wet colors," Statler said.

For the White River, he wants a sowbug that has more olive and brown tones. For the North Fork River, gray is the dominant color.

Color and silhouette are the main points of emphasis on all his patterns. He doesn't worry about the fine details.You'll notice that his sowbug has no tail.

"That's a waste of time," Statler said. He laughed and added, "Besides, you don't want to confuse the fish about which end to eat."

Statler segments the sowbug with thread, but that's done mostly for durability rather than imitation of a real sowbug's segmented body. (He further insures durability with Von Schlegell's Special Formula 251 head cement.)

Now Statler can put his applied math principles to work. He's got a fly the color and shape of a sowbug, one of the most commonly found trout food sources in the White River. And he's got a technique for dead-drifting it near the bottom, where 90 percent of the feeding activity takes place.

"I think 70 percent of fly fishing is in the presentation," Statler said. "And I also think 70 percent is in having the right bug. You can have a fair day with either. But if you can do both, you can really do well."

That adds up to a 140-percent day in the Statler theory of applied mathematics. And that's a good day of trout fishing in anyone's book.

Buffalo National River Remains An Ozark Island Of Time, Space

At one time, it was commonly called the Buffalo Fork of the White River. Its beginning in the Boston Mountains of the Ozarks lies less than five miles from that of the White River, and it eventually joins the White River, 32 miles below Bull Shoals Dam.

But the Buffalo River has met a much different fate than the White River. It has no dams, and it has no trout. After the U.S. Army Corps of Engineers started damming Ozark streams, conservationists drew the line at the Buffalo River.

A series of dams was planned for the Buffalo. A century after the Civil War began, another "civil war" erupted between the federal government and private citizens. Led by Dr. Neil Compton of Bentonville, Arkansas, and the newly-formed Ozark Society, conservationists finally won the battle to preserve the Buffalo River.

Supreme Court Justice William O. Douglas was one those who didn't see the need for dams on the Buffalo River. In a letter, Douglas wrote, in part: "It should be kept in perpetuity as a remnant of the ancient Ozarks unspoiled by man. Its fast waters and its idyllic pools make it a bit of heaven on earth."

In 1972, Congress officially preserved the free-flowing nature of the Buffalo by designating it a National River. It was the first river in the U.S. to gain such status.

And, as Douglas hoped, the Buffalo River remains as an example of the ancient Ozarks. A corridor of more than 95,000 acres of public land now encompasses the Buffalo River. It includes 36,000 acres of designated Wilderness Area.

Most of the public land is monitored by the National Park Service, which is also gathering scientific data on Ozark water and air quality here.

The Arkansas Game and Fish Commission's 9,500-acre Gene Rush/Buffalo River Wildlife Management Area borders the Buffalo River, too.

From a practical standpoint for the angler, the Buffalo River's confluence with the White River provides an opportunity to sample yesterday and today.

The smallmouth bass fishing that characterized the White River before it was dammed can still be found in the Buffalo, which is home to 59 species of warmwater fish.

And the Buffalo National River offers much more than that. Its bluffs are the tallest in the Ozarks, reaching almost 500 feet. Its banks, with a range of soil types and elevations, include over 1,500 plant species.

Whitetail deer, raccoons, possums, beavers and squirrels are the most commonly seen animals along the river, but don't rub your eyes in disbelief if you see an elk. They were stocked by the Arkansas Game and Fish Commission in 1981, and the herd has grown to over 300.

Canoeing, camping and hiking are the most popular activities along the Buffalo River.

The National Park Service offers interpretive programs to give you a better understanding of the Ozarks.

Beginning in 1993, a new way to take a trip back into Ozark history was offered in the form of "Ecotours," many of which are along the Buffalo River. Set up by the Newton County Resource Council, the tours are limited to 12 people and a local guide. Ecotour subjects have included "Native American Sites, Caves and Bluff Shelters," "Pioneer Life at Erbie on the Buffalo River," "Forest Ecology and a Champion White Cedar," and "Outlaw Gangs in Legend and Fact."

If you want to take a trip back in time, the Buffalo River is the place.

Norfork Big Influence At Calico Rock

Jenkins brothers realize benefits from shot of cold water, fish hatchery

Guy Jenkins was operating a small pool hall in Calico Rock, Arkansas, when the dams at Bull Shoals and Norfork turned the White River into a trout stream.

He saw the dams as an opportunity, a chance to live his dream, which was to make a living from fishing. So he opened Jenkins Trout Dock at Calico Rock in 1958.

Terry Jenkins was only seven years old when the dock opened. But it wasn't long before he and his older brother, Danny, were helping their father with the business.

"I didn't know anything else," Terry said. "My life's ambition was to fish the river and guide and work the boat dock."

That's exactly what Guy Jenkins' sons have done. Their father died in 1973. Danny and Terry Jenkins now manage both Jenkins Trout Dock and Jenkins Motel.

Calico Rock is 62 miles downstream from Bull Shoals Dam and 18 miles below the Norfork Tailwater's confluence. Trout anglers here generally work an area 10 miles upstream and downstream from Calico Rock.

With the influence of two dams and numerous tributaries, the White River isn't as subject to the rapid fluctuations that characterize the upper stretches. Terry Jenkins thinks that makes for some easy fishing.

"From Norfork to Boswell Shoals, anybody can catch fish every day," he said. "It's nothing unusual to catch and release 60 to 70 fish a day. The success ratio of people limiting out is probably as good or better than anywhere else on the river."

The trout fishing around Calico Rock is heavily dependent on the Norfork Dam Tailwater, according to Jenkins. The White River's booster shot of cold water from Norfork Dam 18 miles upstream helps maintain river temperatures for trout during the hot months of summer. And the Norfork National Fish Hatchery is critical for maintaining good numbers of fish in the river.

This area is in transition. Like the upper stretch between Cotter and Bull Shoals Dam, the population of big rainbow trout is only a fraction of what it once was.

"Fishing pressure is a 100 times what it used to be," Terry said. "When we first started, a four- to five-boat trip was a big trip. It was nothing unusual to catch six-, seven- and eight-pound fish. We'd catch several 10-pounders a year. Now it's not uncommon to have

Terry Jenkins prepares to land a 16-inch brown trout he caught on a crawfish tail in the White River's Racetrack Shoal.

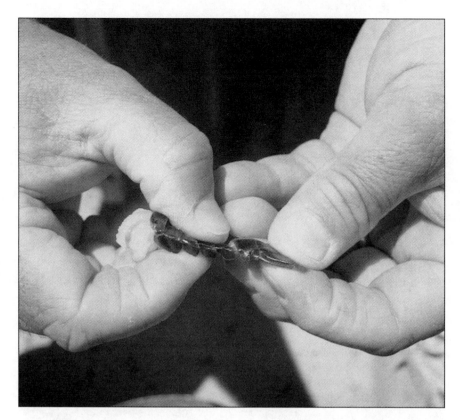

◀▲ **Terry Jenkins demonstrates how to prepare a crawfish tail for trout fishing. After breaking the tail off, you push the meat out "like you would a tube of toothpaste," Jenkins said. The white tail meat is then threaded on a No. 4 hook. Sometimes Jenkins threads two crawfish tails on a hook.**

15- and 20-boat trips. The biggest fish will be under two pounds most days."

Unlike the upper stretch, big brown trout haven't replaced the big rainbows yet. But there are signs that is starting to happen.

"Some of the guides think there are a lot browns up to five pounds in this part of the river now," Jenkins said, as he released a 16-inch brown trout that hit a crawfish tail drifted through Racetrack Shoal.

"We don't fish for browns like they do on the upper end of the river. But we do see some chasing rainbow trout every now and then.

"The river down here is just full of minnows. Any gravel bar you look at will have spots that are just black with minnows. It seems like the browns would do well here."

The beauty of the river remains unchanged. There is less development along the banks than in the upper sections of the Bull Shoals Tailwater. It's rare that you find low water, wade-fishing conditions here, so float trips are the most common method of fishing. The pleasure of a float down the White River brings people back.

"Ninety-nine percent of our busi-ness comes back every year, just like clockwork," Jenkins said.

Most anglers here fish with bait. Worms and salmon eggs are among the top choices, along with the various Berkley Power Baits and Power Eggs. Jenkins, however, prefers crawfish tails.

"Break the tail off and push the meat out like you would a tube of toothpaste," Jenkins said. "Then you thread it on a No. 4 hook.

"Sometimes I'll use two crawfish tails on a hook."

No one can say for sure why trout are attracted to the white meat of a crawfish tail. Whole crawfish are a nat-ural food for White River trout, and they are a popular bait here, too, par-ticularly in the softshell stage.

The appeal of a crawfish tail may be a combination of smell and sight - the crawfish scent and a trout's natural attraction to anything white.

Sometimes a red worm-crawfish tail combination is the bait of choice. Thread the worm over the hook, then cover the hook point and barb with the crawfish tail. Jenkins caught a 14-pound, 10-ounce rainbow trout on this combination in 1980 at Racetrack

Shoal.

"There are probably more big fish caught in Racetrack than any other place around here," Jenkins said.

Rather than the typical White River drift rig, with a bell sinker on a drop-per, bait is usually fished below a small single spinner. A No. 1 Colorado spin-ner above a No. 3 Aberdeen hook is Jenkins' favorite combination.

Because of all the tributaries upstream, the water is more likely to have some color to it; the spinner acts as an attractor.

If extra weight is needed, a split shot is added six inches to a foot above the spinner. When the water is clear, a drift rig without the spinner is a better choice.

The most popular artificial lure is a Countdown Rapala in black-and-silver or black-and-gold color combinations. The preferred sizes are CD5 (1 1/2"), CD6 (2"), and CD7 (2 3/4").

Other popular artificials are Rooster Tails, Blue Foxes, Little Cleos, Mepps spinners and Colorado spoons.

Jenkins recommends 6-pound-test line as the best for bait and artificial lures.

"Four-pound-test is OK, but we

don't have a lot of low water, so six is better," he said.

Unlike most anglers on the upper section of the Bull Shoals Tailwater, Jenkins doesn't care to fish rising water.

"If the water is coming up, we try to stay below it," he said. "If the rise catches you, you're out of luck because the water gets so dirty. When it falls, it clears up, and the fish go to biting."

Jenkins estimates that it takes 18 to 24 hours for Bull Shoals Dam water releases to reach Calico Rock and six to eight hours for Norfork Dam water releases to get here.

On high water levels, Jenkins says the fish move closer to the bank and the gravel bar side is usually the best choice. As the water drops, the trout will move out to the river channel.

"Usually, if you fish about one-third of the way out from a bluff bank, it puts you right at the edge of the river channel at normal flow," Jenkins said. "But the higher the water is, the closer to the bank you fish."

Jenkins prefers fishing the river at normal levels and above. He says you can catch fish at all water levels, but anchoring and bait-fishing at low water is tough on the trout.

"When you anchor, nine out of 10 times the fish are going to swallow the hook," Jenkins said. "That's why I don't like to do it."

He noted that a deeply hooked trout can be released without killing it, if the angler will cut the line as close to the hook as possible and, in the process, be gentle with the fish.

"People mishandle so many fish," Jenkins said. "That's why I don't know if a minimum length limit or a slot limit would help."

It should be interesting to follow the quality of trout fishing on this section of the river. Continued growth in the brown trout population would seem to be the key, as it has been on the upper end of the Bull Shoals Tailwater.

Terry Jenkins should have a feel for that. He's certain to be on the river, taking stock of the trout fishing at Calico Rock, just like he has been for almost four decades.

Calico Rock Scenically Perched On Landmark White River Bluff

Few towns are as scenically perched as Calico Rock, Arkansas. Whether you approach it from a boat in the White River, or an automobile on the Highway 5 bridge, or pass over it in an airplane, Calico Rock will catch your eye and hold it.

From a distance, you'll first notice the city water tower sitting atop a multi-colored limestone bluff. It is this bluff that gave the area its name before there was a town. Fur trappers and early settlers used the distinctive bluff as a landmark for river travel, referring to it as "the calico rock."

Henry Rowe Schoolcraft explored the Ozarks in 1818-19. In his journal, he described the distinctive bluff as a "lofty smooth wall of stratified limestone, presenting a diversity of color in squares, stripes, spots or angles, all confusedly mixed and arranged according to the inimitable pencil of nature."

When approached from the river on a foggy morning, Calico Rock seems to sit in the sky, like an Ozark version of the Land of Oz. For a true sense of awe, try to imagine the White River in such a raging torrent that it rose to flood the town, as it did several times between 1897 and 1927. (Floods in 1916, 1915, 1927 and 1898, respectively, mark the four highest White River levels in recorded history.)

That's the bad side of this give-and-take relationship with the river that dominates the history of towns like Calico Rock.

Of course, the river put these towns on the map in the first place. The first steamboat reached Batesville in 1831 and soon began making the trip upstream to Calico Rock during the rainy seasons when the White River was high.

Later, smaller steam-powered packets would make year-round river transportation possible and could go as far north as Forsyth, Missouri.

"The calico rock" got a post office in 1851 and became a town in the 1870s. By then, the steamboat business had made Calico Rock an important docking point and distribution center for Izard, Stone and Baxter counties.

When the St. Louis and Iron Mountain Railway was completed in the early 1900s, it gave Calico Rock another avenue of commerce and made it a boom town. In 1923, a passing train sparked a fire that destroyed many of the Main Street businesses.

Today, Calico Rock's downtown area, which is listed on the National Register of Historic Places, features buildings from the early 1900s boom and the reconstruction period after the fire.

Earl Brown was born just across the White River from Jack's Resort, and he has guided anglers there since 1965.

White River Regains Some Of Its Mystery

Less is known about trout fishery near Mountain View, Sylamore

At Jack's Resort, almost 80 miles downstream from Bull Shoals Dam, the White River, as a trout stream, is more of a mystery. Little scientific research has been done by the Arkansas Game and Fish Commission here. The river is wider, there is less development along the banks and commercial operations are widely spaced.

The White River's personality has been filled out by numerous tributaries, including rivers like the North Fork and Buffalo, and significant creeks like Crooked and Piney. Just below Jack's, another major tributary, Sylamore Creek, makes its way into the White.

Because of distance from Bull Shoals and Norfork dams and the influence of so many tributaries, the White River here doesn't have the frequent and substantial rises and falls of the upper river. But it does have its ups and downs. Jack Hinkle built his boat dock here in 1961. He and his wife, Mary Hale, operate the second-largest resort on the Bull Shoals Tailwater. Only Gaston's Resort can accommodate more people.

Earl Brown was born and raised just across the river from Jack's Resort, and he has guided here since 1965. Hinkle and Brown have seen all the fluctuations of the White River since it became a trout stream.

Hinkle was on the dock when Jim Miller of Memphis brought in the 19-pound, 1-ounce Arkansas record rainbow trout. Miller, now deceased, also had a home on the North Fork River. He said he caught the fish near Mount Olive, upstream from Jack's Resort. It broke the old state mark by one ounce.

"It died and he kept it in the livewell all day long or it might have weighed more," Hinkle said. "The trout was 30 inches long and 30 inches around. I remember it well because it was as big around as it was long."

Miller said he caught the fish on the combination of a Rooster Tail and a nightcrawler. Gaudy combinations like that are still common on this part of the river, particularly when water levels are high. Brown frequently uses a No. 2 spinner with a couple of small orange beads, plus a No. 3 hook baited with either a nightcrawler, salmon eggs or Berkley Power Eggs.

Artificial lures with a lot of flash are popular, too. The Panther Martin is Brown's favorite. He prefers the yellow with black dots 1/4-ounce Panther Martin. He also uses Rooster Tails, Mepps spinners and small Countdown Rapalas (rainbow trout is his favorite color pattern).

"I guess they've tried everything for trout around here, including dynamite," Brown said with a laugh. "When the fish are biting, I've seen guys catch them with the filter tip off a cigarette. In fact, I've cleaned fish and found a cigarette filter tip in them."

As Brown floated through one of his favorite fishing holes down river from Jack's Resort, he hooked a trout on his spinner and nightcrawler rig. Judging by the bend in his rod, it looked to be a decent-sized fish.

"Sometimes a little mule will pull harder than a big one," Brown said. And he was right, as the fish turned out to be a 1 1/2-pounder.

Although Brown will run upstream as far as Calico Rock and downstream as far as Guion, he usually fishes no more than eight or nine miles in either direction from Jack's Resort. You'll see people fishing from the banks on this lower stretch of the White River trout waters, especially around the Sylamore Creek mouth. But, because of its width and depth, the river is more suitable to float fishing. The times when it gets low and wadable are rare.

Bait, by far, is the lure of choice. Boaters usually choose between two fishing methods: 1) drifting downstream, bouncing a worm off the bottom; or, 2) anchoring above a deep hole, fishing with corn.

Fly fishing opportunities are usually limited to the feeder creeks. In late fall, winter and early spring the creeks can be loaded with trout.

"I love to fly fish," said Hinkle, who has caught steelhead in Oregon and Alaska. "I just like fishing rivers for rainbow trout."

Sylamore Creek and Rocky Bayou Creek are his favorites for fly fishing here. Trout have been caught several miles up Sylamore Creek in the winter. During the summer, you are likely to catch a smallmouth bass. This far downstream, the White River still shows some signs of its former self, before Bull Shoals and Norfork dams were built.

"There are a lot of smallmouth bass in the river here," Hinkle said. "October, November and December are probably the three best months for smallmouth."

> ## "They've stocked more brown trout here in the last three years, and we're starting to see some nice German browns."

As far as trout are concerned, this is mostly rainbow territory. But reports of brown trout are more frequent than ever before.

"They've stocked more brown trout here in the last three years, and we're starting to see some nice German browns," Hinkle said.

AGFC trout biologist John Stark suspects there may be some brown trout spawning activity in the area. He has heard unconfirmed reports of brown trout spawning in Sylamore Creek.

But this far from the dams' cool currents, high water temperatures become a summertime problem. If the power generators at both dams are shut off for more than a day during hot weather, the water warms quickly.

No one knows how the trout in this part of the river react. Do they move upstream to cooler water, or do they find deep thermal refuges, or do they just get trapped and die?

Hinkle has seen high water temperatures and dead fish. He thinks he knows a remedy.

"I've seen water surface temperatures of 83 degrees right in the middle of the river," Hinkle said. "There were fish floating everywhere. We need to put in a minimum flow regulation. If they could just leave one unit running at Bull Shoals, it would make a big difference."

Just like everywhere else in these Ozark tailwater trout fisheries, the number of five-pound-plus rainbow trout has declined significantly in recent years. Hinkle and Brown have seen the days when a five-pound rainbow was common.

It is the one-time presence of those big rainbows that proves the fish-growing potential in this section of the river. Brown thinks it will take a combination of minimum flow and catch-and-release for the river to reach its potential.

"Over the last few years, people have fished it to death," Brown said. "The trout don't have a chance to grow."

With so many miles and so many tributaries between here and the dam, there are limitations to how much trout habitat can be controlled.

"I tell you when we lost a lot of big trout here," Hinkle said. "It was in the flood of '82. The river was 60-something-feet high here. Before that flood, you could get out and catch five- and six-pound rainbows."

That's the way it goes this far down river. Highs and lows are less frequent but more dramatic than they are upstream. Fishing's up-and-down cycles take longer to develop. Hinkle thinks another upswing has begun.

"There were more big fish caught (in 1993) than there were the year before and the year before that," Hinkle said.

The scenery is just as spectacular as anywhere else on the White River. There are high bluffs around almost every bend.

It just seems wilder here, less affected by man's heavy hand. This last section of the Bull Shoals Tailwater offers both trout fishing and the best chance to duplicate that Ozark tradition of the float trip, the way it was done before the dams were built.

Hugh Shell's explorations of Blanchard Springs Caverns led to U.S. Forest Service development. Water exits the cavern system and flows into White River.

Heart Of The White River System Found Underground In Caverns

To get at the heart of the White River System, you have to go underground. There are plenty of places to do that. Over 6,500 caves have been discovered in southern Missouri and northern Arkansas since the 1950s, when the modern era of cave exploration began.

This is one of the richest cave regions in the world, and the crown jewel is Blanchard Springs Caverns. You'll understand why when you enter the cave's Cathedral Room. It is four football fields long, 180 feet wide and lavishly decorated with rock formations, including a 65-foot floor-to-ceiling pillar in the middle, called "The Giant Column."

"I like to listen to people's first impressions," said Joel Breeding, a guide at the caverns. "You can hear them gasp. It takes their breath away."

Over six miles of rooms and passageways have been explored in Blanchard Springs Caverns. Hugh Shell of Batesville, Arkansas, was the primary explorer of the caverns in the 1960s.

"I knew there was a lot of cave," Shell said. "But little did I know of the beauty and majestic grandeur I'd see."

His underground journeys helped spur U.S. Forest Service development.

Two trails are open for tours. The Dripstone Trail, which includes the Cathedral Room, is less than a half-mile long. It was opened to the public in 1973. The Discovery Trail, 1.2 miles long, was opened four years later.

At one time, this huge hole in the ground was full of water. Geologists estimate the cavern system began to form 50 to 70 million years ago. Formations like The Giant Column had their start after water subsided, two to five million years ago.

"Someone is always asking how much of this we built," said Tony Guinn, a U.S. Forest Service information specialist. "They can't believe the water did all this."

Blanchard Springs Caverns is still alive and, therefore, wet. From it flows 7,000 gallons of water per minute. It feeds Mirror Lake, which is annually stocked with rainbow trout by the Arkansas Game and Fish Commission. The cavern's water eventually flows into Sylamore Creek, which empties into White River.

It is the clear water flowing from this underground system that allows trout, a non-native fish, to seem natural here. Air and water temperatures inside the cavern hover around 60 degrees year-round.

Ozark Folk Center Preserves Music, Crafts Of The Hills

In some ways, little has changed around the Stone County Courthouse. The courthouse anchors the town square in Mountain View, Arkansas. Musicians still gather here with their fiddles, banjos, guitars, mandolins and dulcimers to play the music of the hill country.

It is the music of a bygone era, but it's guaranteed to remain for generations to come in Mountain View. The Ozark Folk Center State Park was built in 1973 to preserve lore and crafts that were destined to disappear from the Ozarks.

Located one mile north of Mountain View, the Folk Center features include individual cabins where daily demonstrations of blacksmithing, basket weaving, wood carving and quilting are a few of the dozens of Ozark pioneer skills on display.

An herb garden, now said to be the largest of its kind in the South, attracts increasing interest. It is highlighted during the annual Herb Harvest Fall Festival and during seminars on the medicinal and culinary aspects of herbs.

But it's the music, like that played around the Stone County Courthouse, that is the main focus here. The annual lineup of Folk Center special events includes fiddle contests, dulcimer workshops, autoharp jamborees, folk dance workshops and various music concerts. Another feature of the Folk Center is a 1,000-seat auditorium, where a regular program of Ozark music is played, amplifier-free. Mountain View also serves as the host for the annual Arkansas Folk Festival.

All of this adds up to give Mountain View, Arkansas, the unofficial title of "folkways capital of the nation."

Lock and Dam No. 1 at Batesville was built in 1903 and maintained until 1951, but now serves as a city park fishing pier.

Railroad Delivered Knockout To Locks

Only three of 10 locks and dams were built before they were obsolete

Buffalo Shoals is one of the most scenic spots on the White River. Located upstream from Buffalo City, it features clusters of water-smoothed rock strewn the width of the river. If you've enjoyed the natural beauty of Buffalo Shoals, you can thank the St. Louis, Iron Mountain and Southern Railroad for preserving it, even though unintentionally.

The U.S. River and Harbors Act of 1899 included plans for a system of 10 locks and dams between Batesville and Buffalo Shoals. They were designed to facilitate river transportation that was interrupted during low water periods.

Zinc and lead mining along the Buffalo River created a need for reliable year round boat traffic up and down the White River.

The first lock and dam was built at Batesville in 1903. But only two more were constructed upstream before an extension of the St. Louis, Iron Mountain and Southern Railroad from Batesville to Cotter was completed.

The railroad killed the steamboat industry and rendered the lock and dam system useless. There was no need to build the other seven locks and dams, which would have put Buffalo Shoals, and every other shoal and low-water landmark between it and Guion, underwater.

The U.S. Army Corps of Engineers maintained the three locks until 1951. Lock and Dam No. 1 then became city property of Batesville, and now serves as a landmark and fishing pier at Riverside Recreational Park. All three locks and dams remain in place but are inoperable.

Lock and Dam No. 2 is located about 10 miles upstream from Batesville, near the Independence and Stone counties border. Lock and Dam No. 3 is 12 more miles upstream. It is nine river miles from Lock and Dam No. 3 upstream to Guion.

The Arkansas Game and Fish Commission considers Lock and Dam No. 3 the end of the White River trout waters. It is located 101 miles below Bull Shoals Dam.

Summer temperatures frequently make the river unsuitable for trout this far downstream from the cool-water releases of Bull Shoals and Norfork dams.

But during cooler months, some trout will be found all the way to Batesville. And the White River between the three locks and dams is gaining a reputation for excellent winter walleye fishing.

Highlights Of Bull Shoals Tailwater Trip

("Left" and "right" directions assume the angler is facing downstream.)

The 101 miles of trout habitat in the White River from the Bull Shoals Dam to Lock and Dam No. 3 below Guion can be divided into four sections:

1) Bull Shoals Dam to Cotter, 18 miles;

2) Cotter to the White River's confluence with the North Fork River at the town of Norfork, 26 miles;

3) Norfork to Mount Olive, 30 miles;

4) Mount Olive to Lock and Dam No. 3, 27 miles.

The following description of 101 miles of river is intended to be used as a general guide of major landmarks, rather than for specific details on how to fish these areas. But you also should keep in mind that most of these holes and shoals got their names because they've been good fishing spots.

BULL SHOALS DAM TO COTTER: Most of **Bull Shoals State Park**'s 725 acres lies along the White River below Bull Shoals Dam. Not only is there a wealth of public access for bank fishing and wading, but there's also a state-owned trout dock and a boat ramp in the park.

The White River from Bull Shoals Dam to the downstream boundary of the park is the largest winter spawning area for brown trout in the Ozarks. In 1990 special brown trout regulations went into effect that require catch-and-release, artificial lures and single barbless hooks in this area from Nov. 1 through Jan. 31. Beginning Jan. 1, 1995, a year-round, one-mile catch-and-release zone for all species of trout was established from 100 yards below the dam to 100 feet above **Rivercliff Trout Dock**, which is located across the river from the park. **Big Spring**, once called Dew Spring, is near the lower boundary of the park and a major shoal below it is known as **Dew Eddy Shoal**.

Downstream from the park, the left bank is lined with commercial operations, including **Newland's Lodge**, and the deep pool here is commonly called **Newland Hole**. Below it is **Cane Island**, located about three miles from the dam. It features a long shoal down its left side. **Gaston's Resort**, the largest on the Bull Shoals Tailwater, dominates the left side of the next long, straight, shallow pool. Just before the river makes a sharp right turn, **Bruce Creek** enters from the left. It has a shoal above it, **Partee**,

When all eight hydropower generators at Bull Shoals Dam are shut off, the White River is reduced to a trickle.

and one just below it, called, appropriately, **Bruce Creek Shoal**. It was in this area where Troy Lackey caught a 31-pound, 8-ounce state record brown trout in 1972.

A steep bluff rises and lines the left bank for the four miles. **Baxter County Road 9**, also known as **Denton Ferry Road**, follows the river from here to Cotter, providing walk-in access to many of the fishing spots over the next 13 miles. (There is private land between Baxter Co. 9 and the river, too. When in doubt, ask for permission to cross from nearby landowners.)

Stetson's Resort is just below Bruce Creek, on the opposite side of the river. The shoal below it is called **Three Chutes**, which drops into a pool called the **Blue Hole**. The left side of Blue Hole includes a long, narrow strip of land that becomes an island at high water levels, but usually features a one-way entrance from below it to some water called **Turkey Bottom Slough**.

The Arkansas Game and Fish Commission's **White Hole Public Access Area** marks the top end of the next river bend. The **White Hole** area includes shoals above it and below it, plus several commercial operations down the right side.

The river starts to bend back to the left, after you pass **Sportsman's Lodge** on the right, then **Fulton's Lodge** on the left. **The Narrows** is a series of shoals and an island or two, depending on the water level. If you are boating, stay to the right of the islands. If you are wading, keep a close watch for rising water, or you'll find yourself trapped on an island.

Tucker Shoal follows the Narrows. Below Tucker, two culverts from Denton Ferry Road on the left mark the spot where Carl Jones hooked the 20-pound, 12-ounce brown trout that set a 2-pound-test line record.

Wildcat Shoals Public Access is 12 river miles from Bull Shoals Dam. An AGFC-built boat ramp here can be reached from Denton Ferry Road (Baxter Co. 9). **Wildcat Shoals** is farther downstream, after the river makes a sharp left turn. This is one of the

The White River, as seen from an overlook in Cotter. An AGFC boat ramp near the rainbow-arched highway bridge is a popular access point.

longer and better-known shoals on the river. At low water, it's a favorite of fly fishers and a nightmare for inexperienced boaters. Access to the shoals for wading anglers is off a spur road from Baxter Co. 9, east of the AGFC's Wildcat Access. A trail leads to the river.

Rainbow Drive Resort is on the left, below Wildcat Shoals. The deep pool in front of it was formerly known as **Craven Hole**, but is usually called **Rainbow Hole** now. **Hightower Creek** (also called **Tool Creek**) enters from the left. Several private residences line the left bank before the river starts a gradual turn back to the right. The next landmarks are **Hurst Fishing Service** and **Lithia Creek** on the left. At low water, there is a rock island just above Hurst and a gravel bar that juts out below Hurst. Boaters should stay to the right.

Chamberlain's Resort dock is now visible on the left, as is the Highway 412 bridge downstream. On the right, below Chamberlain's is an area called **Hardy Bar**, named after Hardy Huddleston, the former owner and a long-time White River guide.

Just below the **Highway 412 bridge**, **Bayless Island** begins on the left side and **Fallen Ash Creek** enters on the right. At low water, a long gravel island extends down past the mouth

of Fallen Ash Creek. Below the gravel on the right, where the chunk rock and small boulders begin, marks **McBee Landing**, which used to be a steamboat stopping point.

Past Bayless Island, an unnamed island begins and extends downstream to the railroad bridge and rainbow-arched highway bridge at Cotter. At low water, boaters must go down the right side, and the island is accessible to waders from the park and AGFC access at Cotter. At high water, boaters can go down the left side of the island. With a city park, AGFC boat ramp and **Cotter Trout Dock** here, this is one of the busiest places on the Bull Shoals Tailwater. In addition to the bank fishing opportunities, this is the take-out point for many one-day floaters from the dam, and the put-in point for boaters going to Buffalo City and Norfork.

COTTER TO NORFORK: At Cotter, the White River makes a sharp bend to the left. Just around the bend on the left is **Miller's Float Service** dock. A steep bluff lines the right side of the river and this deep pool is often called the **Miller Hole**. Below it is a medium length shoal with an island in the middle. It's called **Roundhouse Shoal**, because of a nearby railroad roundhouse. For the remainder of the

Bull Shoals Tailwater's 80 miles, and beyond, all the way to Batesville, a railroad track follows the river down the left side.

The main river channel goes to the left of the island in Roundhouse Shoal. At low water, waders can gain access from a pulloff on Baxter County Road 315. Fishing is good on either side of the island, but if you're wading on the right side, a slight rise in the water level will leave you stranded on the island.

The pool below Roundhouse is called the **Armstrong Hole** and it includes a slough on the right side, behind what is almost a second island below Roundhouse. A long gravel bar follows on the right side. Some anglers call this area **Spout Springs**.

Redbud Resort on the left is the first commercial dock below Cotter. There are also some private homes here. Just past them, **Jenkins Creek** enters on the left side. The shoal here is called both **Redbud Shoal** and **Jenkins Creek Shoal**. It marks the beginning of a 1.5-mile year round catch-and-release zone established by the AGFC beginning Jan. 1, 1995.

Baxter County Road 58 leads to the **Rim Shoals** area. **Brainerd's Bend Guide Service** is located on the left bank, followed by **Rim Shoals Resort**, which allows wading anglers access for a daily fee. This is one of the most popular areas on the Bull Shoals Tailwater for fly fishers. There are two

islands at Rim Shoals. At low water, boaters should go down the right side of both islands. Both sides offer riffles and runs for fly fishers. The first island is often referred to as "**upper Rim**" and the second island "**lower Rim**," or **White Shoals**. The power line that crosses the river below the second island marks the end of the catch-and-release zone. This area is accessible for waders from Baxter County Road 60. Some anglers refer to the area as **Farmhouse**, in reference to the white house near a vehicle parking spot just off BC 60.

A long pool leads to the mouth of **Crooked Creek** on the right. At one time there was a commercial dock here, Highway 101, but it is privately owned now. Crooked Creek's best stretches of smallmouth bass fishing are far from here, above Yellville, but the mouth holds some smallmouth, too. There is a long gravel bar on the right below Crooked Creek, a high cut bank on the left and a short riffle. The river turns back to the left and goes into **Shoestring Shoal**, which features big boulders down the right side. **Dry Creek** enters from the left side and has a railroad bridge over it. At the end of this pool stands **Fletcher Mountain**. **Michael's Point** is on the right. The mountain on the left creates a long, deep pool, one of the deepest between the dam and Norfork. It is lined with boulders on the left.

The **AGFC's Ranchette Access** is

the next landmark. Just below it begins the **Rough Hole**, so named because of a series of ledges and rough bedrock bottom. Below it, in low water there is a gravel island in midstream. Boaters should go to the right, near **Crane Island**, which is marked by private campground signs.

Buffalo Shoals starts at the bottom of Crane Island. This is one of the most scenic spots on the White River. In addition to the long series of shoals featuring some large water-worn rocks, a high bluff stands at the end of this stretch of river, serving as a backdrop for the shoals. It's possible for wading anglers to reach this area by walking up the railroad tracks from **Buffalo City**, but a boat is by far the best way to experience this spot. The **AGFC's Buffalo City Access** includes two concrete boat ramps.

Buffalo City is dominated by the sheer bluff across the river from it. There are many stories about a white cross placed high on this bluff, but it seems no one claims to know the absolute truth. For a daily fee, **White Buffalo Resort** offers bank fishing and wading access to the Smith Island area, located at the mouth of the **Buffalo River**. The main river channel runs to the right of **Smith Island**.

With the influence of the Buffalo River, the White River changes significantly here. It is wider and there are many shallow, graveled-in areas, reflecting the heavy water flows that

Photo by Russell Cothren

Fly fishers frequently congregate at Rim Shoals, where wading access can be gained by paying a daily fee.

rush down the Buffalo at times.

Below Smith Island, **Cunningham Creek** enters from the left. It's marked by an unnamed shoal. The opposite bank is a long gravel bar.

The next riffle is called **Nellie's Apron**. As with the cross at Buffalo City, there are many stories about how this place was named, including one about how Nellie was picking berries on the high bluff on the left and fell into the river. Only her apron was found, so it goes.

Nelson Creek enters on the left and offers some good fish habitat below it. Just downstream on the right is the **AGFC's Cartney Access**, which can be reached from Baxter County Road 72. (On some maps, Cartney is marked on the left side of the river, but public access point and boat ramp are on the right.)

Barren Creek is one of the larger creeks in this section of the river. It enters on the left, and features a railroad bridge over it and a shoal below

it. The next landmark downstream is **Shipps Ferry**. The old ferry boat landing is still visible on the right side, but the AGFC public access and the best fish habitat (boulders, ledges) is on the left.

This next six miles from Shipps Ferry to Norfork is one of the prettiest stretches of the Bull Shoals Tailwater, but it's not known for its trout fishing. It looks like classic smallmouth bass habitat, with an abundance of chunk rock bottom, and there are some smallmouth in this stretch. But high water temperatures in the summer can be a problem for trout in this last stretch before the cooling influence of the Norfork Tailwater.

The first landmark below Shipps is **Big Creek**, which enters on the left and has a railroad bridge over it that can be seen from the river. Downstream on the right is the old Matney campground, followed by **Red Bluff**, which is marked by a huge slab of stone that appears ready to fall into

the river. The river bends to the left and the bluff side shifts to the left in the form of sheer, white rock, appropriately named **White Bluff**. This is classic White River float trip scenery.

The river bends back to the right, bringing the **Highway 341 bridge** and the town of **Norfork** into view. There is a small gravel island in midstream below the bridge. Houses line the right bank.

NORFORK TO MOUNT OLIVE: With AGFC boat ramps on both sides of the White River at Norfork, plus Rose's and Norfork commercial docks nearby, this area offers almost everything the angler needs. The Norfork Tailwater and the Norfork Trout Hatchery nearby fulfill a couple more needs of the trout angler - cold water and stocked trout.

Like Cotter upstream, Norfork is a town centered around trout fishing. The large public access area at the confluence of the White and North Fork

Looking upstream, White Bluff stands tall behind the Highway 341 bridge, which crosses White River near Norfork.

City Rock Bluff marks the White River where Racetrack Shoal begins, just upstream from Calico Rock.

rivers attracts many bank fishers, plus it is a popular boat launching site for trips on either river.

As mentioned about the previous stretch from Cotter to Norfork, the railroad tracks serve as a constant landmark down the left bank of the river, particularly with bridges over the tributaries entering the river from that direction. A large railroad bridge over the North Fork River is visible from the White River. After a break at the town of Norfork, **White Bluff** stands tall again as you head downstream. (This is also called **Norfork Bluff**.) The river bends to the right. Just before it starts a sharp bend back to the left, **Job's Island** marks the left bank. The sharp bend in the river includes **Steamboat Shoal**, where manmade rock structure to facilitate river traffic is evident. The long ridge of rock extending from the bottom of an island here is commonly described as looking like a dinosaur's back.

After Steamboat Shoal, the river turns back to the left into a long straight stretch. **Dead Man Hole** is the first pool below it. **P.J.'s Resort** and **Red's Landing**, an AGFC public access, are on the left bank. Below Dead Man Hole, the right bank features a strip of river bottomland that was at one time planted in pumpkins,

hence the name **Pumpkin Patch** for this stretch of river.

Mathis Island on the right marks the beginning of a river bend back to the right, which turns into **Chastain Eddy**. It's one of the deepest holes of this White River section, and it extends all the way to **Monkey Island**. **Sneed's Creek** enters from the right, near Monkey Island. The river then makes a left turn into what is called **Berry Eddy**.

The next stretch of river is marked by two creeks entering from the left, first **Moccasin Creek**, with **Moccasin Shoal** below it, then **Tan Trough Creek**, and a shoal below it. **Mill Creek** enters on the right side, below Tan Trough Shoal, and also has a shoal below it. You have now left Baxter County. The Baxter-Izard county line on the left bank is located at Berry Eddy. On the right side of the river, the Baxter-Stone county line is just below Moccasin Shoal.

Lindsey's Trout Dock and the **AGFC's Chesmond Ferry Access** mark this next section as the river starts a bend to the left. Both are on the left bank and you can see evidence of the old ferryboat landing on the right, just above **Jack's Creek**. **Chesmond Shoal**, marked by several small boulders, starts here, just above

City Rock Bluff. This scenic bluff line extends down the river to **Racetrack Shoal**. This is one of the best-known fishing spots in the area. It's called Racetrack because the shoal surrounds a small island, which is shaped like the infield on a track. You can boat down either side of Racetrack Shoal at most water levels, but the left side is the main channel and the right side gets too shallow for a boat when the river is dead low.

Herd Island begins on the right, about midway down Racetrack Shoal. After you pass it, you can look downstream to the next bend in the river and see the bluff that gave Calico Rock its name and the city's water tower perched on top of it. **Jenkin's Fishing Service** dock is on the left, just before the **Highway 5 bridge**. There's an AGFC public boat ramp here, too. **Calico Boat Dock** is on the left, just past the bridge.

Calico Bluff extends downstream toward **Creswell Island** on the left. A long pool here is called **Slick Rock Hole**. The land to the left has a slough behind it and is labeled Creswell Island on some maps, but there is actually an island below here that most people call Creswell Island. This is followed by a long, straight pool known as **Whitehouse Eddy**. It is named after

Old Whitehouse Creek, which enters a the end of the pool from the left.

There are several springs along the river below Whitehouse, including one that can usually be seen from the river, and this area is called **Twin Springs**. Below it, a major tributary, **Piney Creek**, enters from the left and is squeezed through a rough, swift area called **Piney Chute**.

The community of **Boswell** is on the left, followed by **Boswell Shoals**, one of the more prominent shoals in this section of the river. It can also be reached by land from the right side of the river at the **Optimus Access**, a U.S. Fish and Wildlife Service walk-in area without a boat ramp. Canoes and small johnboats can be launched and taken out here. The river starts to bend to the right.

Soldier Rock Eddy got its name from a Civil War story about a Confederate soldier who escaped, or tried to escape and died, depending on your source, while avoiding Union troops. The soldier is said to have jumped his horse from the rock into the river. It is a long deep pool that extends down to **Bone Island**, on left, which is an island only at high water levels. This area is also marked by a large boulder in the river, on the right, near Bone Island, that is called **Split Rock**, as it seems to have split from the bluff bank near it.

The river bends to the left and **Landers Island** begins on the right, just above the **AGFC's Mount Olive Public Access Area**, and extends past **Mount Olive**.

MOUNT OLIVE TO LOCK & DAM NO. 3: The center of activity on this stretch of river is near the towns of Sylamore and Allison, where Sylamore Creek enters the White River. Several commercial operations are located here.

With so many tributaries feeding the river to this point and Lock & Dam No. 3's stabilizing influence 27 miles downstream, this section of the White River is characterized by wide sweeping bends and bottomland.

After you leave Mount Olive, a large section of White River bottomland -

Harris Bottom - dominates the right side of the river. After the river bends back to the left, **Jack's Resort** is on the right, just below Harris Bottom. **Sylamore Creek**, a major White River tributary, joins from the right downstream from Jack's. The town of Sylamore is on the opposite bank. A ferryboat used to transport cars across this section of the river. The landings on either side now serve as public boat ramps. A bridge spans the river just below Sylamore Creek. **Brickshy's**

Resort is located here. It's in the middle of a gradual river bend to the left. The land on the left is called **Sylamore Bottom**.

After the river straightens, **Buck Island** dominates the next stretch of water. The main river channel runs to the left of it. The river starts to make a gradual bend back to the right. The small community of **Twin Creek** is on the left, just above it is a railroad bridge over **East Twin Creek**. The bottomland on the inside of this river

From Cotter all the way to Batesville, a railroad track runs along the river.

bend is called **Round Bottom**. It is the first of three big bends in the river. **Handford Bluff** marks the left bank after Round Bottom. It's easy to see the railroad track, which runs along a narrow strip between Handford Bluff and the river.

The river then bends back to the left, where the bottomland on the inside of this curve is called **Greasy Bottom**. **Rocky Bayou** enters from the right side below Greasy Bottom. (There's more than one Rocky Bayou in this area, but this is the most significant White River tributary.) A smaller tributary, **Lyons Creek**, enters from the left, past Rocky Bayou, and the river starts another bend back to the right. The inside curve here is called **Jones Bottom**, and as you come around it, you can see the town of

Guion (pronounced GUY-on) downstream on the left. **Lovelady's Trout Dock** is on the left, just below **Hidden Creek**. The Guion Ferry was one of last in Arkansas to be replaced with a bridge. As at Sylamore upstream, the old ferryboat landings here now serve as public boat ramps on either side of the river at the **Highway 58 bridge**.

The **AGFC's Wild Haw Landing** is on the left. That name dates back to settlers in the early 1800s, and by 1877 Wild Haw Landing was one of 14 steamboat landings between Batesville and Calico Rock.

After you pass under the bridge, another stream named **Rocky Bayou** enters from the left. The silica sand mining operation dominates the left side of the river. It began operation in 1909.

This long straight stretch of river, which begins at Lovelady's Trout Dock, extends about four miles to **Pruitt Island**, on the right, where the river makes a gradual left turn. **Penter's Bluff** lines the left bank as the White River turns due south.

The **AGFC's Younger Access** is across the river from Penter's Bluff, just before the southerly turn. The next landmark is **Lafferty Creek**, which enters from the left.

Lock & Dam No. 3 is about one mile downstream from Lafferty Creek. Buoys mark the dam, and boaters should use caution here. The only way to venture past the dam is to portage. The **AGFC's Martin Public Access** is two miles downstream from Lock 3, on the right.

Bull Shoals Tailwater Mileage Chart

River Access	White Hole	Wildcat Shoals	Cotter	Rim Shoals	Ranchette	Buffalo City	Cartney	Shipps Ferry	Norfork	Red's Landing	Chesmond Ferry	Calico Rock	Mount Olive	Sylamore	Guion	Younger	Lock & Dam #3
Bull Shoals Dam	7.0	12.0	18.0	24.5	28.5	32.0	36.0	38.0	44.0	49.0	59.0	62.0	74.0	79.0	92.0	98.5	101
White Hole		5.0	11.0	17.5	21.5	25.0	29.0	31.0	37.0	42.0	52.0	55.0	67.0	72.0	85.0	91.5	94.0
Wildcat Shoals			6.0	12.5	16.5	20.0	24.0	26.0	32.0	37.0	47.0	50.0	62.0	67.0	80.0	86.5	89.0
Cotter				6.5	10.5	14.0	18.0	20.0	26.0	31.0	41.0	44.0	56.0	61.0	74.0	80.5	83.0
Rim Shoals					4.0	7.5	11.5	13.5	19.5	24.5	34.5	37.5	49.5	54.5	67.5	74.0	76.5
Ranchette						3.5	7.5	9.5	15.5	20.5	30.5	33.5	45.5	50.5	63.5	70.0	72.5
Buffalo City							4.0	6.0	12.0	17.0	27.0	30.0	42.0	47.0	60.0	66.5	69.0
Cartney								2.0	8.0	13.0	23.0	26.0	38.0	43.0	56.0	62.5	65.0
Shipps Ferry									6.0	11.0	21.0	24.0	36.0	41.0	54.0	60.5	63.0
Norfork										5.0	15.0	18.0	30.0	35.0	48.0	54.5	57.0
Red's Landing											10.0	13.0	25.0	30.0	43.0	49.5	52.0
Chesmond Ferry												3.0	15.0	20.0	33.0	39.5	42.0
Calico Rock													12.0	17.0	30.0	36.5	39.0
Mount Olive														5.0	18.0	24.5	27.0
Sylamore															13.0	19.5	22.0
Guion																6.5	9.0
Younger																	2.5

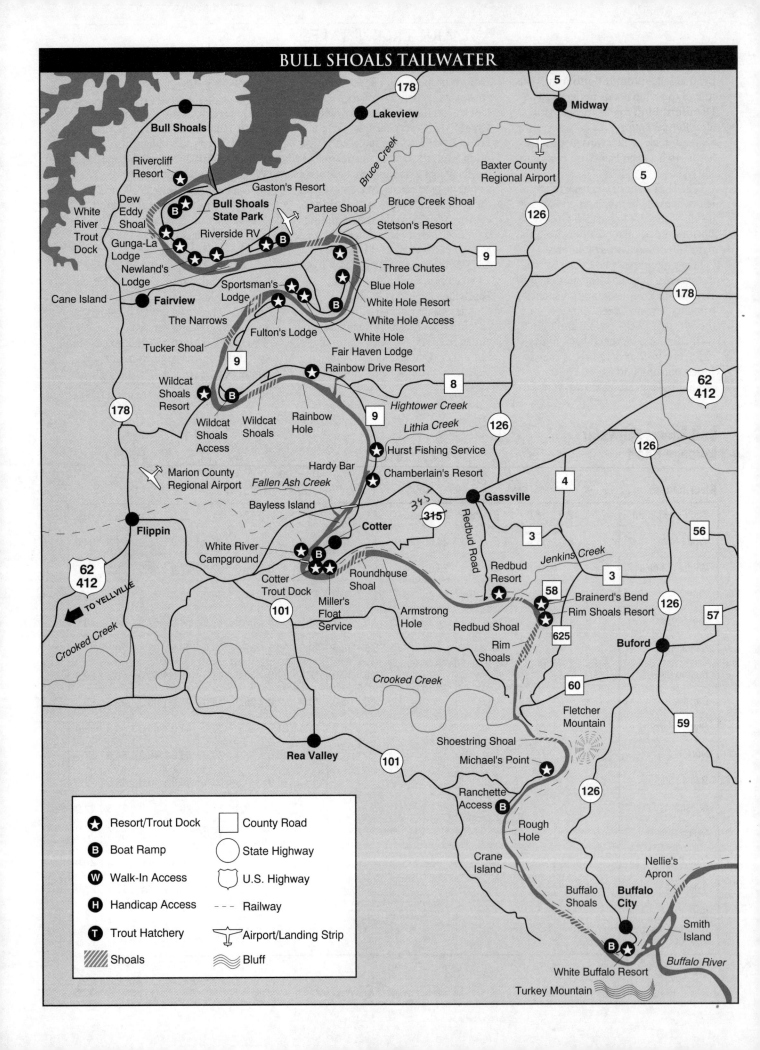

BULL SHOALS TAILWATER

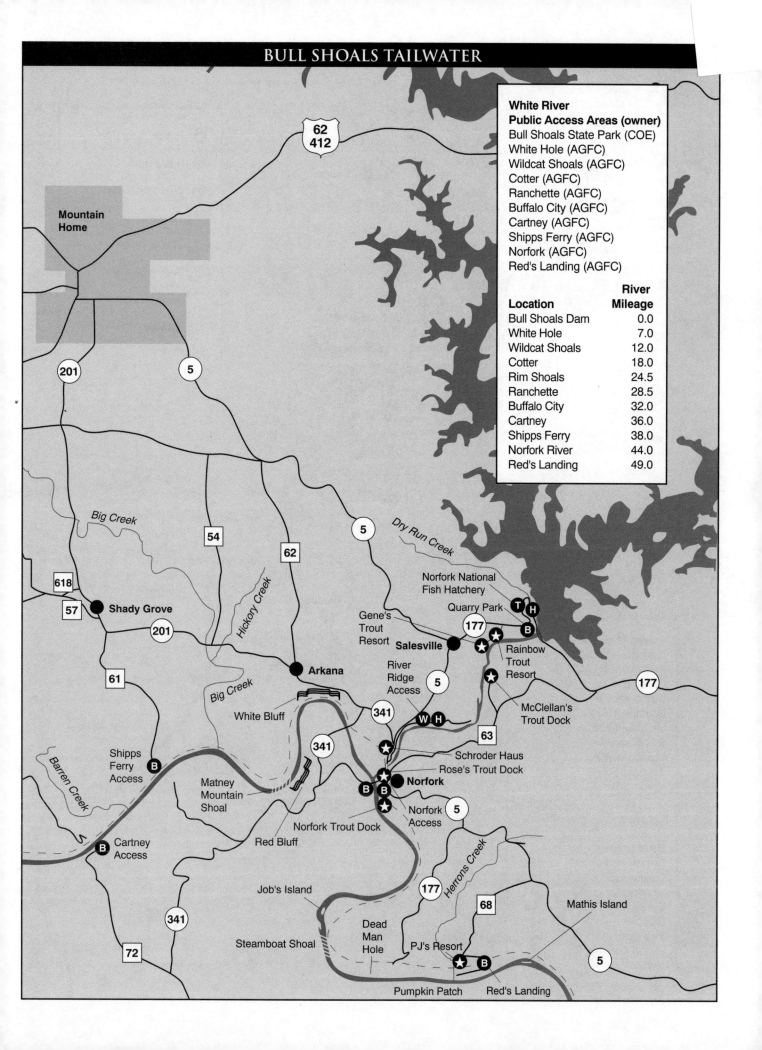

BULL SHOALS TAILWATER

White River
Public Access Areas (owner)
Bull Shoals State Park (COE)
White Hole (AGFC)
Wildcat Shoals (AGFC)
Cotter (AGFC)
Ranchette (AGFC)
Buffalo City (AGFC)
Cartney (AGFC)
Shipps Ferry (AGFC)
Norfork (AGFC)
Red's Landing (AGFC)

Location	River Mileage
Bull Shoals Dam	0.0
White Hole	7.0
Wildcat Shoals	12.0
Cotter	18.0
Rim Shoals	24.5
Ranchette	28.5
Buffalo City	32.0
Cartney	36.0
Shipps Ferry	38.0
Norfork River	44.0
Red's Landing	49.0

BULL SHOALS TAILWATER

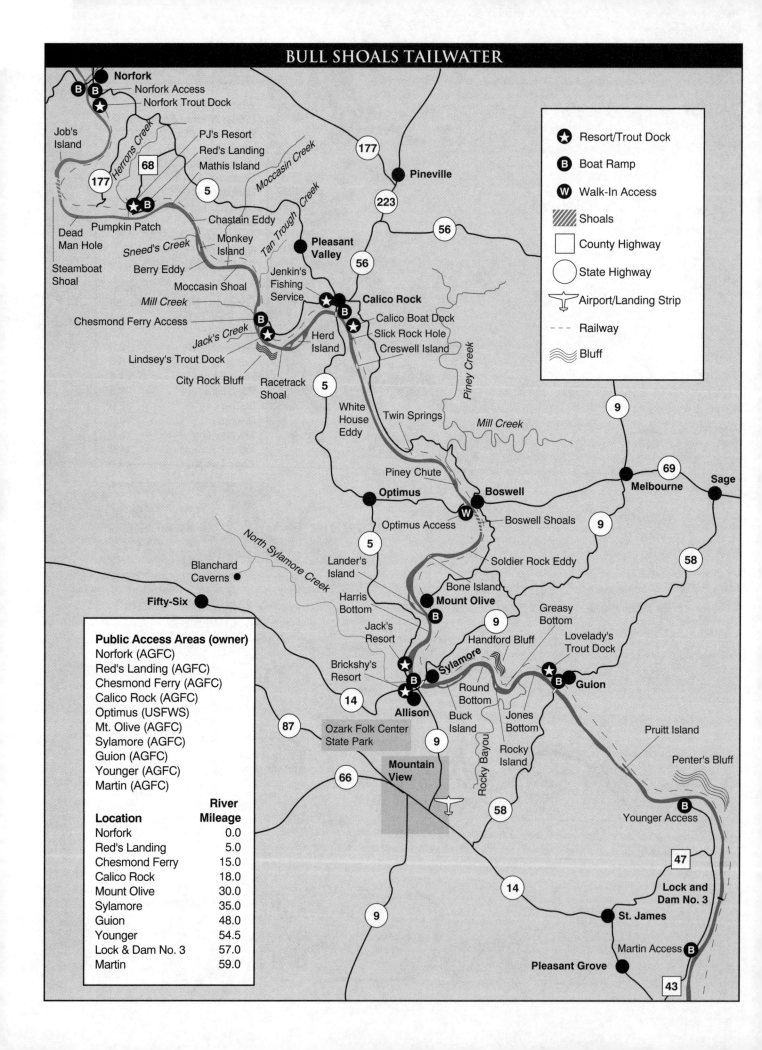

Legend:
- ★ Resort/Trout Dock
- Ⓑ Boat Ramp
- Ⓦ Walk-In Access
- ▨ Shoals
- ☐ County Highway
- ◯ State Highway
- ✈ Airport/Landing Strip
- --- Railway
- ≈ Bluff

Map labels:

Norfork
Norfork Access
Norfork Trout Dock
Job's Island
PJ's Resort
Red's Landing
Mathis Island
Herrons Creek
Moccasin Creek
Tan Trough Creek
177
68
5
223
Pineville
177
56
Chastain Eddy
Dead Man Hole
Pumpkin Patch
Monkey Island
Sneed's Creek
Berry Eddy
Moccasin Shoal
Mill Creek
Chesmond Ferry Access
Jack's Creek
Lindsey's Trout Dock
City Rock Bluff
Racetrack Shoal
Herd Island
Jenkin's Fishing Service
Pleasant Valley
Calico Rock
Calico Boat Dock
Slick Rock Hole
Creswell Island
Piney Creek
56
5
Steamboat Shoal
White House Eddy
Twin Springs
Mill Creek
Piney Chute
Optimus
Boswell
Melbourne
Sage
9
69
58
Optimus Access
Boswell Shoals
9
Blanchard Caverns
North Sylamore Creek
Lander's Island
Soldier Rock Eddy
Bone Island
Fifty-Six
Harris Bottom
Jack's Resort
Mount Olive
5
Greasy Bottom
Handford Bluff
Lovelady's Trout Dock
9
Brickshy's Resort
Sylamore
Round Bottom
Buck Island
Jones Bottom
Guion
14
Allison
Rocky Bayou
Rocky Island
87
Ozark Folk Center State Park
9
Mountain View
66
58
Pruitt Island
Penter's Bluff
Younger Access
47
14
Lock and Dam No. 3
9
St. James
Martin Access
Pleasant Grove
43

Public Access Areas (owner)
- Norfork (AGFC)
- Red's Landing (AGFC)
- Chesmond Ferry (AGFC)
- Calico Rock (AGFC)
- Optimus (USFWS)
- Mt. Olive (AGFC)
- Sylamore (AGFC)
- Guion (AGFC)
- Younger (AGFC)
- Martin (AGFC)

Location	River Mileage
Norfork	0.0
Red's Landing	5.0
Chesmond Ferry	15.0
Calico Rock	18.0
Mount Olive	30.0
Sylamore	35.0
Guion	48.0
Younger	54.5
Lock & Dam No. 3	57.0
Martin	59.0

Photo by Russell Cothren

Great blue herons are the most commonly seen bird along the Bull Shoals Tailwater, where they fish for trout, too.

BULL SHOALS TAILWATER FLOW CHART

The figures listed are general estimates and shouldn't be relied upon to predict water conditions. All anglers should be constantly aware of changing water conditions. Pick out objects at the water's edge and refer to them often to note rising water.

"Always act like there are eight generators of water on the way," advised one veteran Bull Shoals Tailwater fishing guide. "Then you're not surprised by anything that happens."

Again, the figures listed are just general estimates of what some veteran White River guides think water flow rates to be. There is no consensus or official chart of water flow rates because there are too many variables involved.

Bull Shoals Dam	4-8 generators
Gaston's	45 minutes
White Hole	90 minutes
Wildcat Shoals	3 hours
Cotter	5 hours
Rim Shoals	6 hours
Buffalo City	9 hours
Shipps Ferry	10 hours
Norfork	14 hours
Calico Rock	24 hours
Sylamore	35 hours

NORTH FORK RIVER

NORFORK TAILWATER

The Key To Trout Success In The White River System

There are only 4.8 miles of trout stream from Norfork Dam to the North Fork River's confluence with the White River. But in many ways, this is the most important section of trout water in the entire White River System.

If nothing else, it has the longest history as a trout stream. Norfork Dam, completed in 1944, was the first of the five major hydropower projects in the White River Basin and the first to undergo the transformation from a warmwater to a coldwater fishery.

In July 1948, five years before any hydropower generation began at Bull Shoals Dam, the Arkansas Game and Fish Commission made an experimental stocking of 600 rainbow trout in the Norfork Tailwater. These four- to six-inch fish grew to two and three pounds within a year; six- and eight-pound trout were caught the second year. The experiment was officially a success.

Trout stocking increased in the

◀ **John Gulley, at the "Blue Hole" of the Norfork Tailwater during low water conditions.**

A view of the Norfork Tailwater from Highway 5, which runs along the river above River Ridge Access.

North Fork, then, in 1952, stocking began in the White River below Bull Shoals. Word quickly spread about the quality of trout fishing in these streams and created a need for increased trout stocking. The AGFC was dependent on the U.S. Fish and Wildlife Service for about 10,000 pounds of fingerlings each year, and that was the extent of

the stocking.

In 1955, Hugh Hackler, who served as both a representative to the state legislature and an Arkansas Game and Fish Commissioner, led a movement requesting Congress appropriate funds for a trout hatchery.

Congressman Jim Trimble and Senator J. W. Fulbright sponsored the bill that resulted in the Norfork National Fish Hatchery, which was completed in August 1957.

The hatchery was deemed necessary as mitigation for the loss of the warmwater fisheries. By 1962, approximately 1.8 million trout from the Norfork Hatchery were being stocked in the White and North Fork rivers.

Less than 30 years later, this 4.8-mile stretch of river would produce a world record trout.

On August 7, 1988, Huey Manley landed a 38-pound, 9-ounce brown trout while fishing from McClellan's Trout Dock, and the legend of the North Fork River as a trout stream shot to a new level. Manley's fish was recognized as a new world record by the National Fresh Water Fishing Hall of Fame.

NORFORK TAILWATER AT A GLANCE

Location: The 4.8-mile tailwater runs into the White River at the town of Norfork, Arkansas. Mountain Home, Arkansas, is located 14 miles northwest of Norfork. The White River flows 44 miles from Bull Shoals Dam to its confluence with the North Fork River.

Road Mileages to Norfork Dam

Little Rock, Ark.	173
Tulsa, Okla.	268
Shreveport, La.	411
Memphis, Tenn.	190
Kansas City, Mo.	311
St. Louis, Mo.	256
Dallas, Texas	545
Chicago, Ill.	577

Length of Trout Waters: Unlike the other White River System tailwaters, which gradually become warmwater fisheries, depending on air temperatures and time of year, the Norfork Tailwater trout habitat has a definite end - its confluence with the White River - 4.8 miles from Norfork Dam. However, the North Fork's boost of cold water is the main factor that extends trout habitat another 57 miles down the White River to Lock & Dam No. 3 near Guion.

Dam: Commercial power generation began in 1944. The overall project, which forms a 22,000-acre lake at the power pool level of 554 feet above sea level, was completed in October 1949 at an estimated cost of $28.6 million. There are two hydroelectric power generators in Norfork Dam. It was the first of the U.S. Army Corps of Engineers dams built in the White River System.

Trout Stocking: The 1994 stocking schedule called for 53,000 9-inch rainbow trout, 32,000 12-inch rainbow trout, 10,000 brown trout, 25,000 cutthroat trout and 20,000 brook trout. The browns, cutthroats and brookies were 6- to 8-inches long when stocked.

Fishing Regulations: Daily limit is 6 trout, including not more than 2 browns or cutthroats. Brown trout daily limit is 2 with a 16-inch minimum size limit. Cutthroat limit is 2 with a 16-inch minimum size limit. No size restrictions on rainbows.

Catch-and-Release Zone: (As of January 1, 1995) Catch-and-release fishing only with barbless-hook artificial lures in the Norfork Tailwater from Otter Creek to 100 yards upstream from River Ridge Access.

Scenic Views: For a quick overview of the Norfork Tailwater, start at the dam and take Highway 177 past Quarry Park and the Norfork National Fish Hatchery to Salesville. Go south on Highway 5 at Salesville. There is a scenic overlook off Highway 5 near Goat Ridge Bluff. Highway 5 then crosses the North Fork River near its confluence with White River at the town of Norfork.

Power generation information: Call U.S. Army Corps of Engineers Bull Shoals Dam powerhouse at 501-431-5311 for a recorded message of current conditions on the Norfork and Bull Shoals tailwaters. For a 24-hour forecast, call the Southwest Power Administration recorded message center at 918-581-6845 and press #15 for Norfork Dam.

Norfork, North Fork, etc.: The names Norfork and North Fork get tossed around interchangeably, but there are some differences. Norfork Dam was named for the nearby town of Norfork, Arkansas. The dam is on the North Fork River. It is not the Norfork River or the North Fork of the White River. (The sign on the Highway 5 bridge is incorrect.) To make matters a little more confusing, a tailwater (the stream below a dam) is called by the name of the dam. So North Fork River below Norfork Dam is Norfork Tailwater.

When David Wooten of Jordan, Arkansas, caught a 34-pound, 8-ounce brown trout six days after Manley landed the new world record, Norfork's legendary status took another leap.

There are arguments about whether or not those two big brown trout spent parts of their lives in the White River. But those arguments are irrelevant. While five tailwaters are included in the "White River System," only the Bull Shoals Tailwater and Norfork Tailwater truly function as one. The other three are separated by warmwater fisheries.

A symbiotic relationship exists between the Bull Shoals and Norfork tailwaters. Each has qualities that multiply the trout-producing capability of the other.

> "If you added artificials-only and catch-and-release regulations, it would produce 12- to 18-inch fish better than any river in the world."

The best example of this is found in White River water temperature. Particularly after the Buffalo River joins the White River, 32 miles from Bull Shoals Dam, warmwater tributaries are starting to seriously compromise trout habitat. But the Norfork Tailwater supplies a booster shot of cold water 44 miles downstream from Bull Shoals Dam and helps extend the White River trout waters another 57 miles to Lock and Dam No. 3 below Guion.

On the other hand, the Norfork Tailwater doesn't have anywhere near the brown trout spawning activity found in the Bull Shoals Tailwater.

Norfork Dam seldom operates with four floodgates open, as shown here. Usually, water flows only from the two hydroeclectric power generators.

Wolf House Holds Nearly 200 Years Of Local History

Standing high on a hill above the confluence of the White and North Fork rivers, the Wolf House remains a testament to early settlement in the Ozarks. In 1809, Major Jacob Wolf was appointed by President Thomas Jefferson as the Indian agent for the Arkansas district of the Louisiana Territory.

Wolf, accompanied by black slaves, brought a flatboat up the White River to its confluence with the North Fork. Aided also by Native American workers, a two-story log house was built here. The logs were dovetailed and notched, then sealed with mortar made from mussel shells. A blacksmith shop was built nearby, where Wolf forged iron hinges and nails.

When the house was complete and the fields cleared, Wolf went back to Kentucky and brought his wife to their new home. Wolf's friends included Sam Houston and Davy Crockett

Now, closing in on two centuries later, the Wolf House serves as a museum. It has been in use almost every day since Wolf built it - as a courthouse, post office, hospital and boarding house after it was Wolf's home.

The Wolf House is listed on the National Register of Historic Places. It is considered the oldest two-story log structure in Arkansas.

The settlement at the confluence of the White and North Fork Rivers was known as Liberty shortly after Wolf came here. It was an appropriate name because Liberty was jumping off spot for entering the Ozarks. When the railroad came, the name of the town was changed to Devero in honor of a construction engineer.

In 1907, a townsite was platted and Devero became Norfork - a contraction of North Fork, the nearby River.

Through the use of implanted radio transmitters, AGFC fisheries biologists have documented two-day brown trout movements up to 30 miles long during the spawning season.

So it is quite conceivable that the two 30-plus-pound browns caught in the Norfork Tailwater in 1988 could have spent part of their lives in the White River, at least on a spawning run or two.

When evaluated on its own, apart from the connection to the White River, Norfork has its distinguishing characteristics, as do the other four White River System tailwaters.

For instance, Norfork National Fish Hatchery, which empties into Norfork from Dry Run Creek, supplies highly-oxygenated, nutrient-rich water. In this short, relatively narrow tailwater, that has a dramatic effect.

The effect is enhanced by the fact that Norfork Dam has only two power generators (versus eight at Bull Shoals).

Aquatic vegetation has a chance to grow and, most importantly, remain in place rather than being scoured away by powerful water flows.

The Norfork Tailwater provides a near-perfect trout growing environment.

"If you added artificial-only and catch-and-release regulations, it would produce 12- to 18-inch fish better than any river in the world, just because of that hatchery," said Mark Hudy, a former AGFC trout biologist who left Arkansas to work as fisheries biologist for the U.S. Forest Service in Virginia. "The hatchery is putting tons of food in per day. So you are basically fertilizing the system."

The Norfork Tailwater can also be credited with another significant contribution to trout fishing in the White River System. It was here where Ozark tailwater fly fishing took hold.

The myth about these trout not taking flies didn't die easily, but men like Dave Whitlock, Chuck Davidson and Art Hempstead helped cast some holes in the myth - enough holes that other fly fishers were encouraged to try it.

It's easy to see what attracts the fly fisher here. The Norfork Tailwater has all the characteristics of a classic trout stream. The various ledges, drops and splits in the bedrock that lines much of the river give the riffles and pools a special character.

When the Norfork Dam power generators are off, this is the ultimate place in the White River System for a wading fly fisher.

And it's the last place you want to be with a boat. At dead low, only the mouth of the Norfork Tailwater is navigable by boat.

Gulley Tied To Norfork Trout History

Through years of living along the river, fly fishing guide has seen it all

As part of their honeymoon, John and Betsy Gulley took a float trip. They got in a canoe at McClellan's Trout Dock on the North Fork River and floated down to Sylamore on the White River.

When a group of transplanted fly fishers, led by Chuck Davidson, made the North Fork River their hangout, John Gulley listened and learned from them.

When three young men banged on his door at midnight, shouting something about a big brown trout, John Gulley got out of bed and took them to a Mountain Home grocery store, where Huey Manley's 38-pound, 9-ounce fish officially became a world record in 1988.

When Jim Miller caught the Arkansas record 19-pound, 1-ounce rainbow trout in the White River in 1981, John Gulley was one of the first to hear Miller's story. Miller and Gulley were neighbors on the Norfork Tailwater.

When the Gulleys' cabin burned to the ground in 1992, taking all John's fishing equipment in the flames, they moved to the other side of the North Fork River and built a house.

It seems that John Gulley's life is one of the interlacing strands of the trout fishing history here.

"How do you like my creek, boys?" It's a question Gulley often asks his customers after a day of fishing on the North Fork or the White rivers.

Gulley has been guiding since 1973. He has been a member of the Orvis-endorsed guide program since 1991 That fire may have destroyed his fishing tackle, but it couldn't didn't touch the memories that Gulley has accumulated here.

Since Gulley's father put a cheap, Japanese-made bamboo fly rod in his 10-year-old son's hands, John's fishing equipment of choice has been a fly rod. There aren't many trout in southwest Arkansas, where John grew up. Bream and bass provided his initial fly

When John Gulley first started fishing the Norfork Tailwater, many people said these trout wouldn't hit a fly. Gulley quickly learned they were wrong.

rod catches. Although his fly fishing experiences now include everything from bream to tarpon, it's a love for catching trout on a fly in the Ozarks that occupies Gulley most of the time. It wasn't that long ago when common theory stated that Ozark tailwater trout wouldn't hit a fly.

"They hit a fly just as good or better then than they do now," Gulley said. "It was great. Fly fishing is starting to boom here now. It has increased beau-

coup over the years."

You don't have to take Gulley's word on that. He'll drive you a few miles to Art Hempstead's home and let you hear a second opinion. Hempstead is a native upstate New Yorker. He trout fished with some of the all-time fly fishing greats, like the late Lee Wulff, before he ever knew about trout in Arkansas. When a friend told Hempstead of the trout fishing here, he said, "Where do you fish, in rice paddies? That's the only part of the state I'd seen."

Hempstead came here to die in 1969. After a serious car accident, doctors diagnosed him with sclerosis and gave him eight months to live.

"I figured if I only had eight months to go, I'd go get in some good fishing." Hempstead said.

When he first came to the White and North Fork rivers, he was skeptical of his friend's fishing report. These didn't look like trout waters to Hempstead. Soon he was catching "trout I used to have to lie about." Hempstead's eight months passed quickly. He did not.

"I kept getting in better fishing," Hempstead said. "I figure that's the reason I didn't die."

> ## "I kept getting in better fishing. I figure that's the reason I didn't die."

Hempstead was a loner. How many friends do you need with trout fishing on your mind and death staring you in the face? It took awhile, but Hempstead finally accepted Gulley's efforts at friendship. That never would have happened if Gulley hadn't been a good fly fisherman.

Hempstead eventually started sharing his secrets with Gulley, like how to catch trout on a Black Nose Dace pattern at night.

"You couldn't catch a rainbow trout at night in New York and Vermont," Hempstead said. "But night was often the time they shut the generators off here, so I started fishing at night. It's unbelievable the trout you can catch here at night. One night I caught a 31-inch rainbow. It might have weighed 20 or 21 pounds. It was a beautiful fish."

It's a testament to their friendship that Hempstead showed Gulley a "secret" fly pattern passed down to him several years ago. He made Gulley promise he wouldn't reveal it, and Gulley hasn't.

"It worked so well, Art was afraid it would hurt the river if everybody knew about it," Gulley said.

By 1993, Hempstead's vision had weakened to the point he could no longer drive a car. "Oh, I can drive," Hempstead joked. "I just can't see where I'm going." He reluctantly gave up the independence of driving after a few close calls. During the brown trout spawning run in '93, Gulley took his old friend fishing. Hempstead hadn't lost his touch with a fly rod. He landed trout up to 26 inches that day.

Chuck Davidson moved to the Ozarks in 1975. Hempstead had been catching trout here for six years by then. They became friends because of their common passion for fly fishing.

On a wall in the Baxter County Library, there is mounted a 6 1/2-pound cutthroat trout, which was caught by Hempstead. On a small metal plate beneath the trout the inscription reads: In the memory of Chuck Davidson, "The Old Man of the River" who brought cutthroat trout to Arkansas.

Just like with Hempstead, Gulley spent many hours with Davidson, listening to his stories about fishing and his theories on how to make things better and learning how to tie flies.

"That's basically what I did to learn how to trout fish," Gulley said. "Art liked to night fish. Chuck didn't. Chuck's specialty was midge fishing. It made me more versatile."

And it made Gulley appreciate how fly fishing for trout has developed in the Ozarks.

"The North Fork is Chuck Davidson, Art Hempstead and Dave Whitlock," Gulley said. "They started fishing it years ago when people said you couldn't catch a fish on a fly. That's what all the guides and dock owners said - you couldn't do it. They proved them wrong."

Now John Gulley is carrying on that tradition.

Nighttime Fishing Requires Different Patterns, Methods

Two men hired guide John Gulley to take them fly fishing one night on the Norfork Tailwater. The moon was full. Ordinarily, Gulley would have stayed in bed, like his friend Art Hempstead taught him.

"Mostly what Art taught me about night fishing were the signs of nature," Gulley said. "There are nights when he just wouldn't go out. If there are no bugs, a full moon and no cloud cover, he wouldn't leave the house. He would stop fishing five days before a full moon, and he wouldn't go again until five days after, unless it was cloudy."

On this night, there was cloud cover at times, and Gulley witnessed a prime example of Hempstead's advice at work. When clouds covered the moon, Gulley's clients caught fish. When the moon was shining brightly, they didn't catch any. Darkness can multiply the thrills of fly fishing.

"I love to fish at night; 2:30 to daylight is best," Gulley said.

The dangers of being on these tailwaters at night and the discomforts of losing sleep eliminate all but the most dedicated fly fishers.

"You better have a real sensitive fly rod at night," Hempstead said. "You can't see, you fish by feel."

Hempstead taught Gulley a retrieve in which one hand is always in control of the line.

"It's not a strip," Gulley said. "It's a steady, slow retrieve that keeps the slack out of the line."

The bites tend to be bigger at night. Gulley recommends a 3X tippet. His favorite nighttime pattern at Norfork is a Black Nose Dace.

"It's different here at night than on the White River," Gulley said. "On the White River, you try to imitate a sculpin. Here you want to imitate creek minnows."

Photo courtesy of Robert Poole

The late Chuck Davidson will be remembered for his efforts to improve trout fishing in Norfork and Bull Shoals tailwaters.

The Old Man Of The North Fork River

Davidson made numerous contributions as fly fisher, conservationist

Charles L. "Chuck" Davidson died in 1985, but his presence is still felt as strongly among the trout fishers here as any man alive.

If you catch a cutthroat or brook trout in the North Fork or White rivers, tip your hat to Davidson.

If you are a fly fisher who wants to take advantage of rising trout in the North Fork, tie on "Chuck's Emerger," Davidson's creation that remains a popular pattern here.

If you want to read about fly fishing, fly tying, stream ecology or trout, go to the Baxter County Library in Mountain Home and check out one of the many volumes dedicated to Davidson's memory.

If you want to join a fly fishing club, show up at a monthly meeting of the North Arkansas Fly Fishers, which

Davidson founded in 1981 and served as president until his death.

"We called him 'The Old Man of the River,'" said Tom Patterson, a North Arkansas Fly Fishers member. "He taught hundreds of people to fly fish. When he met people on the stream, if they weren't catching any fish, he'd give them what he was using. He was a kind-hearted guy who wasn't looking for glory for himself."

Not everyone remembers "The Old Man of the River" so fondly. If you like to use a drag chain while drift fishing, you can't do it in the North Fork River. Davidson led the effort that resulted in a chain-dragging ban in 1981.

It's still a sore point among some anglers, who don't think chain dragging does any more damage to aquatic vegetation than wading. In many ways,

the chain dragging argument defines the differences between bait fishers and fly fishers here. The two groups tend to be suspicious of each other.

But no one can argue that Davidson didn't think of the rivers first. He also was one of the leaders in the effort to ban trout herding, a practice everyone agrees was damaging the brown trout population in the White and North Fork rivers.

Chuck Davidson was born in Vandalia, Illinois, on Jan. 23, 1907. He was an ironworker by trade. He and his wife, Bess, lived in northern Michigan most of their lives. Chuck fished all over the world. Arkansas' North Fork and White rivers were two of his favorite trout fishing spots. So when Chuck retired in 1975, he and Bess moved into a mobile home on the

North Fork, near McClellan's Trout Dock.

"I could have retired anywhere," Davidson once told Fred Brown of the Memphis Press Scimitar newspaper. "I have fished all over the country. But this is the finest trout stream in America. That's why I came here."

This is where Davidson held court for the next 10 years. If you wanted to talk fly fishing, this was the place to be. Davidson would show beginners everything from how to tie a fly to where to fish it. The only pay he would accept for a successful "guide trip" was a bottle of whiskey, which would be shared with coffee and conversation on his back porch.

The North Fork and White rivers are primarily hatchery-driven rainbow trout waters. Davidson's dream was to prove that the rivers were capable of naturally reproducing various species of trout. There were many doubters, including fisheries biologists.

"They've got the book learning," Davidson said. "All I've got is years of study on the river. And I sample the river every day."

To the doubters, Davidson's dream was just hardheadedness, but the believers lined up behind Chuck's persistence. On February 13, 1982, 75,900 Snake River-strain cutthroat trout eggs from Wyoming were placed in Vibert egg boxes in the White River near Gaston's Resort. The Arkansas Game and Fish Commission traded 50,000 smallmouth bass fry for the Wyoming cutthroat eggs and supervised the placement of the Vibert boxes, which allow fish eggs to develop in a near-natural way. On February 20, 60,000 brook trout eggs were placed in Vibert boxes near Sportsman's Resort.

For the next three years, cutthroat, brook and even a few brown trout eggs were placed in Vibert boxes and North Arkansas Seeder boxes (a creation of Davidson and the North Arkansas Fly Fishers). The AGFC also raised cutthroats up to fingerling and stocker size in hatchery and net pen facilities.

Davidson and the North Arkansas Fly Fishers provided hours and hours of volunteer labor for these efforts. Egg

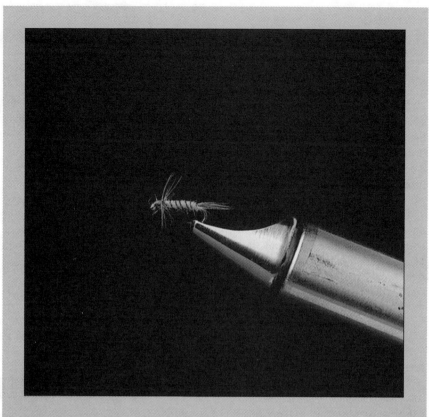

Chuck's Emerger

Hook: Dry fly, sizes 16-20
Thread: Orange 6/0
Tail: Wood duck flank
Body: Yellow wool
Rib: Brown 6/0 thread
Hackle: Ginger

The late Chuck Davidson loved to fish the almost daily midge hatches on the Norfork Tailwater. In the smaller sizes, Chuck's Emerger serves as midge imitation. At the larger sizes, it doubles as a mayfly imitation.

Guide Hank Wilson spent some time with Davidson at the Norfork Tailwater and learned how to tie and fish this pattern.

"Most people fish Chuck's Emerger the wrong way," said Wilson. "They get locked into that upstream dead-drift style.

"When you see fish rising, cast downstream to one side, give the fly a twitch to get it under the surface, then let it swing directly into the rise ring. If a fish doesn't hit, hold it there for six or seven seconds, then recast and try it again.

"This is a good method for someone who is just learning to fish rising fish. There is no mending."

Davidson preferred 7X tippet and a size 18 Chuck's Emerger. Wilson doesn't go quite that light, preferring a 12-foot leader tapering to 6X.

"Chuck could get by with 7X because he favored a seven-foot bamboo rod," Wilson said.

Wilson ties an emerger pattern similar to Chuck's that he calls the Blue Meany. It has a blue body and olive hackle, thread and tail. He ribs it with 2-pound-test brown Maxima monofilament.

boxes need daily maintenance to remove algae from individual eggs.

"Chuck always used an eagle feather to take the algae off the eggs," recalled Verna Cox, the first secretary of the North Arkansas Fly Fishers. "He put an egg in my hand one day when we were checking the boxes. The trout hatched in my hand. I sang 'Happy Birthday' to it, and Chuck got a big laugh out of that. Once that trout hatched in my hand, I was hooked on trout."

Davidson's effort led to an explosion in Arkansas' previously non-existent cutthroat trout record book. In March 1985, the first cutthroat trout was entered as a record and the mark was broken four times in the next six months.

The chronology was as follows:

1) Thomas Eise of St. Louis caught a 3-pound cutthroat in the North Fork River on March 13;

2) Phillip Fournier of Bull Shoals, Arkansas, caught a 4-pound, 4-ounce cutthroat on March 14 in the White River near Gaston's Resort;

3) Ike Brownfield of Conway, Arkansas, caught a 6-pound, 4-ounce cutthroat on July 3 near Tucker Shoals;

4) Scott Rudolph of Ozark, Arkansas, caught a 9.61-pound cutthroat on Oct. 10 near Stetson's Resort.

(In recent years, another strain of cutthroats has been stocked in Arkansas. They haven't thrived like the original Snake River-strain of cutthroats. Increased fishing pressure has also kept cutthroats from growing to state record size. In 1993, the AGFC renewed efforts to bring back the cutthroat by acquiring Snake River-strain eggs and adopting a 16-inch minimum length limit.)

The North Fork and White rivers lost a great friend when Davidson died on July 23, 1985, at the age of 78. North Arkansas Fly Fishers member Larry Woodall of Fayetteville led the fundraising effort that resulted in a $1,556 check being presented to the Baxter County Library.

The fishing books in Davidson's memory now serve to educate another generation of anglers.

Learning to fly fish during high water conditions is a must in Ozark tailwaters. John Gulley says the key is keeping a fly near the bottom of the stream bed.

Gulley Adapted To Fishing With Fly Rod On High Water

John Gulley doesn't fish with bait. He's glad, however, that he was in the boat with a bait fisherman one particular day.

Both power generators were running at Norfork Dam. Gulley is a fly fisherman, and water conditions weren't good for fly fishing this day.

While Gulley was casting a variety of nymphs and streamers and catching nothing, his buddy was catching trout after trout on salmon eggs fished on spinning gear. Make that salmon egg, singular. Instead of loading the hook with three or four eggs, like most anglers do, Gulley's buddy put one egg on the hook. That got Gulley thinking.

"I pulled up to the house and tied a few eggs up, and I caught more fish than him after that," Gulley said. "He thought that was pretty neat. He still makes me tie him some eggs."

Gulley's important discovery wasn't that trout will hit an egg pattern in Ozark tailwaters, but that you can adapt fly fishing techniques to high water and still catch fish. If you've

cussed the U.S. Army Corps of Engineers because the power generators were running on the day you planned to fly fish, you know how important a discovery this was. For someone like Gulley, a fulltime, Orvis-endorsed fly fishing guide, it meant the difference between making a living or not.

"If you fish tailwater streams, you've got to learn to fly fish on high water," Gulley said. "Otherwise, you'll go broke one of those years when we get 200 days of high water."

The purist may turn up his nose at this form of fly fishing. Gulley likes to describe himself as a good ol' boy from Prescott, Arkansas. He doesn't turn up his nose at anything. That's why he was in a position to learn something from his buddy the bait fisherman.

"This is just sophisticated bait fishing," Gulley said. "You've got to think like a bait fisherman. Keep the fly as close as you can to the bottom without it being dead on the bottom."

Gulley has been guiding since

1973. But he didn't start successfully fly fishing in high water until 1987.

"It took me that long to learn it, and I still haven't learned all of it," he said. "It took awhile to get it nailed down pretty good."

He's got it nailed down enough now to catch trout on a fly rod below Bull Shoals Dam when all eight generators are running and the floodgates are open, which he did quite successfully during the brown trout spawning run in December 1993.

Here are the basics of high water fly fishing: a boat, 9-foot fly rod for a 6-weight line (or something close), floating line, 10- to 14-feet of tapered 3X tippet, strike indicator, split shot and three relatively simple fly patterns - egg, San Juan Worm and sowbug.

Gulley uses two-sided foam picture-hanging tape for his strike indicator. He can simply cut off more tape from the roll if he needs to make a more buoyant indicator. He puts a size 3/0 split shot about 18 inches up the tip-pet from the fly. This rig doesn't cast easily. However, long casts aren't important.

Boat operation is crucial. Gulley positions his 20-foot johnboat either at the top or bottom of shoal areas, near deep holes. He keeps the outboard motor running to hold the boat in place or give it a slow downstream drift. The bow is pointed upstream. By making 10- to 20-foot casts out either side of the boat, you can find the current seems that trout are feeding in. The strike will be brief; the hook set must be equally quick.

"What you're trying to do is get a highly visible fly in front of them and get the fish to make a snap decision," Gulley said. "It's not going to sit there long."

On the egg pattern, Gulley varies the size and color with water depth and clarity. In high water that has some murkiness to it, he'll use a big, bright egg. As the water level lowers and clarity increases, he'll go to small-er, more subtle patterns.

"I use all colors," Gulley said. "Whatever egg yarn you can buy will work. Just like the fake salmon eggs, they sell it in all colors."

The egg pattern works all year, but it is most effective in winter months when brown trout are spawning and trout eggs are abundant as a natural food source for trout. Gulley usually ties his egg patterns on a No. 8 hook, but he'll go as small as sizes 14 and 16. He prefers a scud hook, as it seems to add some hook-setting ability.

"Trout will always eat an egg or a worm," Gulley says.

That's why his second choice in high water is the San Juan Worm. He ties them on a No. 10 hook most of the time. It doesn't seem to matter whether it's a long shank or short shank hook.

Color is important. Gulley favors three colors: 1) natural, sort of a gray-ish brown; 2) solid brown; and 3) red.

If the trout are finicky, and water

High-water techniques frequently produce big fish, like this brown trout caught and released below Bull Shoals Dam.

clarity requires a subtle presentation, sowbugs are the choice.

"I probably tie eight or 10 different sowbugs, but they are all gray," Gulley said. "Size is the main thing. Size 14 and 16 work best here. I'll go to a 12 at times on the White River."

When the water conditions are in that intermediate stage - not high, but not dead low either - Gulley changes gear. He adds a 10-foot section of sink tip line, a 10-foot section of tapered 4X tippet and a Woolly Bugger. Gulley anchors the boat, makes a quartering cast downstream and fishes the Woolly Bugger on the swing. He gives it a slight twitch during the swing, then strips it back.

Gulley experiments with the retrieve, varying the length and frequency of the stripping motion. This also works on dead low water. Most of the fish will be found in deeper water, above and below shoals.

Gulley ties three color variations on the Woolly Bugger pattern: 1) olive body, black hackle, black tail; 2) olive body, olive tail, grizzly hackle; 3) solid black. Sizes 8 and 10 are most common. He'll occasionally use size 6 in high water. Gulley brightens this pattern with orange thread at the head of the fly and strips of pearl Mylar down each side of the body.

Gulley says dry fly purists shouldn't give up on Ozark tailwaters. Mayfly and caddis hatches are common on the North Fork and White rivers, beginning about May and continuing through July. Good dry fly patterns include Sulphur Dun (sizes 16-18), Elk Hair Caddis (14-20) and Blue Wing Olive (18-20).

"That's my favorite way to fly fish," Gulley said. "But if there's no low water, the fish don't seem to pay any attention to the hatches."

That's the bottom line here. Do you want to sit around and tie dry flies, waiting on perfect water conditions, or do you want to fish?

"Some people are skeptical at the beginning of the day," Gulley said of newcomers to his high-water techniques. "But, at the end of the day, they like it, and they've learned a little bit."

Woolly Bugger

Hook: Mustad 79580, sizes 6-12
Weight: .035 to .015 lead wire, depending on hook size
Thread: Fluorescent orange
Body: Olive or black chenille, plus 2 strips of pearl Mylar tensil
Tail: Olive or black marabou
Hackle: Black or grizzly

If he were limited to two fly patterns on the Norfork Tailwater, John Gulley says he could get by with Woolly Buggers and sowbugs.

Gulley prefers adding a little flash to the Woolly Buggers he ties. A strip of pearl Mylar down each side and orange thread at the head accomplish this. He is careful not to extend the Mylar too far into the tail, where it could inhibit the marabou action.

Gulley ties Woolly Buggers in three colors - 1) olive body, black tail, black hackle; 2) olive body, olive tail, grizzly hackle; 3) solid black. He ties them mostly in sizes 8 and 10, but for some high-water conditions Gulley steps up in size to a 6. He adds as much lead as he can fit on the hook shank.

There are two ways Gulley fishes a Woolly Bugger on the North Fork River. In a drifting boat, he will cast to structure along the bank and strip the fly back. In an anchored boat, he will make a quartering downstream cast, mend his line, then fish the Woolly Bugger "on the swing."

In this second method, it's important to vary the retrieve and get the fly near the river bottom. Sometimes Gulley twitches the fly as it starts to swing below him. He strips it back erratically - 10 short strips and stop, then five short strips and stop. At times, Gulley feeds line back downstream, then starts the retrieve again. He often adds 10 feet of sink-tip loop-to-loop connection fly line, so the fly will get down near the bottom.

Manley's Record Trout Hit On First Cast

Night of disappointment quickly turned into one for the record book

Huey Manley and his two fishing buddies, Tommy Long and Paul Suddeth, were disappointed when they got to McClellan's Trout Dock on the North Fork River late Friday night, August 7, 1988. They were regular customers at McClellan's. All three usually worked a full day on Friday. They seldom managed to leave North Little Rock, Arkansas, until after 6 p.m., and the dock was always closed by the time they arrived.

"Mr. McClellan always told us we could take a boat out anytime we wanted," Manley said.

But having a dock full of boats didn't help them this night. The Norfork Tailwater was dead low.

"There wasn't even half a generator running," Manley said. "The boats were on sand. We were tired. We didn't feel like trying to push a boat out there. So we just fished from the dock."

Strike two against them was the fact that they didn't bring any worms, their favorite trout bait, which they often dug at home before going trout fishing. There was some corn on the dock.

"We just figured before we went to sleep we'd throw some corn and marshmallows out there," Manley said.

With the water that low, Manley knew of just one deep hole to cast into from his perch on McClellan's Dock. His bait, kernels of corn on each barb of a tiny treble hook, floated off the bottom by a marshmallow, barely settled into the water when Manley felt a strike.

"When I pulled back there was nothing," he said. "Then all of a sudden my line just started singing out."

Manley had just that day filled his Shimano spinning reel with new 6-pound-test line.

"One-hundred-and-five yards is what it held," Manley said. "That fish took almost every bit of it. At one time, I looked down at the reel, and Tommy was yelling at me, 'How much line you got left?' Basically, I just let the fish do

Mike "Huey" Manley of North Little Rock, Arkansas, caught this 38-pound, 9-ounce brown trout on August 7, 1988, in the North Fork River.

what he wanted to do."

Manley wasn't sure what he'd hooked. He had seen some big carp in the area on previous trips. He thought he might have one of those.

"It took 15 minutes to even see the fish," Manley said. "When I finally got him close, he jumped out of the water. Tommy said, 'Man, it's a big brown!' I didn't think it could be, because it was such a huge fish. The lantern was right in my eyes. All I saw was the shadow of the fish."

Not until the third time the fish jumped was Manley convinced he had hooked a brown trout.

Each time Manley worked the fish near the dock, it would make another long run. The pattern continued five or six times.

"I smoked two cigarettes," Manley said. "I had to just let him go where he wanted. I'd light up a cigarette and wait and pant and puff."

Manley estimates the fish fought 30 minutes before he had a chance to land it. Long grabbed one of the many

landing nets hanging from the dock rafters and slipped it over the big brown's head. But when he tried to lift, the weight of the fish collapsed the aluminum net frame.

"Tommy jumped in to grab it," Manley said. "We pushed it up on the dock."

It was near midnight. Manley had a rope with him. He looped it through the trout's mouth and tied the fish to the dock, while they tried to figure out what to do. Long was a fly fisherman and knew that fly fishing guide John Gulley lived nearby. Gulley didn't fully awaken until he put the trout on a scale that measured up to 30 pounds, and the scale bottomed out.

"It seemed like things were happening real fast by this time," Manley said.

Gulley told them to go put the fish back in the water, then he got dressed and came down to the dock in his pickup truck. They filled a 48-quart ice chest with water and tried to lay the fish in it, but the fish wouldn't fit. Gulley took them to a Mountain Home grocery store where the male brown trout weighed 38 pounds, 9 ounces. It measured 41 inches in length and 27 3/4 inches in girth. Manley's biggest trout before that night was a 5-pound rainbow from the White River.

Arkansas Game and Fish Commission fisheries biologist Mark Oliver was on hand at the grocery store to certify the weight. That's when Manley knew he'd caught a new state record brown trout, breaking the 11-year-old mark of 33 pounds, eight ounces, set by Leon Waggoner of Flippin, Arkansas, on March 19, 1977.

It was 3:30 a.m., and Manley wanted to call his wife, Karen, with the big news.

"She said, 'Oh, honey, why would call me at 3:30 in the morning and tell me this?' She thought I was kidding," Manley said.

By the time Manley got back home in North Little Rock on Sunday evening, Karen was convinced the early Saturday morning phone call had been no prank. Big fish news travels fast. Reporters were calling the Manley home, wanting to hear the story of the newest world record brown trout.

Michael Hubert "Huey" Manley's name was entered in the National Fresh Water Fishing Hall of Fame record book as both the all-tackle record and the record for 8-pound-test line.

(In NFWFHF tests, Manley's 6-pound-test line was stronger than the maximum allowed for that class. So his mark was moved up to the next line class - 8-pound-test.)

The International Game Fish Association didn't recognize Manley's fish because it was caught on the combination of a treble hook and bait.

Manley's mark lasted almost four years, until Howard "Rip" Collins caught a 40-pound, 4-ounce brown trout from the Little Red River in May 1992.

Manley said he wasn't disappointed when he heard his record had been broken.

"There are bigger ones out there to be caught," Manley said. "I was glad it was another Arkansan who broke the record."

This rainbow trout couldn't resist one of Jerry Dudley's homemade marabou jigs. Dudley ties jigs in several colors and styles to imitate various trout foods.

Dudley Converted To Jigs After One Trip To Norfork

One conversation changed Jerry Dudley's whole way of thinking about trout fishing. In 1983, Dudley and his son, J.D., were making regular visits to Missouri's Roaring River State Park and catching 30 to 40 trout a day. They were having a good time doing it, too. One Sunday, before services at Fayetteville's University Baptist Church, Dudley was telling a friend, Jim Hall, about his latest successful trout trip.

"Are you catching any big ones?" Hall asked.

"About one- to one-and-half pounds," Dudley said.

"Why don't you let me take you to my place?" Hall replied.

Hall's "place" was the Norfork Tailwater.

"We probably caught and released 150 fish that day," Dudley recalled. "Jim caught a 4-pound cutthroat. We had several rainbows that weighed 2 1/2 to 3 pounds. Brother, I've been hooked ever since."

Dudley was hooked in more ways than one that day. The North Fork River become his trout fishery of choice, and a marabou jig became his trout lure of choice. By the summer of 1994, Dudley's 1983 van was closing in on the 200,000-mile mark, and many of those miles came on trout fishing trips to Norfork. Dudley has put in many hours refining his jig fishing technique and learning the North Fork River.

"Cast right by that rock," Dudley said, one August Saturday afternoon. "There's usually a cutthroat around there."

One cast with a 1/16th-ounce black jig produced a 17-inch cutthroat trout, just as he predicted.

In August 1988, Dudley caught a 6 1/2-pound cutthroat in the mouth of the slough located near McClellan's Trout Dock on the North Fork. Yes, of course, he caught it on a jig. Dudley has three mounted fish hanging on a wall at home - an 11 1/2-pound brown trout, a 6 1/2-pound rainbow trout that his son, J.D., caught, and the 6 1/2-pound cutthroat.

"People look at those fish, and they always go to that cutthroat," Dudley said. "They've never seen one that big."

Dudley spends as much time now on the White River as the North Fork, but he defers to the Norfork Tailwater when it comes to catching "picture" fish.

"The rainbows, especially, just seem to be prettier here," Dudley said. "This river is so different from the White - the tree-lined banks, logs and solid rock. There aren't many gravel bars, like there are in the White."

Jigs seem to work equally well in the two rivers. Earlier, in what would be a 100-fish day, we had caught trout on five consecutive casts in the White River. Dudley makes it seem easy, and he has converted a number of Fayetteville anglers to trout fishing exclusively with jigs. He likes to spread the word.

"Some of my buddies gripe at me because I show so many people how to do this," Dudley said, with a laugh.

The two key ingredients in Dudley's method are lightweight jigs and light-weight line. He prefers a 1/16th-ounce jig almost exclusively. However, depth is important, so in heavier current Dudley will step up in weight to 3/32nds occasionally, and rarely 1/8th.

"You've got to get the jig on the bottom," Dudley said. "But the key is for it to fall as slowly as possible. That's why I don't like 1/8th-ounce jigs, they fall too fast. And I can tell the difference between 1/16th and 3/32nds. If the water is right, you'll catch more fish on 1/16th."

When Dudley first started fishing jigs, he would use 4-pound-test line when the water was high, then go down to 2-pound-test on low water. Now he uses 2-pound test exclusively, specifically Maxima Ultra Green.

In March 1994, Dudley caught an 11 1/2-pound brown trout while fishing with 2-pound line and a 3/32nds-ounce jig below Bull Shoals Dam when all eight generators were running. The key to using 2-pound test is to keep it fresh. Dudley carries three spinning rigs - 6-foot Loomis rods paired with Shimano reels - and nine spinning reel spools loaded with 2-pound-test line. (To keep the spools full, he uses backing of 4- or 6-pound-test before adding 120 yards of 2-pound line.)

Dudley inspects his line for nicks and abrasions after landing a fish. If he finds one, he breaks off several feet of line and reties the jig. After several reties, Dudley puts on a fresh spool of line.

"I don't believe in giving them a chance," said Dudley, about his obsession with new line. "I'm giving them enough of a chance already with 2-pound-test."

Dudley doesn't like to rely on his reel's drag system either, although Shimano spinning reels are noted for having a good one. So Dudley back-reels when a fish is making a run, relying on his own touch for putting on and taking off pressure.

With a trolling motor attached to the front of the johnboat, Dudley can position the boat and control its drift downstream.

Dudley experiments with different colors of marabou for the tail and paint for the jighead, then he brings his jigs to Norfork for some "field testing."

Another important ingredient in Dudley's jig fishing method is an electric trolling motor. He mounts a 36-pound-thrust Minn Kota on the side of a 20-foot johnboat, near the bow. He uses the trolling motor mainly as a way to slow the downstream drift of the boat. He points the boat upstream, then varies the speed of the trolling motor to give him the desired rate of drift.

Dudley can adapt to any rate of current - from eight generators on the White River below Bull Shoals to dead low water at Norfork.

"One generator is perfect at Norfork," Dudley said. "On the White River, four to five generators is my favorite water."

If there is no current, he uses the trolling motor to move around and cast to different areas. Dudley never drops an anchor. He usually stands in the front of the boat, looking for fish, with the aid of polarized sunglasses.

"This is just a fun way to fish," Dudley said. "You don't have to sit around, and you can see more scenery this way, when you're constantly moving."

Much of the time you are sight-fishing - casting to a specific fish - or you'll see a trout follow the jig. This prompts a lot of one-way conversations with fish, along the lines of "take it, take it, take it" as a trout turns to get a closer look at the lure.

That's where Dudley's method gets sophisticated. He has an array of different looks he can give a jig. Some days this will mean the difference in catching fish or not.

"There are a half-dozen ways to fish jigs," Dudley said. "You can hop it slow or fast. Sometimes I strip it in, like you would with a fly rod.

"If the fish are hitting short, you can shake the rod tip while you're reeling the jig. Sometimes that will entice a strike."

Most of the time, Dudley starts with a slow, up-and-down jigging retrieve. The trout usually hit the jig as it falls.

Dudley's other way of adding variety to jig presentation is color. If he had to pick one jig color, it would be black. But he also ties three variations of olive jigs, which he believes imitate sculpins, one of the trout's favorite forage fish.

Dudley orders various other colors of Woolly Bugger marabou from Wapsi Fly, Inc., in Mountain Home. He combines gray, white and pink for a rainbow trout imitation and various amounts of white and gray for imitations of minnows and threadfin shad.

"Burnt orange and brown is probably the most unusual combination I tie," Dudley said. "I think it probably looks like a crawdad."

Dudley owns an independent truck brokerage business. Most of his work day is spent talking on the telephone. Dudley keeps his jig-tying materials handy. When the phone isn't ringing, he works on jigs.

In addition to the marabou experiments, Dudley tries different looks on the jighead. Most often he'll attempt to match the dominant marabou color in a jig with blends of auto body paint.

"My wife has a basic knowledge what colors to blend and get the desired result," Dudley said. He added, with a smile, "This jig business is kind of a family deal."

The auto body paint is expensive, but it won't chip off the jighead, even after repeated contact with boulders and gravel on the stream bed. Sometimes Dudley adds poly-flake, either gold or silver, on the jigheads to give them an extra sparkle.

Dudley has one more secret to his jig-fishing technique - the shape of the jighead. He owns a mold that creates an unusually shaped jig.

The jighead isn't round, and it isn't flat. It's closest to what is known as a tapered head, with the exception that one side is more tapered than the other.

"It's lopsided," Dudley said. "It's almost flat on one side and tapered on the other. I think that's important in giving the jig a different action."

Dudley hasn't been able to find another mold like it. And, in a sense, he has created a monster - teaching more and more people to trout fish with a jig only he can make. But Jerry Dudley is more than happy to feed this monster.

Many of his pupils have been members of the senior high Sunday school class he teaches at church. His love of trout fishing and teaching has led him to work as a parttime fishing guide.

"If I could make a living guiding and tying and selling jigs," Dudley said, "civilization could say goodbye to me."

Meeks Chooses Durable Bait At Norfork

Nightcrawlers get the nod in tailwater known for ledges, logs, lunkers

Carl Meeks pulled a nightcrawler from the peat in a Styrofoam box, then pinched the worm in two pieces. He tossed the bottom section of the nightcrawler in the North Fork River before threading a 1 1/2-inch piece on his hook. He calls this a nightcrawler stub.

"See, there's nothing to this trout fishing," Meeks laughed. "All you've got to do is tear your worm in two."

He had just caught his third rainbow trout on the same 1 1/2-inch nightcrawler stub.

"I like the durability of nightcrawlers," Meeks said. "They withstand a lot of abuse, and Norfork has got a lot of obstacles in it."

Meeks was born in Illinois in 1941 and grew up there. In 1971 he came to visit a friend who had bought a home in Cotter, Arkansas. Meeks liked the area so much he moved to Cotter, too. He quickly became part of the trout fishing scene, starting out as a cook on camp trips, then guiding.

There are many more anglers on the White and North Fork rivers now than there were in the 1970s, but there aren't as many overnight camp trips today as there were then.

"In the old days, there was a lot of camaraderie on those camp trips," Meeks said. "There were a bunch of us that worked a lot of days together."

Meeks' marriage even has a fishing guide connection. His wife, Connie, is Elvin Weaver's sister. Weaver has built a reputation as one of the best guides for catching big trout on the White River. (See story in Bull Shoals Tailwater section.)

Carl and Connie's house stands on a hill that overlooks the Miller Hole of the White River below Cotter. Through a telescope in his den, Carl can look at a particular rock in the Miller Hole and gauge the river flow.

If you're a trout fishing guide in this area, you're going to spend many days on the Norfork Tailwater, too. Meeks enjoys the change of pace in moving back and forth between the White and North Fork rivers.

And the Norfork Tailwater brings back some pleasant memories, including a pair of 12-pound rainbow trout caught in Mill Dam Eddy. One hit a red worm during high-water conditions. The other was caught on a

When Carl Meeks fishes for rainbow trout in the Norfork Tailwater, he uses only half a nightcrawler.

sculpin in low water.

Meeks has been around long enough to witness the decline in the numbers of big rainbow trout.

"At one time, it wasn't uncommon to catch a cooler full of rainbows weighing from three to eight pounds," Meeks said. "There were a lot in the three- to five-pound class.

"There is probably 10 to 15 times the fishing pressure on these rivers now than there was then. That's just a guess. There are more outfitters, more fishermen and the fishermen are more efficient."

Although Meeks fishes with jigs and artificial lures, like Rapalas, at times, he is mainly a bait fisherman. Overall, he prefers red worms, crawfish tails and nightcrawlers, in that order. Nightcrawlers often get the nod on Norfork, as mentioned before, because of their durability.

"I don't like corn, and I don't like Power Bait," Meeks said. "You catch too many stockers."

One reason Meeks likes the Norfork Tailwater is the quality of the rainbow trout here. Although the Norfork National Fish Hatchery is nearby, providing plenty of 9-inch rainbow trout "stockers," it seems there are always good numbers of "holdover" rainbows here. These fish have been in the river long enough to gain some size and some brilliance in the crimson stripe down their sides.

As do most bait fishermen in this area, Meeks usually relies on spinning gear, a drift rig and 4-pound-test line. The drift rig is made from a 30- to 36-inch section of line that has a hook tied to one end and a bell sinker on the other. It is attached to the main line about eight inches above the bell sinker, so the sinker looks like it's on a dropper.

Meeks prefers a No. 10 sinker, "the smallest there is," and a No. 6 hook. "You can use a No. 4 hook, but it catches a lot more moss," he said.

Boat control is the key to fishing a drift rig. On this day, both generators were running at Norfork Dam. Meeks often uses a drag chain for boat control in the White River, but drag chains are banned in the North Fork. Here Meeks uses his outboard motor, keeping it idling and shifting in and out of gear, to both hold the boat parallel to the bank and slow its drift downstream. The drift rig is cast toward the bank.

"I want my line either along side me or slightly upstream," Meeks said. "If the line gets too far behind you downstream, then you are dragging, not drifting."

Water flows slower near the bottom of the stream because it is obstructed by objects in the stream bed - rock ledges, boulders, moss beds, etc. Typically, trout will face upstream behind these objects, out of the swift

> "I want my line either along side me or slightly upstream. If the line gets too far behind you downstream, then you are dragging, not drifting."

current. They will make short darts into the current to pick off food drifting by. Therefore, it is important to get the bait on bottom and keep it drifting the same speed as the current there. The line acts as a gauge, telling you when to slow down or speed up the boat.

"Put your boat in the faster water and fish in the slower water," Meeks said. "That allows you to use the motor. For instance, if you want to fish the middle of the stream, put the boat in the outside edge of the current and cast toward the inside edge."

If there is no water coming from the dam, Meeks will stick with nightcrawlers, especially if he is after a big brown trout, but he changes tactics. Instead of only a part of one nightcrawler, Meeks puts two whole night-crawlers on a No. 6 hook.

"Thread one on, bring the hook out halfway down it and slide the nightcrawler up the line," Meeks said. "Thread another one on halfway and let the tail dangle."

The result is two dangling tails and a hook completely covered in nightcrawlers.

From an anchored boat, this is cast downstream on the same bell sinker rig used for drift fishing.

In August 1994, the Arkansas Game and Fish Commission approved a catch-and-release, artificial-lure-only zone on the Norfork Tailwater from Otter Creek to 100 yards above River Ridge Access, effective January 1, 1995. That area includes Mill Dam Eddy, where Meeks caught the two 12-pound rainbows on bait. In the future, he'll fish that area with jigs, especially when power generation is less than two generators.

"You want to fish a jig as slow as you can fish it," Meeks said. "Work it over moss beds, behind logs, around any of the obstructions where big rainbows tend to lay and wait for food.

"I usually hold the rod tip at about two o'clock and give it a little twitch. You want to fish slow, but vary the retrieve."

Meeks uses 1/16th- and 1/32nd-ounce jigs in olive, brown or brown-and-orange color patterns. Sometimes the trout seem to prefer something with a smaller profile. Meeks wets a jig, then trims the marabou just past the hook bend.

"I like to use jigs when one generator is running and the water is clear," Meeks said. "It's more of a sight-fishing method. You'll see most of the fish take the jig, and that's the hard part - waiting to set the hook.

"If the second generator comes on, you're not done, but there are fewer places to fish a jig. It's tougher to get it down where it needs to be. They won't come up four feet to hit it. You can only raise a fish about 18 inches."

"When the water gets that high, I'd rather put on a Rapala or drift bait."

Then, as Meeks says, the trout fishing becomes as simple as tearing your worm in two.

Norfork Hatchery No. 1 In USFWS For Annual Coldwater Production

Norfork National Fish Hatchery is a key element in understanding both the development of these Ozark tailwaters and their success. In terms of annual production, it is the No. 1 coldwater hatchery in the U. S. Fish and Wildlife Service system. It produces about 500,000 pounds of trout - nearly two million fish - per year, most of which go into the Bull Shoals and Norfork tailwaters.

With the construction of first Norfork Dam, then Bull Shoals Dam, sections of the North Fork and White rivers became unsuitable for the native warmwater fish species. On August 4, 1955, Congress authorized construction of the Norfork National Fish Hatchery as mitigation for these warmwater fishery losses. Two years later, construction was completed. By 1962, the Norfork National Fish Hatchery was producing about 1.8 million trout per year.

Of the state and federal hatcheries primarily supplying trout for the White River System, this was the first. (State-operated Shepherd of the Hills Hatchery on Lake Taneycomo began production in 1958, one year after Norfork.) It is the driving force behind the rainbow trout fishery in the Bull Shoals and Norfork tailwaters, where brown trout natural reproduction is successful but rainbow natural reproduction is limited.

In 1993, the Norfork Hatchery produced 1,965,206 trout. About 75 percent of those, were stocked in Arkansas waters as nine-inch rainbow trout. Another 360,000 five-inch rainbow trout were sent to Arkansas Game and Fish Commission-operated Mammoth Spring Hatchery, where they were raised to 12 inches and then stocked in various Arkansas waters. The Norfork Hatchery also raised some rainbow trout to 12 inches - 22,000 for the Norfork Tailwater and 5,000 for the Beaver Tailwater. Six-inch brown trout and cutthroat trout made up most of Norfork's remaining 1993 production.

As fishing pressure has increased on these Ozark tailwaters, the rainbow trout fisheries have increasingly shifted from put-grow-and-take to put-and-take. When there is an interruption in the Norfork Hatchery stocking schedule, as happened due to water quality and disease problems in the early 1990s, anglers notice it immediately. In that sense, the Norfork Hatchery is more important now than it was 20 years ago, when the carryover population of rainbow trout was much larger.

Through its first 30 years, the Norfork Hatchery included spawning operations, where brood stock were raised and stripped of eggs. The brood fish usually were expended after age five. They were then stocked in local waters. The only big trout in the Norfork Hatchery now are strictly there for show. (Over 200,000 visitors tour the hatchery each year.) As you enter the hatchery, located just below Norfork Dam on Highway 177, the first raceway contains some 10-pound trout.

Norfork Hatchery now raises trout from eggs shipped from other USFWS hatcheries.

"We've found it is more efficient to let smaller hatcheries concentrate on egg production," said Bennie Perry, who became the Norfork Hatchery manager in 1992. "A small hatchery can supply several bigger hatcheries with eggs."

In 1994, the Norfork Hatchery received rainbow eggs from Montana and Tennessee hatcheries; brown and cutthroat eggs came from two hatcheries in Wyoming.

Undeveloped trout eggs become "eyed eggs" after about 20 days. At this stage of development, they can taken out of water and shipped to other hatcheries.

Norfork Hatchery, like the USFWS Greers Ferry Hatchery, raises eyed eggs into adult trout. A nine-inch fish is approximately 18 months old.

Dry Run Creek Ultimate Place For Kids To Learn

Dry Run Creek is the ultimate Ozark "honey hole" for trout. Although the stream is only a quarter-mile long, it typically contains over 2,000 trout, according to Arkansas Game and Fish Commission studies. And there are some lunkers here.

"It's a great place to learn how to trout fish," said Benny Perry, manager of the Norfork National Fish Hatchery. "You can catch 100 fish a day. I see a lot of grandparents with their grandchildren here, teaching them how to fish."

There is a catch to catching fish at Dry Run Creek. You can't keep any. It's all catch and release. And not everyone is allowed to fish here. Dry Run Creek is limited to two groups of people: 1) those under 16 years of age, and 2) properly licensed disabled. Tackle is restricted to single, barbless hooks and artificial lures.

The effluent from Norfork National Fish Hatchery flows out of three outlet pipes into Dry Run Creek at rates up to 22,000 gallons per minute. This produces a cool, nutrient-rich stream that connects the hatchery with the North Fork River.

In addition to trout released from the hatchery, those already in the Norfork Tailwater are attracted to it also. This is especially true in early fall when low dissolved oxygen levels are frequently found in the water released from Norfork Dam.

Rainbow, brown, cutthroat and brook trout are in the creek, but over 95 percent will be rainbows, including some up to 30 inches long.

Dry Run Creek may be fished from sunrise to sunset only. A handicap-accessible wooden ramp, paved walkway and picnic tables are located between the Norfork Hatchery and Dry Run Creek.

Highlights Of A Trip Down The North Fork

("Left" and "right" directions assume the angler is facing downstream.")

With only 4.8 miles to cover, it doesn't take long to reach the White River from Norfork Dam when the power generators are running. However, as mentioned in the introduction of this chapter, the Norfork Tailwater is known as much for its wade fishing opportunities at low water as it is for float-fishing from a boat. Both methods are accommodated with plenty of river access.

Quarry Park below Norfork Dam provides both a concrete boat launching ramp and public access for bank fishing and wading. **Dry Run Creek** enters the Norfork Tailwater in Quarry Park and the mouth of the creek is a popular bank fishing area.

The effluent from Norfork National Fish Hatchery flows into Dry Run Creek at rates up to 22,000 gallons per minute. This highly-oxygenated, nutrient-rich water attracts trout from the tailwater. Anyone may fish at the creek mouth, where no special restrictions apply. But fishing in Dry Run Creek is all catch-and-release and limited to two groups of people: 1) those under 16 years of age, and 2) properly licensed disabled. Tackle is restricted to single, barbless hooks and artificial lures.

Quarry Park extends about three-quarters of a mile down the north bank, and there are several paths from the park to the river. A shoal starts at the boat ramp. A small island, which shows only as a patch of grass at high water, is in the middle of the river near the park boundary. **Rainbow Trout Resort** and **Gene's Trout Resort** are visible on the right, about one mile from the dam, and there some private docks along this section of the river, too.

A shoal marks a left bend in the river, which then makes a slight jog left, then right, and back into a straight stretch called **Long Hole**. At the bottom of Long Hole, a small stream of water cuts into the right bank, then back out a few yards downstream.

Effluent from the Norfork National Fish Hatchery flows into Dry Run Creek, which offers catch-and-release fishing for kids and disabled adults.

There's a shoal between the entrance and exit of this water.

An island that extends past **McClellan's Trout Dock** starts here. The main channel is down the left side, where the dock is located. At the top of the island the river bottom is marked with a series of rock ledges. The lower part of the right side of the island is blocked with fallen trees. Huey Manley's 38-pound, 9-ounce world record brown trout was caught from McClellan's Dock in 1988. On the right side near the end of the island at McClellan's, a large slough extends back upstream.

Past the island, a straight pool marked by a gravel bar on the left and thick cover on the right stretches down to the mouth of, which enters on the left, at approximately the halfway point of the Norfork Tailwater. For a daily fee paid at McClellan's, anglers can park vehicles in the pasture just above Otter Creek and gain walk-in access to this part of the river.

The Arkansas Game and Fish Commission established a year-round catch-and-release zone on January 1, 1995, that begins at Otter Creek and extends one mile downstream to 100 yards above the River Ridge Access.

The next half-mile, from Otter

River Ridge Access features a fishing pier for handicapped and walk-in access for wade-fishing in the North Fork River.

Creek to the beginning of Mill Dam Eddy, includes some of the most distinctive rock features in the Norfork Tailwater.

Right at the mouth of Otter Creek, stands a large sycamore tree. Some anglers call this **Sycamore Pool**. A short shoal leads to another pool, which the late Chuck Davidson, one of the fly fishing pioneers on the Norfork Tailwater, named **Ace in the Hole**, because he could always catch some trout here.

Just before the river begins turning back to the right, a ledge extends all the way across the river. A dropoff behind it forms a waterfall at low water levels and a whitewater shoal at high water levels. At intermediate water levels, this is a particularly dangerous place for inexperienced boaters.

There is a pool below, then an island. The main river channel goes to the right of island, however, you can boat down either side at high water levels, when water flows over the island and splits it in two. During periods of no power generation, the left side goes dry, except for a pool below a V-split ledge and dropoff. Called the **Blue Hole** or **Trap Hole**, this pool lit-

erally is a trap at dead low water levels and usually holds large numbers of fish. However, these landlocked fish aren't easily caught. Davidson called this **Education Hole**.

"He said if you could catch fish here you could catch them anywhere," recalled John Gulley. "These fish will give you an education. They can be pretty smart."

A straight pool stretches 3/10ths of a mile from the end of the island at Blue Hole to a pair of islands below. This is called **Mill Dam Eddy**. The island at the bottom of Mill Dam Eddy is commonly referred to as **Cook's Island**, in reference to Charlie Cook, who lives nearby. The catch-and-release zone ends below this island.

River Ridge Access, which features a handicap fishing pier, plus walk-in access, marks the end of the straight stretch of river that began at Mill Dam Eddy. **Goat Ridge Bluff** lines the right side of the river and Highway 5 runs along the top of it, where there is a scenic overlook of the Norfork Tailwater. At low water, there is a gravel bar in front of River Ridge Access.

The river starts to bend back to the

left. At low water, there is a series of riffles and pockets here. An island is visible downstream. The main river channel goes to the left of it. At high water, a second island forms along the left bank. Baxter County Road 63 roughly parallels the Norfork Tailwater from one end to the other. It runs closest to the river in this last half-mile, from the second island down, along the left side.

The **Schroder Haus** sits atop the bank on the right. The Highway 5 and railroad bridges mark some of the deepest holes in the Norfork Tailwater. David Wooten's 34-pound, 8-ounce brown trout was caught near the railroad bridge in 1988.

Rose's Trout Dock is on the left, just past the bridges. The White River is clearly visible from here. The **AGFC's Norfork Public Access** provides bank fishing on the left. The last stretch of Norfork Tailwater on the right bank is marked by fallen trees that often attract trout.

An aerial view of the North Fork River, as it flows into the White River, 4.8 miles below Norfork Dam. ▶

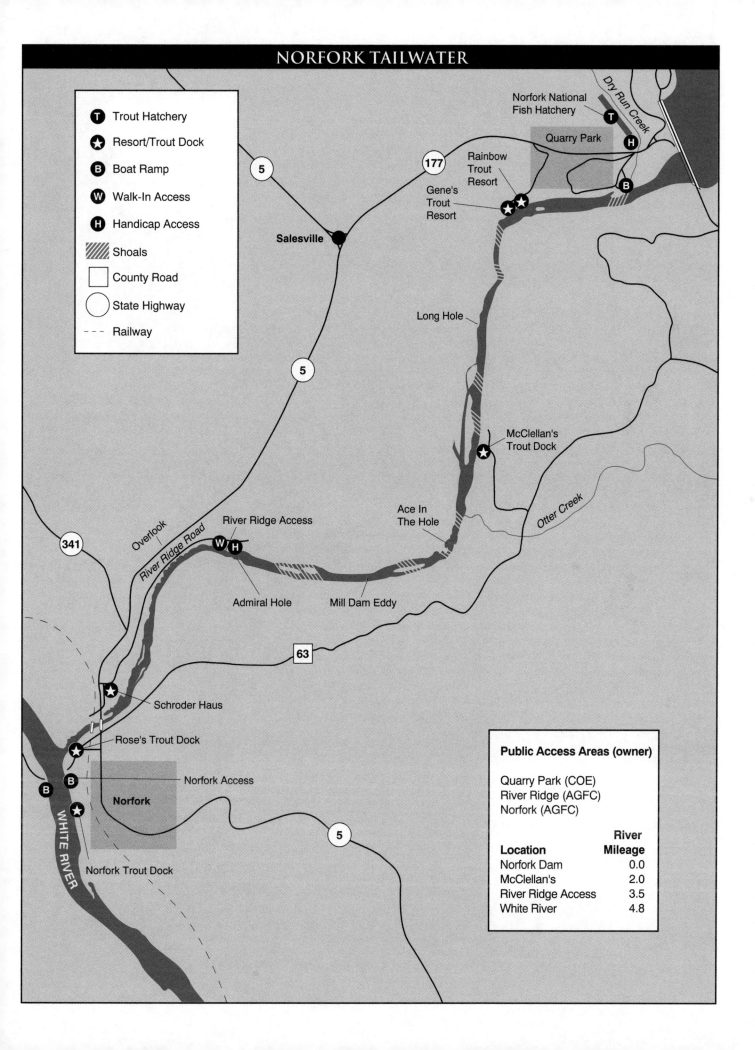

NORFORK TAILWATER

Legend:
- **T** Trout Hatchery
- **★** Resort/Trout Dock
- **B** Boat Ramp
- **W** Walk-In Access
- **H** Handicap Access
- Shoals
- County Road
- State Highway
- Railway

Labels on map:

Norfork National Fish Hatchery
Dry Run Creek
Quarry Park
Rainbow Trout Resort
Gene's Trout Resort
Salesville
177
5
Long Hole
McClellan's Trout Dock
Otter Creek
Ace In The Hole
Overlook
River Ridge Access
River Ridge Road
Admiral Hole
Mill Dam Eddy
341
63
Schroder Haus
Rose's Trout Dock
Norfork Access
Norfork
WHITE RIVER
Norfork Trout Dock

Public Access Areas (owner)

Quarry Park (COE)
River Ridge (AGFC)
Norfork (AGFC)

Location	River Mileage
Norfork Dam	0.0
McClellan's	2.0
River Ridge Access	3.5
White River	4.8

LITTLE RED RIVER

GREERS FERRY TAILWATER

Just Where Are These Big Brown Trout Coming From?

The Little Red River below Greers Ferry Dam, more than any other tailwater in the White River System, illustrates the accidental nature of these world class Ozark trout waters.

Accidental is the wrong word in the sense that at least two fly fishing clubs had every intention of turning the Greers Ferry Tailwater into a brown trout fishery. In 1975, the Arkansas Fly Fishers of Little Rock placed Vibert boxes with approximately 10,000 fertilized brown trout eggs at Cow Shoals. In 1979, the Arkansas Fly Fishers and the Mid-South Fly Fishers of Memphis stocked 5,000 fingerling brown trout from Montana in the river.

But accidental is the right word in relation to the Arkansas Game and Fish Commission's role in the development of this brown trout fishery. The AGFC has never stocked brown trout in the Greers Ferry Tailwater. And it doesn't need to start. AGFC

When brown trout begin their annual spawning run in October, Cow Shoals becomes a popular place.

Photo courtesy of Arkansas Game and Fish Commission

Howard "Rip" Collins caught this 40-pound, 4-ounce world record brown trout on May 9, 1992.

studies show the brown trout population continuing to expand on its own in the Little Red. This isn't intended as criticism of the AGFC, but only to serve as an accurate record of trout history in the Little Red.

All of these Ozark tailwaters were trout experiments that have proven to be hugely successful. And the success

of brown trout in the Greers Ferry Tailwater is at the top of the list.

When Howard "Rip" Collins' caught the 40-pound, 4-ounce world record brown trout in May 1992, it caught many observers by surprise. But the Little Red's ability to produce big browns was documented before that and has been further proven since. In 1988, Melvin Hallmark of North Little Rock, Arkansas, caught a 27-pound, 8-ounce brown trout near Kennedy Park. Dee Warren of nearby Heber Springs caught a 28-pound, 14-ounce brown on August 20, 1993, and seven days later Rick Hart of Conway, Arkansas, landed a 24.64-pounder.

If you need further proof, just go to one of the primary spawning areas, like Cow Shoals, in October and observe the size and numbers of brown trout gathered there.

However, for some people, especially many long-time anglers on the Bull Shoals and Norfork tailwaters, Collins' catch was just too big a surprise to be true. They believe the world record brown trout came, somehow, from the White River.

GREERS FERRY TAILWATER AT A GLANCE

Location: North-central Arkansas, just east of Heber Springs. The first 20 miles of the Greers Ferry Tailwater are in Cleburne County. The Little Red River joins the White River east of Searcy, about 80 river miles from Greers Ferry Dam. But at that point, both rivers are miles away from trout habitat.

**Highway Miles
to Greers Ferry Dam**

Little Rock, Ark.	65
Fort Smith, Ark.	169
Memphis, Tenn.	139
Springfield, Mo.	193
Tulsa, Okla.	299
St. Louis, Mo.	329
Shreveport, La.	287
Dallas, Texas	419

Length of trout waters: 32 miles from Greers Ferry Dam to the Highway 305 bridge, but some trout will be found several miles farther down, especially in winter months when water temperatures are low.

Dam: Construction began in 1959 and was completed in 1964 at a cost of $46.5 million. The dam, which contains two hydroelectric power generators, forms a 32,000-acre lake.

Trout stocking: First trout were stocked in 1966. The 1994 Arkansas Game and Fish Commission stocking schedule called for 214,000 nine-inch rainbows, 80,000 12-inch rainbows, and 50,000 cutthroat trout - a total of 344,000 trout. The AGFC has never stocked brown trout in the Little Red River. The naturally-reproducing brown trout population is apparently the result of stocking and egg planting efforts by fly fishing clubs in the 1970s.

Fishing regulations: (Through December 1994) Daily limit is six, including not more than two browns or cutthroats. Brown trout daily limit is two with a 16-inch minimum size limit. Cutthroat trout daily limit is two with a 16-inch minimum size limit. No size restrictions on rainbow trout. **(As of January 1995)** Daily limit is six, including not more than four browns and two cutthroats. Brown trout measuring 16 to 21 inches are protected by a slot limit and must be released. Daily limit of four can include only one longer than 21 inches; all others must be less than 16 inches. Cutthroat trout daily limit is two with a 16-inch minimum size limit. No size restrictions on rainbows.

Catch-and-Release Zones: (As of January 1995): Catch-and-release fishing only with barbless-hook artificial lures on Little Red River from Dunham Shoal to Mossy Shoal all year. From Oct. 1 through Dec 31 (brown trout spawning), catch-and-release fishing only with barbless-hook artificial lures at Cow Shoals.

Scenic Views: 1) John F. Kennedy Memorial Overlook on the east side of the Little Red River at Greers Ferry Dam; 2) Mossy Bluff Trail Overlook, located at the end of the trail on the west side of the river (enter through the Carl Garner Visitor's Center parking lot); 3) Sugar Loaf Mountain, just south of Highway 110 (a trail leads up the mountain from the parking lot).

Power Generation: For present conditions, call 501-362-5150. For a 24-hour forecast, call the Southwest Power Administration recorded message center at 918-581-6845 and press #16 for Greers Ferry.

Historical Note: John F. Kennedy dedicated Greers Ferry Dam in October 1963. It was to be the President's last public dedication ceremony. Kennedy was assassinated on Nov. 22, 1963, in Dallas.

One theory claims the fish swam down the White River, hung a hard right and swam up the Little Red River during the winter of '91-92, a voyage of 250 river miles. Another theory is that the Arkansas Game and Fish Commission electrofished the big brown from the White River and put it in the Little Red, because it's closer to Little Rock (AGFC headquarters) and to give the area more publicity when the world record fish was finally caught. Neither theory holds water.

Mark Hudy was hired as the AGFC's first fulltime trout biologist in March 1985. He left four years later for a fisheries biologist job with the National Forest Service in Virginia. Hudy can understand how some people were shocked by Collins' world record catch.

Although the Arkansas Fly Fishers claim a four-inch brown trout was caught a year after their Vibert box effort, when Hudy arrived in '85 there was no scientific documentation of wild reproducing brown trout in any of Arkansas' tailwater systems. After spending four years collecting scientific data on Arkansas' trout waters, Hudy wasn't surprised when he heard about Collins' world record catch.

"The Little Red River has got wild reproducing brown trout out the kazoo, far superior to the White River," Hudy said. "It's got better habitat at low flow conditions, which is the limiting factor in most of these systems. Not that the minimum flow is any greater, but there is aquatic vegetation throughout the whole thing.

"Inch-for-inch, the Little Red is putting out more food. There is more productive habitat on a per-area basis. There are no wasted sections."

Hudy claims the Little Red River didn't need the 16-inch minimum length limit on brown trout that was tested in the Beaver Tailwater in 1988-89 and adopted throughout the state in 1990.

"We did not recommend it on the Little Red," Hudy said. "Every year we sampled it, the population was still growing. There was no need to protect it. People on the Little Red complained because they wanted the same protec-

Moss beds, like these above Beech Island, sometimes hamper the angler but provide food and shelter for trout in the Little Red River.

tion the White River was getting."

Recent AGFC studies have documented the need for new regulations on the Little Red River's expanding brown trout population.

But, along with all this attention devoted to brown trout, it should also be remembered that rainbow trout provide the bulk of the Little Red's fish population, just like in the other White River System tailwaters.

In 1968, the Little Red River produced a new state record rainbow trout, which weighed 15 pounds, 8 ounces. In 1994, almost 300,000 rainbow trout were stocked in the Little Red.

That same habitat that Hudy mentioned as being so good for brown trout equally benefits rainbows and cutthroats (50,000 were stocked in '94). But the rainbows and cutthroats are caught from the river before they get the chance to grow like the browns do.

It is the aquatic vegetation that catches your eye when you come to the Little Red River. Moss beds are thick throughout the 32-mile section from the dam to the Highway 305 bridge, which is generally considered the length of the trout waters. None of the other four tailwaters in the White River System has anywhere near the aquatic vegetation of the Little Red.

The moss beds also cause some cussing; it's difficult to drag a lure through them. You'll spend time removing moss from your lures and line. Although some people think the moss beds are getting too thick, it's

wise to keep in mind what Hudy said about productive habitat.

The other feature you'll notice about the Little Red River is the number of private docks along the banks. In the most intensely developed areas, there will be dock-after-dock, separated by as little as 50 feet.

In terms of overall appearance - stream width, water color, aquatic vegetation - the Little Red is similar to the Norfork Tailwater. When you see the areas crowded with private docks, however, you are reminded of the middle section of Lake Taneycomo.

One of the delights of floating down an Ozark stream is the constant change of scenery. About the time you grow tired of looking at boat docks on the Little Red, you'll come to an area with no development in sight, and you'll quickly forget about civilization around the bend upstream.

The Little Red River offers one stretch of scenery unmatched in the Ozarks. Below Big Creek, you'll find the rare combination of cypress trees and trout water. By this point, the Little Red River has moved out of the Ozark foothills and into the Delta.

When I first saw these cypress trees, I couldn't take my eyes off them. So I happened to see the wild turkey fly almost directly over the boat Jerry Rickman and I were fishing from.

Then I felt a tug on my line and reeled in a half-pound rainbow trout. Cypress trees, a wild turkey, a rainbow trout - all at one moment on a float down the Little Red River.

Heber Springs Showing Signs Of Thriving Again

Sugar Loaf was the name of the original Cleburne County seat. In the late 1800s and early 1900s the town's natural springs were touted for their healing powers and Sugar Loaf Springs became known as a health resort, much like another Arkansas Ozarks town, Eureka Springs, only on a smaller scale.

The sulfur springs were proclaimed as a cure for "dyspepsia, headache, biliousness and hundreds of other ailments."

In 1910, the town changed its name to Heber Springs, in honor of Dr. Heber Jones and the springs. Jones was the youngest son of John T. Jones, who had owned the land where the seven springs and Spring Park are located.

Heber Springs' reputation as a resort town grew to include at least 10 major hotels by 1913, and 20 years later doctors were still recommending the spring water as a cure for arthritis, rheumatism and stomach ailments. The resort atmosphere helped swell the population of Cleburne County to 11,903 in 1910. But 60 years later, during Greers Ferry Dam's first phase of construction, the county population was listed at only 10,349.

After the resort town boom subsided, Cleburne County suffered through the first half of the 20th century, just as most of the Ozarks did. But Greers Ferry Dam put Heber Springs and Cleburne County on the map again. The county's population grew 63 percent over the next decade, to 16,909, and it continues to expand.

When Howard "Rip" Collins caught a 40-pound, 4-ounce world record brown trout from the nearby Little Red River in 1992, Heber Springs went on the national map as a trout fishing destination, too.

The Tale Of The World Record Brown Trout

Big fish helped Collins renew strong feelings for the Little Red River

Howard "Rip" Collins had just about lost interest in the Little Red River. On Saturday, May 9, 1992, Collins hadn't planned to fish. He was working on an outboard motor, trying to get it running right, so his son could use it that weekend.

When he thought he had everything in order, he asked his neighbor, Van Cooper, to take a boat ride with him. They put a couple of spinning rigs in the boat; no use being on the Little Red River and not wetting a hook.

Cooper quickly established bragging rights, as he caught four average-size rainbow trout to Collins' none. Collins remembered a tip from fly fishing expert Lefty Kreh about using a lure that is the same color as the bottom and structure in the water. So Collins switched from a white marabou jig to an olive green marabou jig, 1/32 of an ounce.

Collins was fishing a bank about a mile upstream from Swinging Bridge Boat Dock. He placed his third cast with the olive jig near a large, half-submerged log. He was just downstream from an old beaver hut, where Collins had always caught some good fish.

The fish struck and Collins set the hook. "I honestly thought when I set the hook that I had hooked a log, because I'd dropped that jig right by a beautiful log," Collins said.

Then Collins saw the brown trout's tail. "It looked like Shamu the whale," he said.

Collins was fishing with 4-pound-test line on a 4 1/2 foot Browning rod and a Shimano Mark I reel. Although an accomplished fly fisherman, ultralight spinning gear was Collins' first love. Early in his Army career, Collins was stationed in France near Verdun. He noticed a French angler using a tiny, open-faced reel, called an Alcedo Micron, with 2-pound-test line. As much as he could over the next six months, Collins spent time with his

Rip Collins usually has a fly rod in hand when he goes trout fishing on the Little Red, but on May 9, 1992, he took his spinning gear along.

new French friend and learned how to catch trout on the ultralight gear attached to a Mepps spinner or a fly and a plastic bubble.

"That's when I got hooked on trout fishing," Collins said.

Collins retired from the Army as a lieutenant colonel in 1970. When he came back to the U.S., he went back to bass fishing, as he'd done as a boy growing up in southern Indiana.

"But I don't think in my lifetime I've ever used anything over 6-pound-test," Collins said. "I've caught several bass over 10 pounds - 11 pounds, 14

ounces is my biggest. My dad used heavy spinning tackle, 12- to 15-pound test line. He'd tell me that I was sure losing a lot of big fish on that light tackle.

"I like to play a fish. My dad would say, 'Son, the time to play a fish is when it's in the bottom of the boat.'"

Collins would need all his experience in playing fish, plus a good bow-mounted trolling motor on his 14-foot flatbottom johnboat to land the big one this day on the Little Red River. After it was hooked, the fish started upstream. It went around one of the moss beds, which are so common in the Little Red. Collins followed.

"I slacked up and got the boat around the moss bed," Collins said.

Then the fish headed upstream again.

"I backed the drag system off two clicks, so the fish was working against a slack spool," Collins said. "The reel was just singing."

In his experience with ultralight tackle, Collins had learned the best way to adjust a reel's drag system. Before he got to the river, he would thread the line through the guides and then tie it to an immovable object. By breaking the line, backing off the drag system a click or two, then retying and trying to break the line again, you can find the optimum drag setting. This method allows for the friction of the line rubbing against the rod guides, while simply pulling on your line near the reel doesn't allow you to factor this in.

Collins had set his drag system that way on May 9, but he changed during the course of the fight.

"Never in my lifetime have I changed the drag when I was fishing," Collins said. "But if I had left that drag setting the way it was, I would never have landed the fish."

The big brown trout circled moss beds five times, and each time Collins was able to keep up and free his line, thanks to the trolling motor.

"The fish worked upstream the whole time," Collins said. "I'd guess this lasted for about 15 to 18 minutes."

Then came a crucial point. Collins and Cooper had no landing net in the boat. They waved down some other anglers, who had only a small trout landing net. Another boat came by and these men had a full-size net on board. After a miss on the first pass, Cooper got the fish's head in the net, but found he couldn't lift it up. It took both men to pull the big brown trout into the boat.

Collins fishing day was over. He tied the fish to his dock with a section of 3/16ths-inch nylon cord, then spent most of Saturday night on the dock, keeping watch.

On Sunday, Mother's Day, he built a wire cage to put the fish in. He was determined to keep the fish alive, and it seemed to be in good shape.

At this point, Collins still didn't know he had a record fish. He had measured its length at 40 1/4 inches, which was about an inch longer than the 38-pound, 9-ounce brown trout Mike "Huey" Manley caught in the North Fork River in 1988.

The trout Manley caught was a male, so Collins thought the female brown trout he'd landed might be a new record. But most guesses were that the fish weighed about 35 pounds.

That Sunday, word spread across the state about Collins' big fish. But because of his insistence on keeping it alive, the brown trout still hadn't been weighed 24 hours after it was caught. Taking the fish to a place with a certified scale would surely mean its death.

By Monday, arrangements were in place for an U.S. Fish and Wildlife Service hatchery truck to pick up the fish and take it to the Heber Springs Post Office. The postmaster there said he didn't mind a little water on his equipment.

The fish was quickly taken from the truck, brought into the post office, weighed and returned to the aerated tank on the truck.

It's official weight was 40 pounds, 4 ounces. That broke Manley's world record of 38-9, which was recognized by the National Fresh Water Fishing Hall of Fame.

The International Game Fish Association didn't acknowledge Manley's record because it was caught on a treble hook with bait, so Collins' fish easily topped the IGFA world mark of 37 lbs., 7 oz., set by Kurt Stenlund from Lake Storsjon, Lappland, Sweden, October 16, 1991.

Collins got the fish back to its wire cage on the Little Red River in good condition. He hoped the new world record brown trout could be taken to an aquarium somewhere, where it could be displayed for many to see.

But Collins agreed to a 30-minute photo session that afternoon. The stress created by repeatedly pulling the fish out of the water killed it, Collins believes. The fish never revived completely after the photo shoot. Collins still gets teary-eyed when he recalls that day.

"Due to my own stupidity and inexperience, I killed her," Collins said.

But this story has a happy ending. Catching that record fish restored Collins' interest in the river. He was the driving force in organizing a non-profit group, named "Friends of the Little Red River," dedicated to preserving and enhancing the Little Red as a premier trophy trout stream.

In looking back, Collins thinks the record trout hit his jig for a reason on that day in May.

"I was really surprised to catch it," Collins said. "I had no idea there was one in there that big. For a couple of days afterwards, I wondered why I caught the fish.

"I was not the best fisherman on the river by any means. It's darn near impossible to catch a fish that big on 4-pound line. I've lost a lot of fish that broke off in a moss bed or whatever. The 15- to 18-minute fight, the fact that we missed it with the net the first time, everything looked to be luck. Everybody said, 'You're the luckiest guy in the world.'

"I think God intended for me to catch that fish."

Collins pictures it this way. His father, who died at the age of 92, built a reputation in Indiana and Kentucky as one of the best bass fishermen around. While sitting in heaven, watching over his son, Howard, the old man got concerned and went to God with his troubles.

"God, I'm really concerned about my youngest son," Debron Collins said. "He has lost interest in fishing."

"What do you want me to do?" God replied.

"Well, why don't we put him on that big mother brown in the Little Red River," Debron said.

That's the way Collins likes to think it happened, anyway. However it happened, Howard "Rip" Collins and, possibly, the Little Red River will be forever grateful.

Friends Of The Little Red River Growing

Collins, other concerned anglers find enthusiasm for catch-and-release

Since he and his wife, Nancy, moved to the banks of the Little Red River in 1984, Howard "Rip" Collins has put a boat load of energy into the river. First, it was strictly as a fisherman.

"I had a simple schedule," Collins said. "I fished once in the morning and once in the afternoon. I broke only for lunch and a 30-minute nap."

Collins became concerned about the river and a perceived lack of attention it got from the Arkansas Game and Fish Commission. He says he butted heads with AGFC officials and got no results. That was part of the reason he had lost interest in the Little Red River, until catching a world record brown trout renewed that interest.

"I am known, affectionately, I hope, as that cantankerous old fart on the Little Red River," Collins said with a smile. "I am a totally obnoxious S.O.B., but I've been that way for so many years, it's too late to change."

Collins, however, has changed his tactics in fighting for the river. He is looking for strength in numbers. Friends of the Little Red River was formed in October 1993. Its mission is to maintain and enhance the Little Red River as a premier trophy trout stream.

With an initial goal of 1,000 members, Friends of the Little Red River had signed up 500 members by early 1994 and upped its goal to 5,000 members.

"A thousand was going to be too easy," said Collins.

One step toward maintaining and enhancing the river is to encourage the release of trophy fish. You've heard of CPR - cardio-pulmonary resuscitation; Friends of the Little Red River emphasizes LTR - live trophy release.

For anyone who wants to keep a fish to be mounted, Friends of the Little Red River will pay the cost difference between a skin mount and a fiberglass mount to any angler releasing a trout 21 inches or longer.

Collins put together a Live Trophy Release kit that is available free at most area tackle stores and boat docks. It includes an application blank, with instructions on how to measure trout and identify species and sex, a 60-inch water-resistant measuring tape, and a pencil.

By taking one length and two girth measurements (a photo helps, also), an angler can release any trophy-size fish and still get a fiberglass reproduction of it to hang on the wall.

Collins, by the way, knows something about making reproductions of

> ## "Current taxidermy technology does not require that a fish be killed in order to have 'bragging rights' on the catch."

trout. He's had five fiberglass reproductions made of his 40-pound, 4-ounce world record brown trout, and Collins carved a wooden reproduction of a 30-inch male brown trout he landed on a fly rod and released back into the Little Red in October 1990.

If you don't want a reproduction, you can fill out the application blank and receive an embroidered patch indicating the length and species of the released trout. By October 1994, FLLR had received 40 Live Trophy Release applications. Seven requested fiberglass replicas.

The released fish included browns and rainbows from 21 inches to 31 inches. A 29-inch brown trout reported on a Live Trophy Release application by Collins was certified as the National Fresh Water Fishing Hall of Fame catch-and-release world record on a fly rod and 6-pound tippet.

"We feel that little can be done to prevent large fish from being harvested for food," Collins said. "We wouldn't even consider an objection if food is the reason for harvest.

But we also feel that many of these 'trophies' are being taken just for that reason - a trophy to be hung on the wall. Current taxidermy technology does not require that a fish be killed in order to have 'bragging rights' on the catch."

Other points of emphasis for the Friends of the Little Red River include:
■ cooperation with the Arkansas Game and Fish Commission to evaluate the prospect of slot limits, artificial only and/or catch-and-release only areas;
■ education on improving water quality and reduction of trash on the river;
■ encouraging all other conservation measures that will assist in accomplishing the goal of preserving and enhancing the Little Red River as a premier trophy trout stream.

The initial seven-member Friends of the Little Red River board of directors included: chairman Bob Brown, a guide on the river and the owner of Brown Spots Recording in Little Rock; Carol Walker, executive director of the Heber Springs Chamber of Commerce; Billy Lindsey, owner of Lindsey's Rainbow Resort and a member of the Arkansas Parks and Tourism Commission; Abe Vogel, owner of Lobo Landing Resort; George Heine, owner of Swinging Bridge Resort; Carl Garner, resident engineer at the Greers Ferry Lake Corps of Engineers office; and Wendel Stacey, sportscaster for KARK-TV in Little Rock.

Friends of the Little Red River is a non-profit organization. Membership is $5 per year. For more information, write: Friends of the Little Red River, P.O. Box 1003, Heber Springs, AR 72543.

Portrait Of The Artist As A Fly Fisherman

Duane Hada has combined a passion for painting with the outdoors

As he approached the Little Red River's Libby Shoal, Duane Hada could see a man fishing from one of the rock out-croppings there. A can of corn was beside the fisherman, who had caught a few small rainbow trout. But he just couldn't coax the big rainbow trout in the pool to hit a piece of corn.

"I watched for awhile," Hada recalled. "The big trout was ignoring the corn, but he was cruising slowly through the moss picking off sowbugs."

When Hada asked the man for permission to drift a sowbug imitation through that pool, the man said, "Go ahead, but what's a sowbug?"

A few minutes later, Hada hooked and landed a four-pound rainbow trout on a size 16 sowbug. Both he

and the other angler had learned something about the Little Red River.

"It was the first big trout I'd caught on the Little Red," Hada said. "It showed me natural foods really are preferred. More and more after that, anytime I could get some free time, I'd come to the Little Red.

"That's when I really started trying to tie some good imitations, based on the samples I would collect from the river."

Hada was then a student at the University of Central Arkansas, working on a bachelor's degree in art. He had grown up in northwest Arkansas and eastern Oklahoma, fishing primarily for smallmouth bass.

The fly fishing bug had already bitten him. While at UCA, Hada roomed with a fly fisherman from Wyoming.

That was in 1981. Still today, most of Duane Hada's time continues to be spent on art, trout and fly fishing.

"That brought it all together for me," Hada said. "It started a love affair."

Hada is one of the better known fly fishermen in the Ozarks. In 1987, his painting of a rainbow trout was chosen for Arkansas' trout stamp. The Arkansas Game and Fish Commission has used Hada's artwork in many of its publications, and he sells numerous paintings and drawings to private collectors.

As a Federation of Fly Fishers-certified instructor at The Woodsman, an outdoors store in Fort Smith, Arkansas, Hada shares his knowledge with all levels of anglers on a daily basis. That is, when he's not guiding.

Duane Hada's interest in trout fishing and the Little Red River began when he was an art major in college.

A Little Red River brown trout swims after a sowbug that it has loosened from a moss bed, as illustrated by Duane Hada.

Hada guides customers on most of the Ozarks' trout and smallmouth bass waters, and he usually puts together an annual saltwater trip to a more exotic location, like Christmas Island.

Hada's wife, Marlene, enjoys fly fishing, too. When they both worked as school teachers in Mena, Arkansas, spring break would consist of an Ozark trout trip - first to the Beaver Tailwater, then Lake Taneycomo, the North Fork River in Missouri, the White River and North Fork in Arkansas, then back closer to home at the Little Missouri River.

But, because of those college years and because The Woodsman tried a two-year experiment with a fly fishing shop that Hada managed in Heber Springs, the Little Red River holds a special place in Hada's heart.

He has strong feelings about the well being of trout in the Little Red. His guide trips are all catch-and-release. He carries a waterproof camera and tape measure, and he photographs the catch for his clients. Many of Hada's clients have had fiberglass fish mounts made from those photos. Hada likes to relate the story of a brown trout with an easily identifiable scar on its back that his clients caught and released six times over a two-year period. The last time caught, the fish measured 26 inches long.

Hada remembers a time when fishing Cow Shoals was almost like a wilderness experience instead of the carnival atmosphere found on fall weekends there now.

And he also remembers a time when he'd guarantee at least one 20-inch rainbow trout from the Little Red River, no matter what time of year you fished it.

"My best rainbow from the Little Red weighed 6 pounds, 4 ounces," Hada said. "I've caught a lot of three-to four-pounders. But I don't dare make that guarantee of a 20-incher anymore.

"The number of people fishing for trout in Arkansas has steadily increased. That increase parallels with the decline in the big rainbows here."

Hada has also witnessed the phenomenal growth of the Little Red's brown trout fishery. He doesn't want to see it end up like the rainbows. So Hada is quick to speak out about protecting the resource.

Quickness, in fact, shows up often around Hada. Once he gets his waders on, there is a quickness in his step that most anglers can't match. He can spot fish before you've even had time to look.

Hada's also quick at the easel. He likes the fast-drying mediums of water colors and acrylics.

"I paint with a blow dryer in one hand and a brush in the other," Hada said. "It seldom takes me more than four or five hours to do a painting from start to finish.

"I can't start a painting, stop and come back to it. It becomes work. I lose the artistic energy. I like to see it build."

For Hada, a painting is like a fishing trip. Putting down the paint brush from a half-blank canvas would be like laying down his fly rod in the midst of a mayfly hatch. For Duane Hada, that just won't do.

How To Catch A Great Big Trout On A Tiny Little Fly

If you want to test an angler's nerves, put a fly rod in his hands and let him drift a size 16 sowbug on 6X tippet in front of a 10-pound brown trout. Most don't pass the test the first time, according to Duane Hada.

There's an old Ozark expression that describes the typical reaction - tree-limbing. You set the hook with enough force to fling the fish up in the tree limbs.

"Most people get so pumped up, they snap the line," Hada said. "They are shaking by the time the fish takes the fly."

It's the trout fishing equivalent of "buck fever."

"One guy had his knees bent, and he came up and set the hook like he was tournament bass fishing," said Hada, who laughed and added, "I keep looking for lighter and lighter rod tips."

Hada has landed brown trout up to 17 pounds on the Little Red River. But, on the surface, his method for going after them doesn't seem to add up. For one, it flies in the face of the old adage about using a big lure for a big fish.

Even Hada admits surprise about some of the discoveries concerning sowbugs and brown trout on the Little Red River. But a friend of Hada's examined the stomach contents of Rip Collins' world record 40-pound brown trout and found it to hold 80 percent sowbugs.

Because there are few sculpins and other baitfish in the upper stretches of the Little Red, everyone expected at least one nine-inch stocker-size rainbow trout to be in the big fish's belly. But none was found.

"Any time I see someone cleaning fish on the river, I try to check stomach samples," Hada said. "I've done hundreds, if not thousands. Sowbugs make up the bulk of discernible food items."

The Little Red River's moss beds

Photo courtesy of Duane Hada

Duane Hada enticed this 29-inch Little Red River brown trout with a size 16 sowbug imitation. Sowbugs are the most abundant trout food in the river.

hold millions of sowbugs. Hada believes all the trout here, not just the browns, have keyed in on this food source. But it is the browns that are growing to world record size, so they have to be slurping sowbugs almost constantly.

Hada knows that big browns do eat smaller trout; he's seen them chasing and catching little rainbows. But he thinks the big browns know they'll expend little energy to tap into this sowbug gravy train.

Hada equates a big brown trout feeding on sowbugs with a 200-pound man, who, although full from a big dinner, will keep reaching into a bowl of M&M candies if the bowl is placed near him.

"Near" is a key word in this sowbug method. Hada stalks big brown trout just like a hunter does deer. He avoids wading, if at all possible, pre-

ferring to walk the banks, watching for trout and observing their paths.

"If big fish aren't spooked, they'll come out of their deep holes and cruise," Hada said. "They'll work a pattern, patrolling about a 50-foot stretch. Once you figure out what the pattern is, then you know where to cast."

Again, it is crucial to keep from spooking the fish. Hada wears dark clothing so he'll blend into the woods and rocks behind him. Polarized glasses are a must, so you can see the fish before it sees you. Once you've got the fish's pattern down, you can position yourself for a cast.

"You don't want to cast on top of the fish," Hada said. "Lead it at least three to five feet. The sowbug better be right in the path of the fish, almost striking his nose. The fish knows there is no need to work for this food. There will be plenty of other sowbugs coming by."

To make up for any Mack Truck tendencies in your hands, Hada recommends a 9-foot, 4-weight rod with a soft, cushioning tip. A No. 14 or No. 16 sowbug is usually tied to a 9-foot 5X leader, plus another three to four feet of 6X tippet. Hada doesn't use a strike indicator when fishing this method.

"Most of the time, you'll know he's seen the sowbug as soon as it settles in the water," Hada said. "It's usually a one-shot situation. You either make it, or you don't. That's what really gets people heated up."

A quick, but soft strike is necessary. The fish can quickly spit out the sowbug imitation.

"It doesn't take much pressure," Hada said. "Just a quick flick of the rod tip. You're not trying to cross his eyes.

"After you've hooked the fish, the first 30 seconds are the most crucial. He's a bull right out of the pen."

If you hook a big rainbow, it's likely to jump. You should lower your rod tip to a jumping fish, so it won't land on a tight line.

But you also want to keep a brown or a rainbow near the surface and keep its head up, so it can't wrap around the base of a moss bed or some other structure.

Once that critical period is over, an experienced angler has the upper hand, even on 6X tippet, according to Hada.

"Most people are surprised how quickly I can bring in a big fish," Hada said. "Once under control, I can take a big fish on 6X tippet and literally roll him over.

"If you totally change his direction, you've probably knocked 10 minutes off the battle. It's like a tug-of-war; use the rod tip as a shock absorber. When he's pulling, don't pull. But don't let the fish rest."

It's easy to see why this method of sight-fishing gives Hada more pleasure than any other type of fly fishing.

"To me, that's a real exciting challenge, going one-on-one like that," Hada said.

Hada's Tips For Little Red River Include Sowbugs, And Much More

As previously noted, if Duane Hada has to pick one fly pattern to fish the Little Red River, it will be a sowbug. But he will never be caught with just sowbugs in his fly box.

"Any good fisherman has to stay flexible," Hada said. "You can't lock into one technique. That's what a lot of people do, lock into a technique because of previous success. You've got to enter the realm of what's going on that particular day."

With that in the mind, Hada offers the following tips that may help you pick up on what's happening at the Little Red River, on different days and in different areas:

Sowbug

Sowbugs revisited: Before leaving the subject of sowbugs, Hada has a couple more tips on fishing them.

Sowbug colors can vary from stream to stream, and they may be different from one point to another in the same stream. Sowbugs have an almost clear exoskeleton, so the color of the food they eat gives them their coloration.

Generally, sowbugs in the Little Red River have a brownish, mottled coloring. Hada equates it with oak tree bark.

When tying his sowbug imitations, Hada uses an Antron blend dubbing. It won't change colors when wet, and it gives the sowbug a more translucent look. He ribs the sowbug with brown nylon thread to make the segmentation more distinct.

Probably because of nutrients from the Greers Ferry National Fish Hatchery, the area near the hatchery outlet pipe in JFK Park has one of the densest populations of sowbugs in the Little Red River. One study document-ed 500 sowbugs per square foot in the river there. So, naturally, a sowbug is a good choice.

Woolly Bugger

Woolly Buggers, of course: JFK Park and Winkley Shoal are excellent places for a beginning fly fisher to take a small Woolly Bugger (#10 or #12) and catch a bunch of rainbow trout, according to Hada. And, as you may have already noticed, the Woolly Bugger is a good pattern on any of these Ozark tailwaters.

Translucence and tail movement are the two areas Hada focuses on when tying Woolly Buggers. He likes tinsel chenille in the body for translucence and sparkle. He prefers a thin body and soft saddle hackle, so the Woolly Bugger won't spin. He doesn't like tinsel in the tail because of its tendency to inhibit movement. Black or olive are the best colors.

"The main thing with a Woolly Bugger or any type of jig is the minnow silhouette and the tail movement," Hada said. "I like a long tail, at least the same length as the body. I think you get more strikes with it, even if you do get some short strikes."

Stripping Woolly Buggers through calm pools is an effective fishing method, especially for small- to average-size rainbow trout.

Midge can make a difference: "The midge seems to fill a niche on these tailwaters," Hada said. "At some point, every fly fisher will encounter a time when the fish are so totally focused on a midge, nothing else will do. This is the fly that saves the day for me a lot of times."

Hada ties the fly in sizes 20 to 24. He prefers a Tiemco curved shank hook because of its strength and wider gap. Those qualities are important because big fish will hit these tiny flies. Hada has landed Little Red River rainbows up to six pounds on a No. 20 midge.

For color imitation, Hada likes grayish-olive with black ribbing. He ties a midge with zelon fibers sticking out the tail and the head. He will fish this pattern sometimes as a deep nymph, or he'll grease the leader and fish it in the film.

Midge hatches are an almost daily occurrence on the Little Red, especially near the dam. A Griffith's Gnat on 7X tippet is also a good choice here.

Egg

Eggs anyone? An egg pattern is hard to beat during the brown trout spawning run. It will catch both browns and rainbows. An egg pattern imitates a natural food source that trout regularly see during the spawning months.

"Some of the biggest rainbows I catch every year come from the deep runs below spawning brown trout," Hada said. "They eagerly take the eggs."

Hada prefers a small tangerine or natural-colored imitation of a brown trout egg. Most of the commercially-tied eggs are too big. Split shot is added to the tippet to get it the egg near the bottom, and Hada relies on a strike indicator.

"I think this is most effective when sight-fished," Hada said. "A good, accurate presentation with a controlled dead-drift is what you are trying to get."

Nymphs, nymphs, nymphs: The sowbug isn't the only nymph pattern you should carry on the Little Red River.

"Most fly boxes ought to have a good number of basic nymphs," Hada said.

For the Little Red River, the basic nymph patterns include: Whitlock Squirrel, Pheasant Tail, March Brown, Blue Wing Olive, Gold-Ribbed Hare's

Ear and a variety of soft hackles. Hada recommends having the Hare's Ear in sizes 10 to 16 in a range of colors, including olive, brown and natural.

"Make some beadhead and some flashback style," Hada said. "I like them tied a little more on the sparse side. I think a lot of people tie nymphs way too beefy."

In addition to standard riffle fishing techniques, Hada likes to float the river in his canoe and sight cast to cruising fish or blind cast into openings around moss beds with a strike indicator.

Hada also suggests a drift-fishing technique. For example, at the very end of Mossy Shoal the water drops into a deep pool with a strong current running through it. Hada takes advantage of that water by putting a Whitlock Squirrel nymph under a strike indicator and drifting it deep along the edge of the current seam.

Hada often uses a strike indicator, usually in the form of brightly-colored yarn because of its sensitivity. Learning to "read" the indicator is important.

Gold-Ribbed Hare's Ear

"Strikes may vary from almost indiscernible pauses in the indicator to violent strikes that move the indicator several feet across the water," Hada said. "The experienced nymph angler learns how to recognize the slightest hesitation and react appropriately."

Dry flies: The Blue Wing Olive represents probably the most consistent mayfly hatch on the Little Red River, according to Hada. He prefers sizes 18 and 20. An Elk Hair Caddis standard adult pattern can be important, especially from April to mid-May. It's common to float the river then and find bushes full of swarming adult caddisflies.

If you see consistent, splashy rises, you may entice more strikes by skit-

Elk Hair Caddis

tering an Elk Hair Caddis across the surface.

"Let the fly make a wake," Hada said. "A lot of times trout will leap and pin it down. It's not a slurp, and it's exciting fishing."

Don't forget the worms: All of the Ozarks tailwaters have aquatic worms that constitute an important food source for trout. And, let's face it, a live worm in the form of a red wiggler or nightcrawler is THE most commonly-used and consistently-producing trout bait in the Ozarks.

A fly fisher can also take advantage of that feeding pattern, and, in fact, do a better job of imitating some of the natural worms in the stream. A San Juan Worm is the best pattern for this. Hada carries a variety of colors ranging from natural to brilliant maroon.

"A lot of times in murky water the fluorescent colors are excellent," Hada said.

He ties them 1 to 1 1/2 inches long.

Hada has another pattern he calls an annelid. (The word "annelid" is derived from the Latin word "anellus," meaning "little ring." The annelid family includes elongated, segmented invertebrates like earthworms, various marine worms and leeches.) He ties it to imitate a tiny worm, about one-inch long, with a translucent, red-tinted body.

"They are all over this river wherever you find a mud bottom," Hada said.

San Juan Worm

Understanding Sowbugs Important For Ozark Anglers

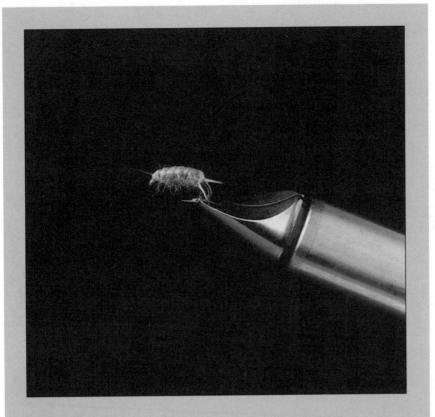

Sowbug

Hook: Tiemco 2457, sizes 14-18
Thread: 8/0, light gray or tan
Body: Gray Antron, plus squirrel or rabbit mix
Tail: Two gray goose biots
Shellback: Freezer bag strip or smoke-colored Larva Lace tubing
Rib: Thin, dark monofilament

Sowbug colors can vary from stream to stream, and they may be different from one point to another in the same stream. Sowbugs have an almost clear exoskeleton, so the color of the food they eat gives them their coloration. Generally, sowbugs in the Little Red River have a brownish, mottled coloring. Duane Hada equates it with oak tree bark.

When tying his sowbug imitations, Hada uses a dubbing blend of gray Antron yarn and either squirrel or rabbit fur. The Antron won't change colors when wet, and it gives the sowbug a more translucent look. He ribs the sowbug with thin brown monofilament to make the segmentation distinct.

Hada prefers the Tiemco 2457 hook because of its weight and wide gap. If he had to tie only one size sowbug for Ozark tailwaters, it would be a No. 16. Hada ties both weighted and unweighted sowbugs. The weighted versions have six turns of .010 lead wire. Before the shellback is brought forward, Hada flattens the body of the sowbug with a pair of hemostats.

"The keys to tying a good sowbug imitation are a flattened silhouette and a translucent body," Hada said. Two common faults, according to Hada, are using muskrat fur dubbing, which turns dark when wet, and making the goose biot imitation antennas much too long.

Even if you've never seen a sowbug, you've probably seen its terrestrial relative in the isopoda order of crustacea, the pill bug or "roly-poly," so you've got a good idea of what a sowbug looks like.

Sowbugs are an important trout food source in all these Ozark tailwaters, but, because of the lack of sculpins and crawfish, sowbugs are more important in the Little Red River than the White or North Fork. The more you know about sowbugs, the better angler you'll be, especially on the Little Red.

Generally, sowbugs inhabit shallow unpolluted water. They are much more common in springs, streams and subterranean water than in ponds or lakes.

Most sowbugs found in the Ozarks are about a quarter-inch long. Coloration can vary from black to gray to brown, depending on characteristics of the particular stream sites.

Sowbugs are scavengers. They eat both dead and injured aquatic animals and dead and living aquatic vegetation.

Although sowbugs can be seen drifting in the water, they can't swim. They have seven pairs of legs, and their movement is restricted to slow crawling. For this reason, sowbugs at times are found in huge concentrations, mainly as a result of stream flow.

Where the current is swift, sowbugs will be swept from the stream bottom and deposited where the current slows downstream.

One of the main characteristics of the sowbug is its flattened shape. It's easy to tell the difference between a sowbug and scud because of this difference in shape.

The location of the legs adds to this disparity, as a sowbug's legs stick straight out from its sides, while a scud's legs hang down, underneath its body.

Jack Jones usually goes after trout with ultralight spinning gear, 4-pound-test line and a small marabou jig.

Panama Jack Would Rather Fish A Jig

Pockets in moss beds provide perfect place to put bug-like lure

They call him "Panama Jack" and he is one of the most recognizable anglers on the Little Red River. Jack Jones never gets in his boat without first grabbing the wide-brimmed white straw hat and fingerless white gloves from his tackle locker at Lindsey's Rainbow Resort boat dock.

Jack couldn't care less if people recognize him or not. The hat and the gloves are to shield his face and hands from the sun and any more bouts with skin cancer.

"I had seven skin cancers cut off me (in 1993)," Jones said. "I can't afford to get out in the sun too much anymore. I also use a lot of sunscreen."

Staying indoors is out of the question. Jones was in the restaurant business in Memphis for almost 30 years. He's already logged more time indoors than he cares to admit. Jack and his wife retired and bought a place near Greers Ferry Lake and the Little Red River in 1979.

When the power generators aren't running at Greers Ferry Dam, you'll find Jones fishing a jig in the Little Red River, usually between Lindsey's and the dam. The moss beds are thick here. Jones likes to attach a bobber about three feet above a 1/64th-ounce jig on 4-pound-test line and work the holes in the moss beds.

"The idea is to use as small a jig as you can, so it will fall slower," Jones said. "Fish like anything falling."

Jones uses only two jig colors - black and brown.

"Ninety-percent of a trout's diet is insects," Jones said. "How many insects do you see that are any colors other than black or brown?"

Jones "sweetens" the jig by sliding a waxworm on the hook. He makes sure the point and barb of the hook are covered completely by the waxworm. In addition to adding scent to the jig, Jones thinks the waxworm helps in the visual aspect of the presentation also.

"What I've done in essence is make a bug - with the head, the hackle and the body," Jones said.

Jones has hunted and fished all his life - for just about every species of game and fish. He didn't start guiding until 1984. Jones says he got conned into his first guiding trip by an outfitter, who had a big company booked for a weekend trip and needed all the guides he could find.

"The guys I was with had this big ol' cooler of beer," Jones said. "All I did on that first guide trip was pass out beer to people wearing blue and white hats. We never went fishing."

But Jones did start guiding on a regular basis and he says he likes the challenge of catching fish on demand. Like most guides, he has accumulated a group of regular customers. Jones knows various methods of trout fishing that will produce under various water conditions, so his fishing time isn't limited by the power generation schedule at the dam. But many of his regulars want to go jig fishing or they don't want to go fishing at all.

"And I just enjoy fishing this way," Jones said. "It gives you something to do and you aren't anchored up. You are mobile and you can cover a lot of territory."

Jones prefers a 6 1/2-foot rod with a spinning reel. The longer rod is important for both casting distance and ease of casting a jig and bobber

separated by three to four feet of monofilament. Jones will move into a spot, cast the jig to moss pockets all the way around the boat, then move a short distance to new water.

Big trout tend to hang out in the moss beds, which provide both cover and an abundance of food in the form of sowbugs. As Rip Collins proved with his world record brown trout, casting a small jig doesn't mean you're going to catch a small fish.

"I think nine out of 10 times you'll catch bigger fish using a jig," Jones said.

But you won't catch big trout on a consistent basis like you did a few years ago on the Little Red River.

"That's been the vast change, the availability of big fish," Jones said. "A whole generation of fish is gone. People are mounting 3 1/2-pound trout now."

Again, as Collins' record shows, there are still some huge trout in the river, especially brown trout. It's the rainbows that get worked over heavily. They remain vulnerable, no matter what the water conditions.

"Once they start running water, you can't fish this way," Jones said of his jigging method. "The fish go into a different mode."

When power generation at the dam begins, Jones switches to a Carolina rig baited with salmon eggs for catching rainbow trout. If he's after browns, Jones prefers artificial lures like Rapalas or Shad Raps or Rogues with some orange coloring on them.

"I used to paint Rapalas orange," Jones said. "One guy I fish with takes Little Cleos and paints one side of them orange."

Another good all-around lure Jones likes is the Rebel Crawfish. He takes the front treble hook off and adds a split shot to his line, about one foot in front of the lure.

"You fish it like you would a Countdown Rapala, with a slow retrieve," Jones said. "It's the same old principle of letting something fall. There are so many ways of catching trout. It's all a matter of how you like to fish."

And, when water conditions allow, Jones would rather fish jigs.

By using a paddle to scull his johnboat, Jones keeps moving until he finds a place where trout are congregated.

Lindsey's Rainbow Resort - First Dock On The Little Red

When you visit the Little Red River now, evidence of good trout fishing is everywhere. There are six major commercial docks. All of them have some kind of "brag board" featuring pictures or lists of big trout. And there is usually a picture of Rip Collins' world record brown trout somewhere handy.

But Billy Lindsey was here before there were trout in the river and before there were any commercial docks. Bill and Mavis Lindsey, Billy's parents, are both from Arkansas, but the family was living in Orange, Texas, in 1964 when Bill bought the property along the Little Red River where Lindsey's Rainbow Resort now stands.

"Those were lean years," Billy recalled. "We moved here in the spring of '65. They were supposed to start stocking trout in the fall, but, because the moss didn't take hold, it was almost two years before the hatchery started putting any fish in here. There were still some small-mouth and largemouth bass, crappie and bream. We had a few fishermen.

"We were on the river seven years before any other operators came here. In those days you could leave the dam and go all the way down the river to Pangburn and not see another soul for 20 miles."

The Lindseys' first office was a 4' x 8' room built on the dock. Billy would come home from elementary school and do his homework there. Interruptions were few.

In the years since, besides the influx of commercial and private docks, there has been a big change in the look of the Little Red River itself. When Greers Ferry Dam water releases are low or stopped, huge beds of aquatic moss are visible. When the Lindseys first came here, there was none.

"My dad helped Jim Collins, a fisheries biologist, sprig the moss," Billy

Billy Lindsey grew up on the Little Red River and so will his sons, Jared (left) and Nathan. The Lindsey family moved here in 1965, before trout fishing began.

said. "They did it just like sprigging grass."

The moss was brought in from Mammoth Spring on flat-bed trucks, further illustrating the manmade nature of these Ozark trout fisheries.

Moss and trout have since taken hold in the Little Red River. This 32-mile stretch of trout stream became popular long before Collins took the world record brown from it in 1992, which then brought a new wave of anglers here.

Lindsey's Rainbow Resort has grown from one cabin, a dock and a half dozen boats to include 31 cabins that can accommodate over 100 people, a heated swimming pool, a restaurant, a campground with recreational vehicle hookups and, of course, all the trout fishing services - from guides to bait to boat and motor rentals.

Billy doesn't get to spend much time down on the dock anymore. He's either working in the office or working as a member of the Arkansas State Parks, Recreation and Tourism Commission, to which Lindsey was appointed in 1987.

With that appointment, trout fishing in Arkansas got its second voice

on the commission. Jim Gaston, owner of Gaston's Resort on the White River, has been a Parks and Tourism commissioner since 1973. Gaston and Lindsey, reappointed in 1994 for his second term, wouldn't have been able to remain on the commission if they were simply one-issue commissioners. But when an issue involving Arkansas trout fishing does come up, Lindsey and Gaston are in a position to defend their interests, and, most importantly, the interests of the two rivers where their businesses are located.

"Contrary to what some people might say, not that many people are looking out for the White River and the Little Red River," Lindsey said.

Just how important is trout fishing in Arkansas tourism? A 1988 study revealed that trout fishing accounted for 6.8 percent of the state's then $2.1 billion dollar travel industry. As a reminder, Lindsey and Gaston distributed political campaign-style buttons with a simple message - 6.8%.

Billy Lindsey has witnessed the Little Red River's part in that trout fishing equation grow from 0.0 percent to a place that can boast of a world record brown trout.

Big Lures Can Attract Big Brown Trout

Largemouth bass stickbaits prove to be effective for trout, too

When Abe Vogel starts thinking about catching big brown trout, he rummages through his bass fishing tackle.

"I don't think there's a bass bait made that, if you chunked it long enough, wouldn't catch a brown trout," said Vogel, who owns Lobo Landing Resort.

Sam Lester and Michael Brown think the same way, but they didn't always. Lester and Brown have guided fishing trips on the Little Red River for over 20 years. They used to fish a lot of bass tournaments, too. Lester works for the Arkansas Game and Fish Commission as a fisheries technician. He has been on enough AGFC electrofishing surveys of the river and fished it enough to gain a special feel for seasonal changes.

"In the spring, when warm water starts running in from the creeks, there are places in this river where you can fill a boat up with everything but trout," Lester said. "You can catch bass as long as you want to."

Lester and Brown started making it a habit of carrying their bass fishing gear when they fished the Little Red River creek mouths in the spring. Stickbaits were one of their top-producing lures. "Stickbait" is a general term used to describe any long, thin wooden or plastic baitfish imitation. The lures usually include two or three treble hooks.

"Pretty soon we started catching some brown trout on stickbaits," Lester said. "Then we started fishing the shoals in the main river with them. That's when we really started to catch big brown trout."

The method of using heavy, bass fishing tackle and what are considered primarily bass fishing lures for brown trout made headlines in 1993. In August, Dee Warren of Heber Springs landed a 28-pound, 14-ounce brown trout on a Bandit stickbait.

The fish was certified as a 20-pound-test world record by the

Photo courtesy of Arkansas Game and Fish Commission

In August 1993, Dee Warren of Heber Springs, Arkansas, caught this 28-pound, 14-ounce brown trout from the Little Red River on a Bandit stickbait.

International Game Fish Association. It is the second-largest brown trout recorded from the Little Red River.

Warren is a guide on the Little Red River. He specializes in this method of fishing for browns, and the publicity he received for catching that 28-pounder has made it an increasingly popular technique.

Lester gets excited just talking about it.

"Until you get out there and do it and get a lot of response to your lure, you don't understand," Lester said. "But when those fish start chasing that stickbait and flashing at it, and you catch a few, it will just knock your socks off."

Lester says it was about 1987 when he and Brown happened upon their

stickbait success. Vogel says he learned about it from Lester. They have some common ground in their particular methods, but they differ on some points. For instance, Vogel prefers 12-pound test line and spinning tackle, while Lester uses baitcasting gear and 18- or 20-pound test.

Smithwick Rattlin' Rogues and Bomber Long A's are their favorite stickbaits. They both like a Bomber Long A color pattern that Vogel has named "the green ugly." It has a black stripe down the side, like a largemouth bass, but the dominant overall color is fluorescent green. It wouldn't seem to imitate any of a brown trout's natural forage.

"It's so ugly, I think it just pisses them off," Lester said.

In the Rogue, Vogel prefers a rainbow trout pattern. It's the stickbait angler's version of "matching the hatch."

"There was a guy fishing from our dock who was reeling in a small rainbow trout when a brown trout bit it in two," Vogel said. "It happened right there in front of several people."

One observer thought the brown trout weighed about 15 pounds. That same week, Vogel said, another angler brought in a 6-pound brown trout that he caught on a rainbow trout-colored Rogue. The brown also had a stocker-size rainbow trout in its mouth.

When Lester casts a Rogue, he prefers one with a black back, gold sides and orange belly. If you are going to carry only two stickbaits, according to Lester, make sure one is a "green ugly" Bomber Long A and the other is a black-gold-and-orange Rattlin' Rogue.

"Just forget that you are trout fishing," Lester said. "Get out there and bass fish."

Lester uses the medium-billed stickbaits. He casts right next to the shoreline and quickly gives two or three quick jerks to get the lure down in the strike zone. Once there, he starts retrieving it as quickly and erratically as possible.

"Some people worry about reeling too fast, but speed is important," Lester said. "You don't want them to get a good look at it. The fish are reacting to the flash and the movement. And when a brown trout comes after it, there's no possible way you can reel it in too fast."

Lester, his wife, Jan, and their three kids live on the Little Red River, near Charlie's Island. That proximity to the river has given Lester special insight into the behavior of brown trout.

"I've sat in my yard and watched two or three brown trout gang up on another trout," Lester said. "They'll literally knock it out of the water, then another one will grab it in midair.

"They say that if a largemouth bass was human, it would get beat up or kick ass every night of the week. A brown trout is no different."

Greers Ferry National Fish Hatchery Specializes In Raising Rainbows

When you catch a rainbow trout from the Little Red River, it most likely came from the Greers Ferry National Fish Hatchery. This is one of three U.S. Fish and Wildlife Service hatcheries (Norfork, Arkansas, and Neosho, Missouri, are the others) that supplies trout for the White River system. State hatcheries provide the remainder.

Only rainbow trout are raised here, no browns or cutthroats. The Greers Ferry Hatchery receives eggs primarily from two other U.S. Fish and Wildlife Service hatcheries, then raises them to five-, nine- and 12-inch lengths. An average year of production here equals rainbow trout weighing a total of 225,000 pounds.

> ## "Our maximum production here is 200,000 to 250,000 pounds of trout per year."

The relationship between federal and state hatcheries is illustrated with a typical year at Greers Ferry, which includes production of almost one million trout:

■ 315,000 trout are raised to five inches and sent to Arkansas' Spring River Hatchery for further growth to 12 inches;

■ 610,000 trout are grown to nine inches for stocking mostly in the Little Red River, but some other trout fisheries in Arkansas and some in other states, primarily Texas, in places like the Brazos and Guadalupe rivers, receive these fish;

■ 30,000 trout are grown to 12 inches for stocking in the Little Red River.

Michael Cleary was named the Greers Ferry Hatchery manager in 1988. He knows that anglers want more 12-inch trout stocked in the

Little Red River, but Cleary says any increase in that figure would have to be correlated with a significant decrease in the number of trout raised to shorter lengths.

For instance, Cleary says the Greers Ferry Hatchery used to provide 180,000 six-inch fish to the Spring River Hatchery annually. Greers Ferry now gives the state hatchery 315,000 five-inch trout.

The state gets more fish to work with, but production from Greers Ferry is actually the same because 180,000 six-inch trout weigh the same as 315,000 five-inch trout.

"Our maximum production here is 200,000 to 250,000 pounds of trout per year," Cleary said. "Some years it may be a little less, but not more. At one time there was talk about adding raceways. There are 36 now and we have space and water supply for 12 more.

"Twelve more raceways would increase production to about 300,000 pounds annually, but there are no plans to do that."

The hatchery's water supply comes from three intake pipes in Greers Ferry Dam - one at 410 feet sea level elevation, another at 370 feet and another at 331 feet.

It's possible to mix water from the three intakes; usually about 70 percent of the hatchery water comes from the middle intake.

The water is aerated before it goes in the raceways, but no chilling is needed.

The optimum water temperature for rainbow trout is 58 degrees.

"We try to keep it in the low 50s here," Cleary said. "There's a little bit more oxygen in the colder water, plus parasites and bacteria don't grow as well."

The hatchery uses 9,000 to 10,000 gallons of water per minute. As much as 15,000 gallons per minute is available through the intake system.

Too Loose La Trek To The Little Red

Women gather on the river for a less-serious form of networking

Opening day of the muzzleloader deer hunting season was less than a week away. The fishing guides were thinking about hunting deer, not fishing for trout.

"How do you shoot those things?" asked Cathy Slater.

"With the knowledge that it's a wildlife management tool," replied guide Mike Brown.

"Oh, bull****!" said Bev Lindsey.

That's the way it is when "The Loose Group" gets together for an outing. A variety of subjects are cussed and discussed.

These once- or twice-a-year group ventures into the outdoors usually center on trout fishing out of Lindsey's Rainbow Resort on the Little Red River. History of the group also includes a trout fishing trip to Gaston's on the White River and a duck hunting trip to Stuttgart, Arkansas.

The Loose Group is all women. In fact, it includes some of the most politically powerful women in Arkansas, especially on the conservation front. Slater serves as the state's historic preservation officer. She was appointed by then-Governor Bill Clinton after a stint of environmental work on Clinton's staff. Lindsey is the director of the Department of Arkansas Heritage. She has been involved in the Carter, Mondale and Clinton presidential campaigns; her specialty is advance work. Lindsey's husband, Bruce, is a senior adviser to President Clinton.

The Loose Group was formed in 1988 after a lunch conversation between Kay Kelley Arnold and Julie McDonald Cabe.

Cabe is the executive assistant to the president/governmental affairs at the University of Central Arkansas.

Arnold is the director of federal regulatory affairs for Entergy Corporation, was the founding director of the Arkansas Field Office of the Nature Conservancy, has served as the director of the Department of Arkansas

Heritage, and is a board member of the U.S. Fish and Wildlife Foundation and the Arkansas Game and Fish Foundation.

But the bottom line here is trout fishing.

"Julie and I had lunch together," Arnold said. "We didn't know each other liked to fish. We started talking about it and said, 'Let's go.' I told her I wanted her to meet an old friend; she said she wanted me to meet a friend of hers. We just started inviting people. It's a less-serious form of networking, if you will."

> "When I woke up this morning, knowing I was going to be on the river this afternoon, I said, 'Praise Jesus, I know I can get through the rest of the day.'"

A seriously less-serious form of networking. The key ingredients, generally, are a river, trout fishing, beer, wine, Bloody Marys, a pound of fudge, cigars and a poker game. (Arnold's husband, Richard, who serves as the chief judge of the U.S. Court of Appeals 8th Circuit, taught the group the fine arts of poker-playing and cigar-smoking.)

This particular outing didn't include some of those ingredients, like the cigars and the poker game, as it was only a one-afternoon adventure.

There is one more key element - conversation. Lots of conversation.

"The more time a man spends in the woods or on a river, the more ani-

malistic a man gets," said guide Tom Bly.

"It's the same for women," Lindsey replied.

"When my husband comes in from the woods or fishing, he looks tired and helpless," said Marilyn Porter, the newest member of The Loose Group. "I like them dressed up in hunting clothes and dirty."

"Your interpretation and my interpretation of the outdoors experience have the same results," Bly noted with a smile.

No, the conversation about sex is not why this is called The Loose Group.

"We did not want it to be exclusive; we wanted it to be inclusive," Arnold said. "We wanted it to be a way to meet new people and see old friends. If someone called and said, 'I'd really like to go fishing with you,' they go on the list. It's just a loose group."

Other members of The Loose Group have included Nancy DeLamar, director of the Arkansas Nature Conservancy; Kathy Gardner, vice president and general counsel for Arkansas Louisiana Gas Company; and Diane Gilleland, director of the Arkansas Department of Higher Education. There have been others; newcomers are always welcome.

"Most of these women had never been fishing before," Arnold said. "That's kind of a subtext here. This was a safe, fun way to try it. In my opinion, one of the greatest elements of friendship is being introduced to new things."

Arnold grew up in nearby Heber Springs. She is the veteran angler of the group. The guides she hires for these trips are mostly long-time Heber Springs buddies. Brown guides part-time and builds houses for his full-time job. Gary Cresswell played football with Lindsey's Resort owner Billy Lindsey at Heber Springs High School and is now a parttime Baptist preacher and parttime fishing guide. Sam Lester is a fisheries technician for the Arkansas Game and Fish Commission. He guides parttime, but spends most of his free time on his artwork. His pen and ink drawings with a Southwest theme were exhibited in 1993 at the Greers Ferry Dam Visitor's Center. Tom Bly is one of two AGFC fisheries biologists for the district that includes Greers Ferry Lake and the Little Red River. He does some guiding on the side. Brown, Bly, Cresswell and Lester go to deer camp together every fall.

Although they aren't members of The Loose Group, the guides have become an integral part of these outings. They enjoy the conversation, which usually includes plenty of male opinions quickly followed by female perspectives on those opinions. Like when Lindsey shot down Brown's attempt to put man's reason for deer

hunting into some higher plane like "a management tool." No, that dog just won't hunt with The Loose Group.

"I think women like to fish for the same reason men do," said Slater, bringing the conversation back to the task at hand. "It's a good reason to drink beer in the middle of the day."

The guides, except for Cresswell, the Baptist preacher, nodded in agreement. The guides admit they enjoy these outings as much as The Loose Group.

Part of that comes from the lack of pressure to catch fish. Being outdoors with friends is No. 1. If the fish are biting, so much the better. Porter, the newcomer, caught the only fish on this late afternoon trip. It was a small cutthroat that was immediately released back into the river.

"Some people don't know how to relax," Bly said. "They bring their

portable phones with them in the boat. They want to fish like they do business - get out and get it done."

The Loose Group knows how to relax. After Porter caught her fish, most of the time was spent with boats pulled together, watching the river flow and sharing stories.

"When I woke up this morning, knowing I was going to be on the river this afternoon, I said, 'Praise Jesus, I know I can get through the rest of the day,'" Arnold said.

"The river restores you. It's hard to come out here and be mad or carry a grudge. It can alter your mood in a way that is very positive."

Added Lindsey, "Water has that effect on people. It always has. There's nothing new there. But it's nice to share it with somebody."

That is what The Loose Group is all about.

Photo courtesy of Nancy DeLamar

The Loose Group, after a day on the river: (l to r) Mike Brown, Kathy Gardner, Nancy DeLamar, Bev Lindsey, Sam Lester, Kay Kelley Arnold, Diane Gilleland and Julie McDonald Cabe.

Abe Vogel caught a state record chain pickerel from the Little Red River in 1979. The fish weighed 7 pounds, 10 ounces.

Chain Pickerel Unchanged In Little Red

One thing that didn't change when Greers Ferry Dam altered the Little Red River from a warmwater stream to a cold one was the presence of chain pickerel. In fact, as Abe Vogel will tell you, chain pickerel seem to be thriving in the Little Red River now.

Vogel and his wife, Lesa, own and operate Lobo Landing Resort, located 17 miles downstream from the dam. Abe's grandfather, the late George Choate, was one of the fishing legends of this area. He became one of the first guides on Greers Ferry Lake, and he also guided trout fishermen at most of the major docks on the Little Red.

Choate lived by the motto, "If I don't fish every day, I have a headache." Choate was 89 years old when he died in 1991. Based on that motto, Vogel says Choate shouldn't have had any headaches until the last six months of his life.

Choate also helped teach Vogel to be a pretty good fisherman, good enough to make Arkansas' record book. On January 5, 1979, roads were iced and sleet was falling. It was 12 degrees and no one was thinking about fishing, except Vogel. He was casting an L&S jointed Mirror Lure off the back of the dock.

After every four or five casts, Vogel went back inside to thaw the ice from his rod guides and baitcasting reel. He had the frog-colored, metal-lipped Mirror Lure attached to 20-pound test line, which proved invaluable when Vogel hooked a 7-pound, 10-ounce chain pickerel on one of his casts into the bitter cold. Most Arkansas chain pickerel weigh in the 2- to 3-pound range.

"The previous four state records came out of this river, so I'd kept up with what the current record was," Vogel recalled.

His fish broke the previous mark by seven ounces. Two weeks later, Vogel lost his lucky lure to another chain pickerel.

"I have no doubt there is a world record chain pickerel in this river," Vogel said. "I've hooked bigger ones, but always on a jig and 2- or 4-pound test. They just saw it off."

The all-tackle record chain pickerel, according to the National Freshwater Fishing Hall of Fame, is 9 pounds, 6 ounces (Homerville, Ga., 1961). Chain pickerel have a mouth full of needle-like teeth, and they tend to take a lure deeply. That makes it difficult to land them after they get a chance to rub those teeth across monofilament line.

Chain pickerel are easily identified by their long, slim bodies and a black chain-like color pattern on their sides. The main body color varies from green to yellow.

All the moss beds in the Little Red River provide excellent habitat for chain pickerel, which prefer to hide near underwater vegetation and pick off prey as it swims by. Adult chain pickerel feed mostly on other fish, therefore minnows, stickbaits and jigs are good choices for the angler.

Chain pickerel aren't common in the Ozarks. They are found only in the southeastern part of Missouri and throughout the Coastal Plain area of Arkansas. Their U.S. range includes Atlantic Coast and Gulf Coast states from Maine to Louisiana.

Highlights Of A Trip Down The Little Red

("Left" and "right" directions assume the angler is facing downstream.)

Just like all the other parks just below the dams on Ozark tailwaters, **John F. Kennedy Park** below Greers Ferry Dam is a popular spot and includes a variety of facilities, like a public boat launching ramp and campsites. This is where the first big brown trout was caught from the Little Red. In 1988, Melvin Hallmark of North Little Rock, Arkansas, landed a 27-pound, 8-ounce brown using fish intestine for bait.

The **Greers Ferry National Fish Hatchery** outlet pipes provide a constant flow of nutrient-rich, highly-oxygenated water near the park. The park is a stocking site for rainbow trout. In addition, the outlet pipes attract mature rainbow trout during the spawning period, which can range from October through April for rainbows. There are two small shoals within the park boundaries and that provide good wade fishing during low flow. Boaters will find good drift fishing from the park down to Beech Island.

From the powerlines that cross the river below JFK Park down to Cow Shoals, fishing is almost exclusively by boat. This is a popular area for drifting with bait during high water and fishing with jigs under bobbers during low water. **Beech Island** does provide shoals on either side for wade fishing during low water. However, access is by boat only. Boaters should stay on Beech Island's left side as they travel downstream from the park.

Just below the island are **Lindsey's Rainbow Resort** on the left and **Red River Trout Dock** on the right. Past Lindsey's and Red River docks, the river bends to the right and there is a small shoal. This is the original Cow Shoals. But when the AGFC walk-in access area was created in 1988, the name "Cow Shoals" moved downstream.

Although brown trout spawning has spread to many other shoals in the Little Red, **Cow Shoals** was the first and it remains by far the most popular for fly fishers. In 1988, the Mid-South Fly Fishers of Memphis and the Arkansas Fly Fishers of Little Rock raised $4,000 to purchase property, then donated it to the AGFC, which established a walk-in public access area here. You can reach the access area by turning off Highway 110 at Highway 210, which will lead you due east down a paved road that turns to dirt before you see the green AGFC sign marking the site. Beginning in 1995, the Cow Shoals area was declared catch-and-release only from Oct. 1 to Dec. 31 to protect spawning brown trout.

Below Cow Shoals, **Wilburn Creek**

Long, deep stretches, like this one at Egypt Slough, provide good fish habitat during low flow on the Little Red River.

The old Pangburn bridge was left in tact, minus its middle section, and provides fishing piers from both sides of the river near the new Highway 110 bridge.

enters from the east. After a heavy rain, Wilburn Creek significantly alters the water clarity of the Little Red. There is a stretch of flat water and moss beds that holds good numbers of trout. It leads to the top of an area known as **John's Pocket**, which includes a couple of slough-like spots that, especially in high water, hold good numbers of fish. Access is by boat. **Ritchey Shoals** is located at the bottom of John's Pocket. It is another popular fishing spot.

Most boaters get to Ritchey Shoal and John's Pocket from downstream at **Barnett Access** and **Swinging Bridge Trout Dock**. Long after a new concrete-and-steel bridge was built over the river on Highway 110 here, the old suspension bridge remained, hence the name Swinging Bridge. With Swinging Bridge Trout Dock on the north side of the river and the AGFC's Barnett Access Area on the south side, this is one of the more popular areas on the river. About a mile upstream from here is where Rip Collins caught the 40-pound, 4-ounce world record brown trout. Rick Hart caught his 24.64-pound brown trout

in this area, too. With **Winkley Shoals** below the Highway 110 bridge and **Sugar Loaf Mountain** nearby, this is also one of the most scenic spots on the river.

It's a seven-mile float between Barnett Access and the AGFC-built public ramp at Lobo Landing. The river makes a 180-degree turn from Barnett Access to the top of **Scroncher Shoals**. The land to the east is called **Cooter Neck Bend**. At one time, Cooter Neck Bend Trout Dock was located here, but it is no longer in operation. **Charlie's Island** is the next landmark downstream, the cut bank to the right of the island is called **Red Banks**. **Sulphur Creek** enters the Little Red River from the right just below **Charlie's Island**. It carries the effluent from the Heber Springs wastewater treatment plant. The shoal below it is called **Baker's Ford** and a deep pool called **Round Hole** follows.

Scroncher Shoals and **Moss Dam Shoal** mark the next section of the Little Red River. The shoals provide good wade fishing in low water. The pool between the two shoals is a good area for boat fishers during high

water. Below Moss Dam Shoal, there is another deep pool, called **Egypt Slough**.

The river begins a left turn, which features **Libby Bluff** standing high on the right with a **Libby Shoal** below it, making this one of the most scenic spots on the Little Red. The AGFC owns the land between Highway 337 and Libby Shoals and has established a walk-in access area. A railroad came to a quarry site here many years ago. Libby Shoals offers good wade fishing at low water. There is a deep hole below it that also provides good trout habitat.

The AGFC-built public boat launching ramp at **Lobo Landing** marks, roughly, the halfway point of the Little Red's trout waters. It's 17 miles from the dam to Lobo Landing and 15 miles from Lobo Landing to the Highway 305 bridge. With **Lobo Landing Trout Dock** here and **River Ranch Resort** located just upstream on the opposite bank, this is one of the most popular areas of the river for boaters.

There is a long straight stretch of river from Lobo Landing to **Dunham Shoal**, which is more like one big, propeller-eating rock than a shoal. There is a deep hole just below the big rock. The river veers north, then starts to curve back south into **Mossy Shoal**. The area between Dunham and Mossy shoals has few houses along the shore and no docks. It's another of the more scenic stretches of the Little Red, and it holds good numbers of trout. Beginning January 1, 1995, this one-mile stretch from Dunham Shoal to Mossy Shoal became a year-round catch-and-release area.

Rainbow Island is the next major landmark. The island is a private housing development. The main channel goes to the right here; on the left-hand side, a bridge connects the island to the bank. A 180-degree turn in the river below Rainbow Island is called **Horseshoe Bend**. Just below it is the **AGFC's Dripping Springs Access** and the **Dripping Springs Trout Dock**. Road signs off highways 110 and 16 in Pangburn will guide you to Dripping Springs.

Highway 110 crosses the Little Red River just north of Pangburn. The **Pangburn bridge** area includes an old low-water bridge that has been converted by the AGFC into a public fishing pier. There's also access for the handicapped. The middle section of the low-water bridge was removed, making two fishing piers - one accessible from each side of the river. **Pangburn Shoal** below the bridge is accessible to waders from the south side of the river and usually holds good numbers of trout.

The largest tributary in the first 32 miles of the Greers Ferry Tailwater is **Big Creek**, which enters the river from the north, about a mile below Pangburn Bridge. It's here that you'll see the most dramatic changes in the Little Red's scenery. Cypress trees are common along the banks below Big Creek. It's here that the foothills of the Ozarks give way to the Delta. During winter months, trout can be found several miles up Big Creek, and it's also a good stream for black bass during warmer months. Further downstream, signs on either bank mark an underwater pipeline, which signals the halfway point between Big Creek and Ramsey Access. There are no houses along the banks in this area. There are several small shoals in this stretch during low-water periods; they are accessible only by boat.

Ramsey Access marks the last AGFC public access point on the trout waters of the Little Red River. It's 29 miles from the dam. Many people consider this the end of the trout waters. Summer temperatures can cause problems for trout this far from the dam. Almost all of the trout caught here will be rainbows. Bank fishing is popular.

It's another three miles to the **Highway 305 (Dewey) Bridge**, but there is no public access at the bridge. Depending on time of year and water temperatures, you can catch trout several miles downstream from the Highway 305 bridge. While the trout numbers are nowhere near that of the upper section of the Little Red, fishing pressure is nowhere near that of the upper section either.

Brown Trout Numbers Continue To Rise

The short history of brown trout in the Little Red River shows why catch-and-release should be considered a management tool, not a way of life. The Little Red River brown trout population has become like a garden planted with too many seeds, according to Arkansas Game and Fish Commission fisheries biologists. They think a few sprouts need to be picked for the rest of the plants to grow.

The 1995 fishing regulations for the Greers Ferry Tailwater doubled the brown trout daily limit from two to four while adding a 16- to 21-inch protected slot limit. (All brown trout measuring 16 to 21 inches must be released; in the four brown trout daily limit, only one may be above 21 inches.)

The new regulations were designed to reduce what is thought to be an over-crowded population of brown trout under 16 inches long. Since brown trout were introduced to the Little Red by fly fishing clubs in the 1970s, the species has thrived. The AGFC hasn't stocked browns in the river because, unlike rainbows, browns have successfully reproduced in large numbers.

From January 1990 through December 1994, brown trout were protected by a two-fish daily limit and a 16-inch minimum length limit. The 16-inch minimum length limit was recommended by AGFC fisheries biologists for all the state's tailwater trout fisheries except the Little Red River, but enforcement concerns resulted in the implementation here, too.

AGFC creel surveys indicated that anglers were releasing brown trout at a rate of 88 percent BEFORE the 16-inch length limit. When the length limit was added, it concentrated brown trout harvest among the 16-inch and longer fish. Combined with their prolific nature here, the result is brown trout as thick as 12,000 per mile in some areas of the Little Red River and an overall average of 6,772 brown trout per mile in the Greers Ferry Tailwater, according to AGFC data gathered in 1993-94.

If simply numbers of fish was the desired goal, the Little Red River would be in unbelievably good shape as far as brown trout are concerned. The problem is most of these browns are under 16 inches long. The new regulations were designed to redirect some of the fishing pressure to those big numbers of small brown trout.

AGFC biologists hope that by thinning out some of the smaller brown trout, the river will maintain the ability to produce a few of the world-class size browns it has in the past.

AGFC data gathered in 1993-94 showed large numbers of small brown trout in the Little Red River.

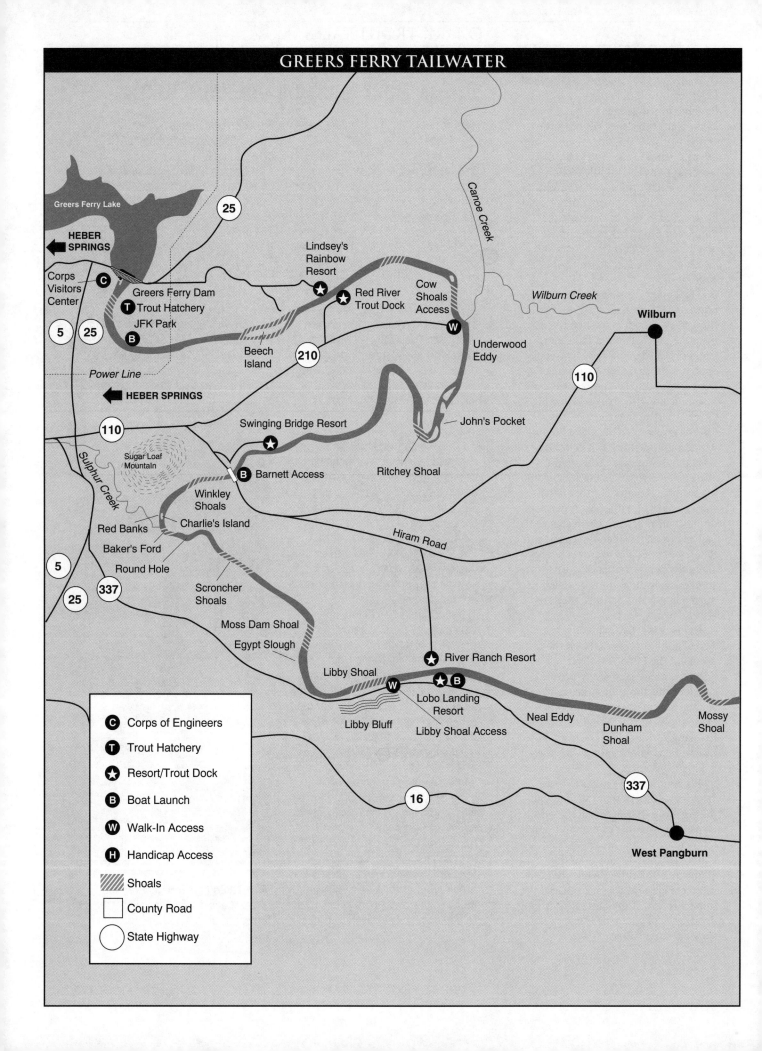

GREERS FERRY TAILWATER

Greers Ferry Lake

HEBER SPRINGS

25

Corps Visitors Center

C

Greers Ferry Dam

T Trout Hatchery

JFK Park

B

5 25

Power Line

HEBER SPRINGS

110

Sugar Loaf Mountain

Sulphur Creek

Red Banks

Baker's Ford

Round Hole

5

25 337

Lindsey's Rainbow Resort

Red River Trout Dock

Beech Island

210

Swinging Bridge Resort

B Barnett Access

Winkley Shoals

Charlie's Island

Scroncher Shoals

Moss Dam Shoal

Egypt Slough

Cow Shoals Access

W

Underwood Eddy

John's Pocket

Ritchey Shoal

Hiram Road

Libby Shoal

W

Libby Bluff

River Ranch Resort

Lobo Landing Resort

Libby Shoal Access

★ B

Neal Eddy

Dunham Shoal

Mossy Shoal

Canoe Creek

Wilburn Creek

Wilburn

110

337

West Pangburn

16

Legend

C Corps of Engineers

T Trout Hatchery

★ Resort/Trout Dock

B Boat Launch

W Walk-In Access

H Handicap Access

▨ Shoals

☐ County Road

◯ State Highway

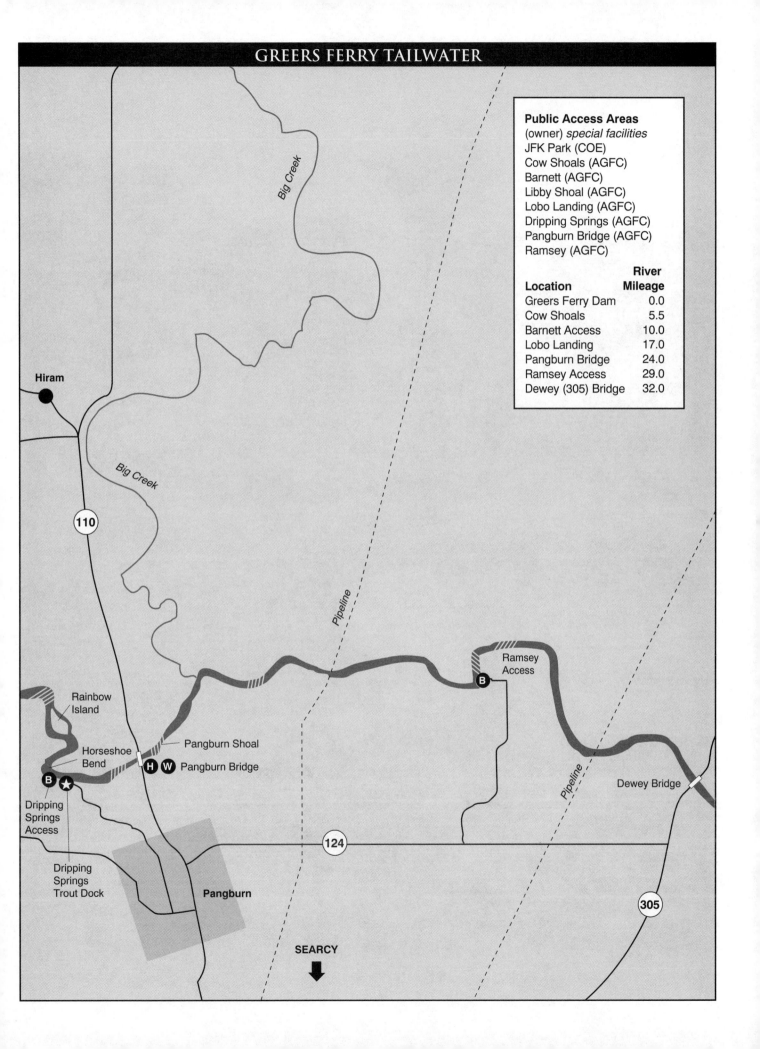

GREERS FERRY TAILWATER

Public Access Areas
(owner) *special facilities*
JFK Park (COE)
Cow Shoals (AGFC)
Barnett (AGFC)
Libby Shoal (AGFC)
Lobo Landing (AGFC)
Dripping Springs (AGFC)
Pangburn Bridge (AGFC)
Ramsey (AGFC)

Location	River Mileage
Greers Ferry Dam	0.0
Cow Shoals	5.5
Barnett Access	10.0
Lobo Landing	17.0
Pangburn Bridge	24.0
Ramsey Access	29.0
Dewey (305) Bridge	32.0

Big Creek

Hiram

Big Creek

110

Pipeline

Ramsey
Access

Pipeline

Rainbow
Island

Pangburn Shoal

Horseshoe
Bend

Pangburn Bridge

Dewey Bridge

Dripping
Springs
Access

124

Dripping
Springs
Trout Dock

Pangburn

305

SEARCY

Tips On Getting The Most Benefits From Guided Trip

John Gulley has worked for over two decades as a fishing guide on the White and North Fork rivers. When he takes some time off, Gulley enjoys traveling and fishing in other places. But even with all the fishing knowledge he has, Gulley doesn't try to figure out a new place on his own.

"I've fished all parts of the world," Gulley said. "I don't ever go anyplace where I don't hire a guide. There's no sense in not hiring a guide. You waste a lot of time finding out how to fish a place."

Just about every resort along the White River System tailwaters can help set you up with a fishing guide. And there are an increasing number of independent guides, who can be booked separately from the resorts.

The next key is communication. Any time spent talking with your guide before the trip is time well spent. Ask questions, tell them exactly what you want to do.

"I used to ask people, do you want to fish for big fish, or just fish?" said guide Paul Jones. "It helps to let the guide know the score."

When you are fishing for big fish, you must realize the chances of not catching anything.

An experienced guide can accommodate a wide range of fishing possibilities. Do you want to see some scenery, or are you determined to spend as much time fishing as possible? Do you want to keep some fish, or are you planning to release them all?

For instance, some fly fishing guides, like Gulley and those at Dale Fulton's Blue Ribbon Flies, offer only catch-and-release fishing.

It's better to get all this straightened out up front, so nothing gets in the way during a day on the river.

Veteran White River fishing guide Pat Perdue, obviously, feels right at home in a johnboat.

WHAT TO EXPECT

When To Visit: These are 12-month trout fisheries. Although there are four definite seasons in the Ozarks, winters are usually mild. In fact, winter probably provides the best opportunities to catch bigger fish. Brown trout spawning runs on the Greers Ferry and Table Rock tailwaters begin in October and last into December. The Bull Shoals Tailwater brown trout spawn doesn't begin until November and continues through January. The late-winter, early-spring shad kills also give the angler a chance to catch bigger than usual fish.

At one time, most Ozark fishing resorts closed in the winter. But that has changed in recent years as word of winter fishing opportunities has spread. Many resorts do offer lower rates in winter.

The busiest season is from Memorial Day through Labor Day, although that is beginning to extend back into early spring, when dogwoods and redbuds bloom, and forward into fall, when the leaves change and fall wildflowers bloom.

It's best to make reservations well in advance if you desire lodging and a fishing guide on May through September weekends.

Weather: Mountain Home is located approximately at the center of the White River System tailwaters. Its 30-year average temperatures and rainfall, month-by-month, are listed below:

	Daily High	Daily Low	Rainfall
January	46	24	2.35"
February	51	28	2.86"
March	60	36	4.09"
April	72	47	4.40"
May	79	55	4.90"
June	86	63	4.16"
July	91	67	3.09"
August	90	66	2.62"
September	84	59	3.68"
October	74	47	2.88"
November	60	36	3.85"
December	50	29	3.19"

Typical Day: Although this book contains many big-fish stories, don't expect to catch one. It's possible, of course, but more realistic expectations for a day on these rivers include a couple dozen 10- to 14-inch rainbow trout and a brown trout or two up to 20 inches.

Guide fees for a party of two generally range from $75 to $150 for a half-day and $100 to $200 for a full day. The wide variation in prices is partly due to meal options available, ranging from a box lunch to a guide-prepared hot shore lunch.

Guided overnight float trips, mainly a feature of the Bull Shoals Tailwater, start at about $175 per day per person, but prices vary considerably, as there is a wide range of float trip options.

Fishing Tackle: The most popular tackle combination includes a 5- to 6-foot rod matched with a spinning reel loaded with 4- or 6-pound-test line. The rod should have a medium to ultralight action.

It's crucial that the reel have a smooth, easily adjusted drag system. It's equally important that the line be new and non-fluorescent. Clear, green or brown are the best line colors.

For fly fishers, a 6-weight, 8 1/2- to 9-foot rod with both floating and sink tip lines is best overall. If you plan to concentrate on brown trout by casting big streamer patterns, you might want to bring a 7- or 8-weight rod. During periods of low water, a 4-weight rod can be useful.

Bring The Shades: Polarized sunglasses are a must for all anglers. You'll see many more fish with polarized sunglasses, plus they will improve your fishing ability - from where to cast to when to set the hook. They also offer protection from the ever-present danger of a fish hook in the eyeball.

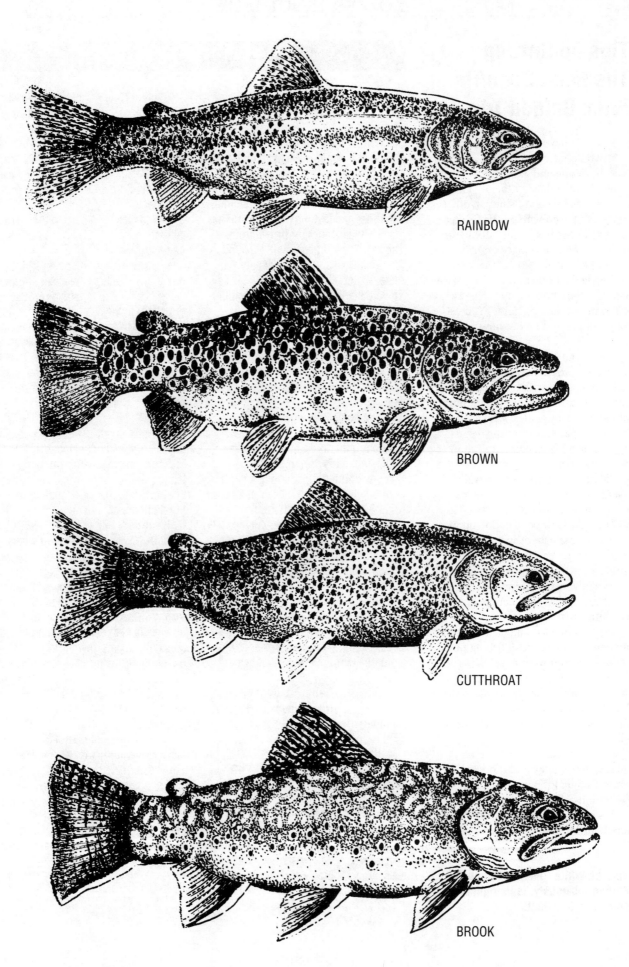

RAINBOW

BROWN

CUTTHROAT

BROOK

Illustrations by Duane Hada

How To Identify White River System Trout

The hooked jaw or kipe of a breeding brown trout males makes it easily distinguishable from the female on the left.

RAINBOW TROUT
(Oncorhynchus mykiss)

Most distinguishing features:
- Pink or reddish streak down sides
- Black spots over entire body, including fins

Other features:
- Olive-green back and upper sides
- Forked tail
- Small mouth

BROWN TROUT
(Salmo trutta)

Most distinguishing features:
- Large black spots with light halos on back and sides
- Usually orange or red spots with halos along lateral line
- Golden brown to silver body color
- Abdomen usually yellow or cream colored

Other features:
- Olive-brown back and upper sides
- Tail slightly forked, faint or no spots
- Breeding males develop a hook or kipe on lower jaw

CUTTHROAT TROUT
(Oncorhynchus clarki)

Most distinguishing features:
- Distinctive red-orange slash marks on the underside of lower jaw
- Black spotting heavier towards rear of fish

Other features:
- Small teeth on midline of tongue
- Olive back and upper sides
- Tail spotted, forked

BROOK TROUT
(Salvelinus fontinalis)

Most distinguishing features:
- Sides usually have crimson spots with blue halos and yellow spots
- Light worm-like markings on dark green upper body
- White edge followed by dark stripe on front of lower fins

Other features:
- Square or slightly forked tail
- Large mouth, jaw extends well behind eye
- Reddish underside in breeding males

Note: Lake trout have been stocked in Bull Shoals Lake and Greers Ferry Lake. Sometimes they are found in the rivers below the dams. The shock of going through the turbines, however, usually kills them. Lake trout are the least colorful of the trout found in the Ozarks. Back and sides are gray to greenish brown with many light-colored spots. Lake trout have a long, slender body, similar to a walleye.

Why, How To Catch-And-Release Trout

Catch-and-release is no longer an option in these Ozark tailwater trout fisheries. Every section of the White, North Fork and Little Red rivers has special regulations that require you to release certain trout.

In 1994, the Arkansas Game and Fish Commission approved 12-month catch-and-release zones on the Beaver, Bull Shoals, Norfork and Greers Ferry tailwaters, effective January 1, 1995. And there are various slot and length limits throughout the White River System.

Catch-and-release is also becoming an increasingly popular personal fishing philosophy.

Bass tournament fishing can take credit for some of that.

Ray Scott, founder of the Bass Anglers Sportsman Society, held his first-ever bass tournament on a White River System lake.

On June 5, 1967, 106 fishermen from 13 states entered Scott's All-American Invitational Bass Tournament at Beaver Lake. Bill Dance launched his highly successful pro bass fishing career by finishing second in the tournament.

The bass caught that day were cleaned at the weigh-in site.

When Scott came back to Beaver Lake in 1992 to celebrate the 25th anniversary of that first tournament, the Bass Anglers Sportsman Society had over half a million members and catch-and-release was a critical part of life tournament bass fishing.

More and more anglers are starting to realize that catch-and-release is as important to trout fisheries management as it is to bass tournament angling.

Catch-and-release won't work as a fisheries management tool if not done properly. If you catch-and-release 50 trout during a day and 80 percent survive, you've killed more fish (10) than the angler who caught and cleaned a daily limit.

If you are going to practice catch-and-release, here are some tips on how to do it correctly:

1. Land the fish as quickly as possible. A fish that is fought to exhaustion is less likely to survive.

2. Wet your hands before handling the fish. Dry hands will remove part of a fish's protective mucous coating.

3. When unhooking and/or photographing the fish, keep it in the water as long as possible. Think about it this way: Don't keep a fish out of water any longer than you would want to be held underwater.

4. Don't let the fish flop around in a boat or on the bank. Barbless hooks make unhooking quicker and easier on the fish and the angler. Cradling a fish upside down seems to tranquilize it for a moment, allowing for easier release.

5. Avoid squeezing the fish or touching its gills. If you must grip the fish, grab the lower jaw and/or tail. For photographs, support the fish with both hands and hold it parallel to the water.

6. If the fish has swallowed a hook, don't try to remove the hook. Cut the line as close to the hook as possible. It's not uncommon to catch a trout and find another angler's hook in its mouth. You will occasionally see a trout that has been hooked on a drift rig, has passed the hook out the anus, and still has the bell sinker hanging from a line out its mouth. The point is this: More times it's the angler's handling, not the hook itself, that kills the fish.

7. Cradle the fish in the water for a moment before releasing, to make sure it has revived. Do not move the fish back and forth in the water, as this backward motion forces water unnaturally through the back of its gills. Instead, hold its head upstream, into the current.

Illustration by Duane Hada

If You Keep A Trout, How To Prepare It

If you partake in a guide-prepared shore lunch, which is one of the main features of a Bull Shoals Tailwater float trip, fried trout will be the main course.

Firewood is gathered from the river bank. After the blaze begins dying to coals, a big cast iron skillet becomes the primary cooking utensil. A mixture of potatoes and onions is fried first, followed by the trout. All the while, a pot of beans simmers next to the frying pan.

"Fried potatoes, fried onions, fried trout - we'd probably fry the beans if we could," laughed one White River fishing guide.

The typical shore lunch does put a pretty heavy dose of cholesterol in your blood. But, as is the case with all foods we're told to avoid on a regular basis, it's worth the indulgence once in awhile.

There are, however, dozens of other ways to cook trout. Ray Horn, a long-time fishing guide on the Little Red River, has assembled a book full of recipes, entitled "Just Trout."

The first secret of enjoying the delicate flavor of a trout, according to Horn, is a fresh fish. On a day-long fishing trip, this requires some extra attention.

"You wouldn't drag a steak around on a stringer half a day and expect it to taste good, would you?" Horn said.

To insure freshness, don't wait until the end of the day to clean the fish. Particularly on a hot summer day, it's best to gut the fish, place it in a waterproof plastic bag and put it on ice immediately after catching it. Don't lay the fish directly on ice, without the plastic bag. The water from melting ice will detract from the taste of the fish.

Horn's next tip is to avoid over-cooking. Trout, especially, need a light touch. Therefore, smoking is one of Horn's favorite ways to prepare trout. He particularly likes the unobtrusive flavor that pecan shells add to the smoking process.

Pecan Shell Smoked Trout

4 to 6 trout about 1/2 lb. each
1 1/2 quarts brine (recipe follows)
3 1/2 cups pecan shells (or more)
1 1/2 cups water
1/3 cup dark brown sugar
1/4 cup lemon juice
2 tablespoons vegetable oil
1/2 teaspoon salt
1/4 teaspoon cayenne pepper

Prepare brine. Rinse trout under cold running water; pat dry. Place trout in brine and refrigerate 4 hours. Soak pecan shells in water 4 to 12 hours; drain well.

In a shallow dish, combine lemon juice, brown sugar, vegetable oil, cayenne pepper and salt; mix well. Pour ingredients in a large zip-top, heavy-duty plastic bag. Remove trout from brine and rinse carefully with cold water; pat dry. Pierce skin of trout with a fork in several places. Roll the trout in the marinade to coat inside and out. Place trout in the bag and refrigerate 2 hours, turning the bag occasionally. Remove trout from bag, reserving the marinade. Set aside.

Meanwhile, prepare charcoal fire in smoke cooker. Let charcoal burn a good 30 minutes or until coated with ashes. Place 1 cup of pecan shells on top of coals and 1 cup of shells circling the outside edge of the charcoal; 1/2 cup of shells should be added to the coals every 15 minutes. Place water

pan in smoker; add reserved marinade. Add hot tap water to fill pan.

Coat grill rack with cooking spray; place rack in smoker. Arrange trout on grill, making sure they are not touching. Cover with smoker lid and cook 2 to 4 hours or until trout flakes easily when tested with a fork.

Brine recipe: Combine 1 cup rock or ice cream salt, 1/4 cup brown sugar and 6 to 8 cups of water in saucepan; heat until the mixture is dissolved. Cool and pour into a 1-gallon glass container; add an additional quart of water and mix well. Cover and refrigerate until needed.

Most trout recipes call for whole trout. However, trout can be filleted as easily as any fish, and many people prefer to eat boneless fish.

Suzie Stephens has owned and operated Nibbles Gourmet Catering, Inc., in Fayetteville, Arkansas, since 1982. She is a certified executive chef and the author of five cookbooks. Plus, Stephens has caught her share of White River trout. She offers the following recipe for trout fillets:

Trout in the House

2 lbs. fresh trout fillets
1/4 cup flour
1 teaspoon Cajun seasoning
1 teaspoon paprika
1/4 cup melted butter
2 tablespoons butter
1/2 cup sliced almonds
2 tablespoons fresh lemon juice
1/2 teaspoon Tabasco
1 tablespoon chopped parsley

Cut fillets in 6 portions. Combine flour, Cajun seasoning and paprika. Roll fish in flour mixture and place in a single layer, skin side down in a well-greased baking dish. Pour melted butter over fish. Broil 4 inches from heat source for 6 to 10 minutes, or until fish flakes easily.

Saute almonds in 2 tablespoons butter until golden brown. Remove from heat. Add lemon juice, Tabasco and parsley. Pour over fillets. Serve.

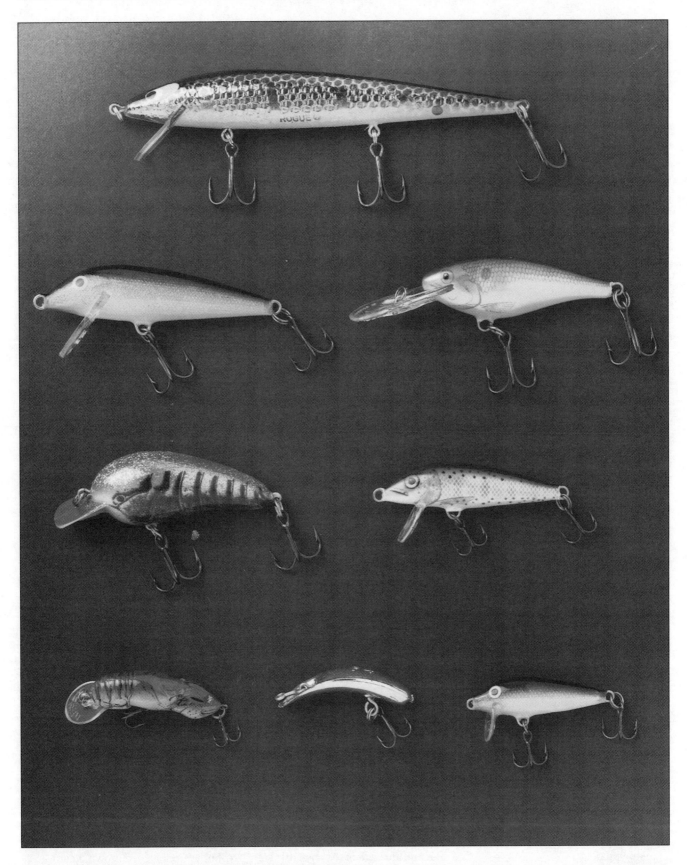

Popular crankbaits in the White River System: (top) Smithwick Rattlin' Rogue; (second row, l to r) Countdown Rapala CD-7 black-and-gold, Rapala Shad Rap; (third row) Norman Baby N, Countdown Rapala CD-5 rainbow trout; (bottom row) Rebel Wee-Crawfish, Worden's Flatfish F4, Countdown Rapala CD-3 silver-and-black.

Spoons and spinners popular in the White River System: (top, l to r) Eppinger Dardevle spoon, Luhr Jensen Krocodile spoon; (second row) Mepps Aglia Long No. 1, Mepps Black Fury No. 1, Blue Fox Vibrax; (third row) Acme Little Cleo, Super Duper, Colorado spoon; (bottom) Rooster Tail, Vibric Trooster Tail, Panther Martin.

THE RECORD BOOK

(Through October 1994)

ARKANSAS TROUT RECORDS

Species	Weight	Date - Place	Bait/Lure	Angler
Brown	40 lbs., 4 oz.	May 5, 1992 - Greers Ferry Tailwater	Jig	Howard "Rip" Collins, Heber Springs, Ark.
Rainbow	19 lbs., 1 oz.	March 14, 1981 - Bull Shoals Tailwater	Rooster Tail, worm	Jim Miller, Memphis, Tenn.
Cutthroat	9 lbs., 9.76 oz.	Oct. 6, 1985 - Bull Shoals Tailwater	Worm-crawfish	Scott Rudolph, Ozark, Ark.
Brook	3 lbs., 10 oz.	Oct. 27, 1984 - Norfork Tailwater	Heluva Jig	Tony Salamon, St. Louis, Mo.

MISSOURI TROUT RECORDS

Species	Weight	Date - Place	Bait/Lure	Angler
Brown	24 lbs., 15 oz.	June 27, 1994 Lake Taneycomo	Shad Assassin	Kevin Elfrink, Jackson, Mo.
Rainbow	16 lbs., 13 oz.	Nov. 21, 1987 - Roaring River St. Park	Jig	Kenneth Smith , Springfield, Mo.
Brook	8 oz.	Nov. 9, 1982 - Spring Creek	Jig	Darryl Ward, Columbia, Mo

PROGRESSION OF ARKANSAS' RAINBOW TROUT RECORD

Weight	Tailwater	Date	Bait/Lure	Angler
11lbs., 3 oz.	Bull Shoals (Cotter)	June 11, 1959	Sonar	Jack Ballew, Gamaliel, Ark.
11 lbs., 12 oz.	Bull Shoals (Rim Shoals)	June 13, 1959	Crawfish	Richard Brainerd, Norfork, Ark.
15 lbs., 1 oz.	Bull Shoals (Rim Shoals)	Sept. 15, 1959	Crawfish tail	Harvey Parnell, Rea Valley, Ark.
15 lbs., 3 oz.	Bull Shoals	Oct. 2, 1959	Minnow	Bo Martin, Lincoln, Ark.
15 lbs., 8 oz.	Greers Ferry	March 4, 1968	Cheese	David Kitchens, Conway, Ark.
16 lbs., 2 oz.	Norfork	June 14, 1970	Mepps	Frank Mandernach, St. Louis, Mo.
16 lbs., 12 oz.	Norfork	July 1, 1972	Crawfish tail	Raymond Sullivan, Des Moines, Iowa
19 lbs., 0 oz.	Bull Shoals (Cotter Shoals)	June 2, 1976	Crawfish	Dick Justus, Bono, Ark.
19 lbs., 1 oz.	Bull Shoals (Sylamore)	March 14, 1981	Rooster Tail, worm	Jim Miller, Memphis, Tenn.

PROGRESSION OF ARKANSAS' BROWN TROUT RECORD

Weight	Tailwater	Date	Bait/Lure	Angler
10 lbs., 13 oz.	Bull Shoals	June 27, 1959	Crawfish tail	Frank Tilley, Norfork, Ark.
12 lbs., 2 oz.	Bull Shoals	July 28, 1959	Crawfish	B.E. Douthitt, Commerce, Okla.
17 lbs., 12 oz.	Bull Shoals	June 9, 1962	Crawfish	Stan Leman, Lakeview, Ark.
25 lbs., 0 oz.	Bull Shoals	Sept. 8, 1963	Little Doc	Tom Gulley, Bull Shoals, Ark.
28 lbs., 3 oz.	Bull Shoals	Sept. 18, 1970	Little Cleo	Dr. Louis McFarland, Hot Springs, Ark
31 lbs., 8 oz.	Bull Shoals	May 24, 1972	Crawfish	Troy Lackey, Lakeview, Ark.
33 lbs., 8 oz.	Bull Shoals	March 19, 1977	Crawfish tail-Worm	Leon Waggoner, Flippin, Ark.
38 lbs., 9 oz.	Norfork	Aug. 7, 1988	Corn-marshmallow	Mike "Huey" Manley, North Little Rock, Ark.
40 lbs., 4 oz.	Greers Ferry	May 5, 1992	Jig	Howard "Rip" Collins, Heber Springs, Ark.

PROGRESSION OF MISSOURI'S RAINBOW TROUT RECORD

Weight	Water	Date	Bait/Lure	Angler
13 lbs., 12 oz.	Bennett Spring State Park	Oct. 23, 1960	White Miller fly	H.N. "Chuck" Branson, Sedalia, Mo.
13 lbs., 14 3/4oz.	Lake Taneycomo (Fall Creek)	Jan. 26, 1970	Little Cleo	Charles Gott, Green Forest, Ark.
14 lbs., 6 oz.	Bennett Spring State Park	July 3, 1974	Tan fur fly (#14)	Robert Lamm, Sedalia, Mo.
14 lbs., 7 oz.	Lake Taneycomo (Hwy. 65 br.)	July 14, 1976	Flatfish	Craig Wolf, Branson, Mo.
15 lbs., 0 oz.	Montauk State Park	March 1, 1977	Jig	David Summers, Salem, Mo.
16 lbs., 12 oz.	Lake Taneycomo (upper end)	Dec. 23, 1984	Salmon eggs	Bill Hecker, Rogersville, Mo.
16 lbs., 13 oz.	Roaring River State Park	Nov. 21, 1987	Jig	Kenneth Smith, Springfield, Mo.

PROGRESSION OF MISSOURI'S BROWN TROUT RECORD

Weight	Water	Date	Bait/Lure	Angler
14 lbs., 1oz.	Current River (below Montauk)	Aug. 15, 1970	Minnow	Michael Whitaker, Montauk, Mo.
15 lbs., 11 oz.	Current River (below Montauk)	July 10, 1977	Corn	Denver Medlock, Rolla, Mo.
16 lbs., 12 oz.	Montauk	Aug. 28, 1990	Jig	Gilbert "Butch" Enke, Salem, Mo.
23 lbs., 4 oz.	Lake Taneycomo	March 29, 1991	Muddler Minnow	Marty Babusa, Hollister, Mo.
24 lbs., 15 oz.	Lake Taneycomo	June 27, 1994	Shad Assassin	Kevin Elfrink, Jackson, Mo.

RECORD BROWN TROUT FROM THE WHITE RIVER SYSTEM

(through October 1994)

INTERNATIONAL GAME FISH ASSOCIATION FRESHWATER LINE CLASS RECORDS

Line Class	Weight	Angler	Place	Date
2 lb.	20-12	Carl Jones	White River, Ark.	9/19/87
4 lb.	40-4	Howard "Rip" Collins	Little Red River, Ark.	5/9/92
8 lb.	33-8	Leon Waggoner	White River, Ark.	3/19/77
20 lb.	28-14	Dee Warren	Little Red River, Ark.	8/20/93
All Tackle	40-4	Howard "Rip" Collins	Little Red River, Ark.	5/9/92

NATIONAL FRESH WATER FISHING HALL OF FAME

Rod and Reel Division

Line Class	Weight	Angler	Place	Date
4 lb.	40-4	Howard "Rip" Collins	Little Red River, Ark.	5/9/92
6 lb.	30-8	Tony Salamon	North Fork River, Ark.	8/31/86
8 lb.	38-9	Michael "Huey" Manley	North Fork River, Ark.	8/7/88
17 lb.	34-0	David Wooten	North Fork River, Ark.	8/13/88
All Tackle	40-4	Howard "Rip" Collins	Little Red River, Ark.	5/9/92

Fly Fishing Division

Line Class	Weight	Angler	Place	Date
4 lb.	15-10	Mike Morris	White River, Ark.	4/15/92

Catch and Release Rod and Reel Division*

Line Class	Length	Angler	Place	Date
4 lb.	32"	John Kalahurka	White River, Ark.	9/19/93
10 lb.	33"	William E. Kaune	White River, Ark.	2/7/94

Catch and Release Fly Fishing Division*

Line Class	Length	Angler	Place	Date
6 lb.	29"	Howard "Rip" Collins	Little Red River	11/25/93
8 lb.	31"	Bill Combs	Little Red River	10/17/93
14 lb.	27"	Bill Combs	Little Red River	10/19/93

* The National Fresh Water Fishing Hall of Fame began a "Catch and Release" section for its record book in 1993.

National Fresh Water Fishing Hall of Fame
P.O. Box 33
Hall of Fame Drive, Hayward, WI 54843
Phone: 715-634-4440

International Game Fish Association
1301 E. Atlantic Blvd.
Pompano Beach, FL 33060
Phone: 305-941-3474

BIBLIOGRAPHY

Berry, Earl. History of Marion County. Yellville: Marion County Historical Association, 1977.

Berry, Evalena. Time and the River - A History of Cleburne County. Little Rock: Rose Publishing Co., 1982.

Compton, Neil. The Battle for the Buffalo River. Fayetteville: University of Arkansas Press, 1992.

Deane, Ernie. Arkansas Place Names. Branson: The Ozarks Mountaineer, 1986.

Pennak, Robert W. Fresh-Water Invertebrates of the United States. New York: The Ronald Press Company, 1953.

Halterman, Skip. Trout Fishing: What Fly Should I Fish Today? Eureka Springs: Old River Books, 1990.

Horn, Ray. Just Trout. Heber Springs: Tumbling Shoals Publishing Group, 1993.

McClane, A.J. McClane's New Standard Fishing Encyclopedia and International Angling Guide. New York, Chicago, San Francisco: Holt, Rhinehart and Winston, 1965.

Messick, Mary Ann. History of Baxter County. Mountain Home: Chamber of Commerce, 1973.

Mid-South Fly Fishers. Home Waters. Memphis: Impressions, Inc., 1993.

Randolph, Vance. Ozark Outdoors: Hunting and Fishing Stories of the Ozarks. New York: The Vanguard Press, 1934/

Schoolcraft, Henry Rowe. Schoolcraft in the Ozarks. Reprint of Journal of a Tour into the Interior of Missouri and Arkansas in 1818 and 1819. Van Buren: Press-Argus Printers, 1955.

Tryon, Chuck and Sharon. Fly Fishing for Trout in Missouri. Rolla: Ozark Mountain Fly Fishers, 1992.

Whitlock, Dave. Guide to Aquatic Trout Foods. New York: Lyons & Burford, 1982.

Wright, Harold Bell. Shepherd of the Hills. New York: Grosset, 1907.

RESOURCES

Department of Energy

**Southwestern Power
Administration**
P.O. Box 1619
Tulsa, OK 74101
918-581-7474

In 1994, SWPA started, on an experimental basis, a recorded message center offering forecasts of power generation schedules. The schedules are subject to change and shouldn't be relied upon to predict safe water conditions. If there is no answer, the message center isn't operating:
918-581-6845
Beaver - #12
Table Rock - #13
Bull Shoals - #14
Norfork - #15
Greers Ferry - #16

U.S. Army Corps of Engineers

Recorded messages for present water conditions:
Beaver/Table Rock: 417-336-5083
Bull Shoals/Norfork: 501-431-5311
Greers Ferry: 501-362-5150

Beaver Lake Office
P.O. Drawer H
Rogers, AR 72756
501-636-1210

**Bull Shoals/Norfork Lakes
Mountain Home Resident Office**
P.O. Box 369
Mountain Home, AR 72653
501-425-2700

Greers Ferry Resident Office
P.O. Box 310
Heber Springs, AR 72543
501-362-2416

Table Rock Resident Office
P.O. Box 1109
Branson, MO 65616
417-334-4101

U.S. Forest Service

Ozark National Forest
P.O. Box 1008
Russellville, AR 72801
501-968-2354

Buffalo Ranger District
P.O. Box 427
Jasper, AR 72641
501-446-5122

Sylamore Ranger District
P.O. Box 1
Mountain View, AR 72560
501-757-2211

Mark Twain National Forest
401 N. Fairgrounds Rd.
Rolla, MO 65401
314-364-4621

Ava District
1103 S. Jefferson
Ava, MO 65608
417-683-4428

National Park Service

Buffalo National River
P.O. Box 1173
Harrison, AR 72601
501-741-5443

State Fishing and Hunting Agencies

**Arkansas Game and Fish
Commission**
2 Natural Resources Drive
Little Rock, AR 72205
For general information, call:
501-223-6300
To report game and fish violations:
1-800-482-9262
To order licenses by phone, charged to Visa or MasterCard:
1-800-364-GAME

**Missouri Department of
Conservation**
P.O. Box 180
Jefferson City, MO 65102-0180
For general information:
314-751-4115
To report violations:
1-800-392-1111

State Parks/Tourism

**Arkansas Department
of Parks and Tourism**
One Capitol Mall
Little Rock, AR 72201
For general information:
501-682-1191
For free vacation planning kit:
800-644-4833

Missouri Division of Tourism
P.O. Box 1055
Jefferson City, MO 65102
For general information:
417-751-4133
For free vacation planning kit:
800-877-1234

**Missouri Department
of Natural Resources
Division of State Parks**
P.O. Box 176
Jefferson City, MO 65102
314-751-2479

Bull Shoals State Park
Box 205
Bull Shoals, AR 72619
501-431-5521
501-431-5557 (dock)

Table Rock State Park
5272 State Highway 165
Branson, MO 65616
417-334-4704

Hatcheries

(All hatcheries are open for public tours.)

**Greers Ferry
National Fish Hatchery**
(USFWS)
349 Hatchery Road
Heber Springs, AR 72543
501-362-3615

Norfork National Fish Hatchery
(USFWS)
Rt. 3, Box 349
Mountain Home, AR 72653
501-499-5255

Shepherd of the Hills Hatchery
(MDC)
P.O. Box 427
Branson, MO 65616-0427
417-334-4865

Spring River State Fish Hatchery
(AGFC)
Rt. 2, Box 37C
Mammoth Spring, AR 72554
501-625-7521

Trout Fishing/Environmental Organizations

Arkansas Chapter Trout Unlimited
P.O. Box 4855
Fayetteville, AR 72702

Friends of Lake Taneycomo
P.O. Box 1734
Branson, MO 65616

Friends of the Little Red River
P.O. Box 1003
Heber Springs, AR 72543

North Arkansas Fly Fishers
P.O. Box 1213
Mountain Home, AR 72653
(Federation of Fly Fishers club)

Beaver Tailwater

**Beaver Lake Office
U.S. Army Corps of Engineers**
P.O. Drawer H
Rogers, AR 72756
501-636-1210
Recorded messages for present water conditions:
Beaver/Table Rock: 417-336-5083

Eureka Springs Chamber of Commerce
P.O. Box 551
Eureka Springs, AR 72632
501-253-8737

(The following list includes only the resorts, guides and attractions mentioned or shown on the map in the Beaver Tailwater section. Check with local chamber of commerce for a more complete list.)

Beaver Dam Store
Rt. 2, Box 419
Eureka Springs, AR 72632
501-253-6154

Charlie's Cabins
Route 2, Box 451
Eureka Springs, AR 72632
501-253-9125

Eureka Springs Gardens
Rt. 2, Box 362
Eureka Springs, AR 72632
501-253-9244

Ferguson's
Rt. 2, Box 450
Eureka Springs, AR 72632
501-253-7326

**Halterman, Skip
White River School of Fly Fishing**
Rt. 6, Box 27
Eureka Springs, AR 72632
501-253-7850

Holiday Island
2 Holiday Island Drive
Eureka Springs, AR 72632
800-643-2988

Riverview Resort
Route 2, Box 475
Eureka Springs, AR 72632
501-253-8367

**Smith, James
Northwest Guide Service**
13965 Hickory Trace
Fayetteville, AR 72704
501-442-2401

Spider Creek Resort
Route 2, Box 418
Eureka Springs, AR 72632
501-253-9241

**Tenison, Bill
Bancroft & Tabor**
603 W. Dickson St.
Fayetteville, AR 72701
501-442-2193

White River Oaks Bed & Breakfast
Rt. 2, Box 449
Houseman Access Road
Eureka Springs, AR 72632
501-253-9033

Table Rock Tailwater
Lake Taneycomo

**Table Rock Resident Office
U.S. Army Corps of Engineers**
P.O. Box 1109
Branson, MO 65616
417-334-4101
Recorded messages for present water conditions:
Table Rock: 417-336-5083

Empire District Electric Company
215 W. Main
Branson, MO 65616
417-334-3174

Branson/Lakes Area Chamber of Commerce
P.O. Box 220
Branson, MO 65616
417-334-4136

Forsyth Chamber of Commerce
Highway 60 Downtown
Forsyth, MO 65653
417-546-2741

Hollister Chamber of Commerce
Hollister, MO 65672
417-334-3050

Rockaway Beach Chamber of Commerce
P.O. Box 1004
Rockaway Beach, MO 65740
417-561-4280

(The following list includes only the resorts, guides and attractions mentioned in the text or shown on the map in the Table Rock Tailwater section. The Branson, Mo., area, in particular, has an abundance of resorts and attractions nearby. Check with local chambers of commerce for complete information.)

Babusa, Marty
3234 State Highway 265
Hollister, MO 65672
417-336-8699

Blue Haven Resort
1851 Lakeshore Drive
Branson, MO 65616
417-334-3917

Branson City Campground
417-334-2915

Branson Trout Dock
305 St. Limas St.
Branson, MO 65616
417-334-3703

Briarwood Resort
P.O. Box 506
Branson, MO 65616
417-334-3929

Cedar Point Resort
261 Cedar Point Road
Forsyth, MO 65653
417-546-3326

Cloud Nine Resort
1575 Lakeshore Drive
Branson, MO 65616
417-334-6241

Cooper Creek Resort & Campground
471 Cooper Creek Road
Branson, MO 65616
417-334-4871
417-334-5250

Del Mar Resort
1993 Lakeshore Drive
Branson, MO 65616
417-334-6241

Eden Roc Marina
Box 674
Rockaway Beach, MO 65740
417-561-4163

Edgewater Beach Resort
2446 State Highway Y
Forsyth, MO 65653
417-546-2721

Fall Creek Resort
One Fall Creek Drive
Branson, MO 65616
417-334-6404
800-872-7899

J.B.'s Dock
Box 297
Rockaway Beach, MO 65740
417-561-4763

Lakeshore Resort
P.O. Box 537-S
Branson, MO 65616
417-334-6262

Lazy Valley Resort
285 River Lane
Branson, MO 65616
417-334-2397

Lilley, Phil
Lilley's Landing Resort
HCR 5, Box 2170
Branson, MO 65616
417-334-6380

Longview Resort
P.O. Box 22
Rockaway Beach, MO 65740
417-561-4179

Main Street Dock
500 E. Main
Branson, MO 65616
417-334-2263

Ozark Beach Resort
245 Kallarney
Forsyth, MO 65653
417-546-4426

Piper's Lakeshore Resort
Highway 176
Rockaway Beach, MO 65740
417-561-4242

Port-0-Call Motel
Highway 176
Rockaway Beach, MO 65740
417-561-4354

Presley, Lloyd
Presleys' Jubilee
2920 76 Country Blvd.
Branson, MO 65616
417-334-4874

Ramsay, Mike
Right Angle Custom Rods & Tackle
Engler Block
1335 W. Highway 76
Branson, MO 65616

River Run Park
Highway 176
Forsyth, MO 65653
417-546-5142

Riverlake Resort
HCR 2, Box 430 SA
Hollister, MO 65672
417-334-2800

Rustic Acres Resort
417-334-5964

Sammy Lane Resort
320 East Main Street
Branson, MO 65616
417-334-3253

Scotty's Trout Dock
Lakefront
Branson, MO 65616
417-334-4288

Shepherd of the Hills Hatchery
P.O. Box 427
Branson, MO 65616-0427
417-334-4865

Shepherd of the Hills Homestead
5586 West Highway 76
Branson, MO 65616
417-334-4191
800-523-7589

Silver Dollar City
Highway 76 West
Branson West, MO 65616
417-334-4191

Sun Valley Resort
249 Sun Valley Circle
Hollister, MO 65672
417-334-3346

Table Rock Resident Office
U.S. Army Corps of Engineers
P.O. Box 1109
Branson, MO 65616
417-334-4101
Recorded messages for present water
conditions:
417-336-5083

Table Rock State Park
5272 State Highway 165
Branson, MO 65616
417-334-4704

TaCoMo Resort
HCR 2, Box 456
Hollister, MO 65672
417-334-2332
1-800-328-1246 (Reservations only)

Taneycomo Resort
417-334-7375

Tanglewood Lodge
Box 1217
Branson, MO 65616
417-334-1642

Vincent, Charles
P.O. Box 296
Rockaway Beach, MO 65740
417-561-4736

Bull Shoals, Norfork Tailwaters

Bull Shoals/Norfork Lakes
U.S. Army Corps of Engineers
Mountain Home Resident Office
P.O. Box 369
Mountain Home, AR 72653
501-425-2700
Recorded messages for present water
conditions:
Bull Shoals/Norfork: 501-431-5311

Bull Shoals Lake-White River
Chamber of Commerce
P.O. Box 354
Bull Shoals, AR 72619
501-445-4443

Ozark Mountain Region Tourism
Assoc.
P.O. Box 579
Flippin, AR 72634
501-453-8563
800-544-6867

Ozark Gateway Tourist Council
P.O. Box 4049
Batesville, AR 72503
501-793-9316
800-264-0316

Calico Rock Chamber of Commerce
P.O. Box 245
Calico Rock, AR 72519-0245
501-297-8868

Cotter Chamber of Commerce
P.O. Drawer G
Cotter, AR 72626
501-435-6326

Flippin Chamber of Commerce
P.O. Box 118
Flippin, AR 72634-0118
501-453-8480

Mountain Home Chamber
of Commerce
P.O. Box 488
Mountain Home, AR 72653
800-822-3536

Mountain View Chamber
of Commerce
P.O. Box 133
Mountain View, AR
501-269-8068

(The following list includes only the resorts, guides and attractions mentioned in the text or shown on the maps in the Bull Shoals and Norfork tailwaters sections. Check with local chambers of commerce and tourist councils for complete information.)

Blanchard Spring Caverns
U.S. Forest Service
P.O. Box 1279
Mountain View, AR 72560
501-757-2211

Buffalo National River
P.O. Box 1173
Harrison, AR 72601
501-741-5443

Ecotours
Newton County Resource Council
P.O. Box 513
Jasper, AR 72641
501-446-5898

Bull Shoals State Park
P.O. Box 205
Bull Shoals, AR 72619
501-431-5521
501-431-5557 (dock)

Brainerd's Bend
Don Wallace
Rt. 2, Box 597
Mountain Home, AR 76253
501-435-6695

Brickshy's Resort
Hwy. 5-9-14 North
Allison, AR 72560
501-585-2226

Calico Rock Trout Dock
Calico Rock, Arkansas 72519
501-297-8131

Capps, David
Capps Guide Service
P.O. Box 873
Yellville, AR 72687
501-449-5674

Chamberlain's Trout Dock
Route 1, Box 141
Denton Ferry Road
Cotter, AR 72626
501-435-6535

Chatelain, Ralph
Bull Shoals Famous Floats
P.O. Box 44
Bull Shoals, AR 72619
501-445-7160

Cobb, Pete
P.O. Box 391
Cotter, AR 72626
501-435-2028

Cotter Trout Dock
P.O. Box 96
Cotter, AR 72626
501-435-6525

Due, Jackie
Bull Shoals Boat Dock
Box 748
Bull Shoals, AR 72619
501-445-4424

Dudley, Jerry
1146 Columbus Place
Fayetteville, AR 72701
501-442-9801

Fair Haven Lodge
HC 62, Box 88B
Flippin, AR 72634
501-453-2371

Fulton, Dale
Blue Ribbon Flies
Fulton Lodge
P.O. Box 1080
Mountain Home, AR 72653
501-425-0447

Gaston's Resort
#1 River Road
Lakeview, AR 72642
501-431-5202

Gene's Trout Resort
Rt. 3, Box 348
Mountain Home, AR 72653
501-499-5381

Gunga-La Lodge
Rt. 1, Box 147
Lakeview, AR 72642
501-431-5606
800-844-5606

Gulley, John
3012 Riverview Road
Norfork, AR 72658
501-499-7517

Hutchinson, Bob
Bob's Fishing Service
P.O. Box 942
Mountain Home, AR 72653
501-435-2258

Hurst Fishing Service
P.O. Box 129
Cotter, AR 72626
501-435-6414

Jack's Fishing Resort
Box 185
Mountain View, AR 72560
501-585-2211

Jenkins Fishing Service
P.O. Box 303
Calico Rock, AR 72519
501-297-8181

Jones, Carl
P.O. Box 94
Flippin, AR 72634
501-453-2272

Jones, Paul
HC 63, Box 256B
Yellville, AR 72687
501-436-7732

Lindsey's Trout Dock
Calico Rock, AR 72519
501-297-4543

Lovelady's Trout Dock
Highway 58
Guion, AR 72540
501-346-5310

McClellan Trout Dock
Route 2, Box 74
Norfork, AR 72658
501-499-5589

Meeks, Carl
501-435-6335

Miller's Fishing Service
Box 277
Cotter, AR 72626
501-435-6313

Newland's Lodge
Route 1, River Road
Lakeview, AR 72642
501-431-5678

Norfork Trout Dock
P.O. Box 129
Norfork, AR 72658
501-499-5500

Ozark Folk Center
P.O. Box 500
Mountain View, AR 72560
501-269-3851

PJ's Resort Lodge
P.O. Box 61
Norfork, AR 72658
501-499-7500

Perdue, Pat
Bull Shoals Boat Dock
Box 748
Bull Shoals, AR 72619
501-445-4424

Professional Guides Association
c/o Frank Blanton
P.O. Box 664
Flippin, AR 72634
501-453-8916

Rainbow Drive Resort
(White River)
Route 1, Box 1185
Rainbow Drive
Cotter, AR 72626
501-430-5217

Rainbow Trout Resort
(North Fork River)
Route 3, Box 340
Mountain Home, AR 72653
501-499-7214

Red Bud Dock
Route 2, Box 541
Gassville, AR 72635
501-435-6303

Rim Shoals Resort
Rt. 2, Box 597
Mountain Home, AR 76253
501-435-6695

Rivercliff Trout Dock
P.O. Box 150
Bull Shoals, AR 72619
501-445-4420

Riverside Mobile & RV Park
P.O. Box 167
Lakeview, AR 72642
501-431-8260

Rose's Trout Dock
P.O. Box 82
Norfork, AR 72658
501-499-5311

Schroder Haus
P.O. Box 187
Norfork, AR 72658
501-499-7775

Sportsman's Resort
HCR 62, Box 96
Flippin, AR 72634
501-453-2424 or -2422
800-626-FISH

Statler, Fox
P.O. Box 244
Lakeview, AR 72642-0244
501-431-8415

Stetson's Resort
HCR 62, Box 102
Flippin, AR 72634
501-453-8066

Wapsi Fly, Inc.
Rt. 5, Box 57E
Mountain Home, AR 72653
501-425-9500

Weaver, Elvin
P.O. Box 176
Gassville, AR 72635
501-435-6979, or
501-435-6313

White River Trout Dock
Lakeview, AR 72642
501-431-5594

White Buffalo Resort
Route 2, Box 438
Mountain Home, AR 72653
501-425-8555

White Hole Resort
HCR 62, Box 100
Flippin, AR 72634
501-453-2913

**White, North Fork Rivers
Outfitters Association**
P.O. Box 100
Cotter, AR 72626

White River Campground
Highway 62B
P.O. Box 99
Cotter, AR 72626
501-453-2299

Whitlock, Dave
Rt. 1, Box 398
Midway, AR 72651

Wildcat Shoals Resort
Route A, Box 166
Flippin, AR 72634
501-453-2321

Wilson, Hank
P.O. Box 212
Lakeview, AR 72642
501-445-4383

Greers Ferry Tailwater

**Greers Ferry Resident Office
U.S. Army Corps of Engineers**
P.O. Box 310
Heber Springs, AR 72543
501-362-2416
Recorded messages for present water
conditions:
Greers Ferry: 501-362-5150

**Heber Springs Chamber
of Commerce**
1001 West Main St.
Heber Springs, AR 72543
501-362-2444

*(The following list includes only the
resorts, guides and attractions mentioned
in the text or shown on the map in the
Greers Ferry Tailwater section. Check
with local chamber of commerce for
complete information.)*

Bly, Tom
1000 Mill St.
Heber Springs, AR 72543
501-362-8295

Brown, Bob
Friends of Little Red River/guide
1703 Main
North Little Rock AR 72114
800-880-8808

Brown, Mike
501-362-6861

Combs, Bill
Richie Shoal Lodge
P.O. Box 5
Heber Springs, AR 72543
501-362-8655

Collins, Rip
P.O. Box 638
Heber Springs, AR 72543
501-362-6486

Cresswell, Gary
144 Rainbow Road
Heber Springs, AR 72543
501-362-5693

Dripping Springs Trout Dock
263 Dripping Springs Road
Pangburn, AR 72121
501-728-4711

**Greers Ferry National
Fish Hatchery** (USFWS)
349 Hatchery Road
Heber Springs, AR 72543
501-362-3615

**Hada, Duane
The Woodsman**
#153 Central Mall
Fort Smith, AR 72903
501-452-3559, or
501-452-1538

Horn, Ray
Rt. 1, Box 200
Heber Springs, AR 72543
501-362-5802
To order "Just Trout" cookbook:
800-898-7668

Jones, Jack
HC 34, Box 346A
Heber Springs, AR 72543
501-362-3612

Lester, Sam
489 River Dr.
Heber Springs, AR 72543
501-362-8957

Lindsey, Billy
Lindsey's Rainbow Resort
350 Rainbow Road
Heber Springs, AR 72543
501-362-3139

Lobo Landing
3525 Libby Road
Heber Springs, AR 72543
501-362-5802
800-659-8330

Ozark Angler
659 Wilburn Road
Heber Springs, AR 72543
501-362-FLYS

Red River Trout Dock
HC 34, Box 346
Heber Springs, AR 72543
501-362-2197

River Ranch Resort
P.O. Box 292
Heber Springs, AR 72543
501-362-9003

Swinging Bridge Resort
100 Swinging Bridge Drive
Heber Springs, AR 72543
501-362-3327

Vogel, Abe
(See "Lobo Landing")

INDEX